Classical, Renaissance, and Postmodernist Acts of the Imagination

Portrait of O.B. Hardison, Jr. Photo by Stravros Moschopoulos.

Classical, Renaissance, and Postmodernist Acts of the Imagination

Essays Commemorating
O. B. Hardison, Jr.

Edited by
Arthur F. Kinney

DELAWARE

Newark: University of Delaware Press
London: Associated University Presses

Associated University Presses
440 Forsgate Drive
Cranbury, NJ 08512

Associated University Presses
16 Barter Street
London WC1A 2AH, England

Associated University Presses
P.O. Box 338, Port Credit
Mississauga, Ontario
Canada L5G 4L8

The paper used in this publication meets the requirements of the American National Standard for Permanence of Paper for Printed Library Materials Z39.48–1984.

Library of Congress Cataloging-in-Publication Data

Classical, Renaissance, and postmodernist acts of the imagination : essays commemorating O.B. Hardison, Jr. / edited by Arthur F. Kinney.
  p. cm.
Includes bibliographical references.
ISBN 0-87413-583-4
1. Hardison, O. B. 2. Literature—History and criticism.
I. Hardison, O. B. II. Kinney, Arthur F., 1933– .
PN501.C53 1996
809—dc20
96-7748
CIP

PRINTED IN THE UNITED STATES OF AMERICA

Contents

6 CONTENTS

Preface

ARTHUR F. KINNEY

O. B. Hardison was a man of an unmatched range of talents who exercised them with notable warmth, humanity, and good humor through a lifetime unmatched in its range of achievement. He was trained as a scientist, interested in physics and biology, and as a humanist, drawn to the classics, to poetry and poetics, and to drama and the theater. A poet and scholar himself, he was also a teacher, a musician, and the administrator of the library housing the world's largest collection of Shakespeareana, the Folger Shakespeare Library in Washington, D.C., which he helped to transform into one of the leading intellectual communities and facilities in the nation's capital. Early in life he was concerned with Christian rite and ritual and the role of the church fathers in Western poetics and in the formulation of drama; later in life he was just as obsessed with computers and technology generally; when he died early (at the age of 61) he was working to combine these interests in a trilogy of works concerned with the evolution, history, and unavoidable future of man whose life on this planet as we now know it would one day, he prophesied, disappear through the skylight.

Like the challenge of this last project—combining aesthetics with eschatology—all of his ventures held two things in common: the exercise of courage in doing something different, and the dynamics of the imagination in conceiving what might, and could, be done when man combined vision with hard work and guts. All of this, however, was graced with generosity, tact, and a pervasive, intractable sense of humor—often with and at himself. Early in a career at the University of North Carolina at Chapel Hill, where according to *Time* magazine, he was one of the nation's top ten teachers and his stimulating, organized classes and his unending stream of publication showed much scholarly promise, he took off for leave with his wife and six children in a new camper and spent his time writing a detective novel under a pseudonym. He probably wanted to do this because he hadn't before, because he liked mystery novels, and because it was, if an unpredictable act, yet predictably a new, risky act of the imagination. When, after the directorship of the Folger, he moved on to become a University Professor at Georgetown University, he turned from Sidney and Spenser and Milton to teaching Shakespeare and from classroom lectures to student performances: on the East Coast, he was discovering for himself what Homer Swander, with ACTER, was discovering on the West Coast. He hadn't done that before. And he doubtless saw it, too, as he saw all other things: as ways to awaken the intellect and the imagination of others, since the life of the mind was always a participatory and, as often as not, a communal, life.

How could anyone hope to commemorate adequately and suitably a life and a man like that? His wife Marifrancis Hardison, who had been his partner through most of his intellectual and imaginative experiences, knew the answer instinctively: by calling on those whose minds and works touched his. But they would hardly be a community that would have precedent elsewhere, in any other anthology or *festschrift:* they would have, instead, to include physicists and poets, scientists and teachers of humanities, colleagues and former students, men and women both, of great distinction and of distinction yet to come. She was right, of course: and when we asked such an array of persons to contribute, no one declined. Everyone in this volume has contributed something that represents his or her own interest and perspective, their own acts of imagination to commemorate so many dimensions of his, by writing or choosing from their writing works that, for them, find resonance in O. B. Hardison's own life and work. This book opens with explicit perspectives on O. B. Hardison himself—on the man, on the young but nationally-famous teacher at Chapel Hill, on the later administrator and educator and poet in Washington, D.C., and on the professor whose strikingly original pedagogy is working through a second generation and on into the next. But, truth to tell, every contribution here is a special memoir of its kind: each of them and all of them in the aggregate do not merely reflect O.B.'s interests and his commitment to their own work but become themselves acts of imagination: imaginative recreations and representations of what most fascinated O.B. That has been the intention from the start. It began with Marifrancis's suggestion, continued with the counsel and encouragement of Jerry Leath Mills, and results, now, some four years later, in a unique collection of statements and poems. We hope this collection will recall and recover O. B. Hardison, too, for its readers who knew him as well as introduce him to those readers lucky enough to be at the moment of discovery.

Classical, Renaissance, and Postmodernist Acts of the Imagination

Part 1
Remembering O. B. Hardison, Jr.

O. B.

Paul Trachtman

Friend, you made living a mystery.
You took large steps, mouth agape, eyes wide,
sharing your amazed love of it all,
holding your days like exotic fruits
never before described by science,
always biting into a surprise.
And nothing was too ordinary
to hide its mystery from your eyes.
You would talk with the same excitement
of discovering a medieval text
or taking your tractor through tall grass.
You knew the art of explaining things
without obscuring their mystery.
You could split words like firewood
and burn the sentences as you talked
so that your voice was full of warm light.
You were a farmer whose crop was seeds,
a scholar digging with a real spade,
a poet who named everything but himself.
Your smile was always there, always new,
leaving its gay creases on your face.
You knew the voices of many centuries
but never heard the voice in your bones,
and when your time came there was no time.
Dying, you held out a mystery:
Eternity is always just beginning.

O. B. Hardison, Jr. at Chapel Hill

Jerry Leath Mills

Upon O.B.'s untimely death in 1990, the Raleigh, N.C., *News and Observer* asked me, as his former student and colleague, to write a memorial article for the Sunday edition. Going through my files in preparation, I rediscovered a photograph, now more than twenty years old, that says perhaps even more than the proverbial thousand words about what O.B. meant to the academic community in Chapel Hill during the dozen years he graced its faculty, ultimately as professor of English and Comparative Literature and editor of *Studies in Philology.*

The photo is of three men facing the camera in my living room. In the center, smiling broadly, is David Richardson, now a professor and scholar in his own right but then a proud and relieved young man fresh from passing his final doctoral exam in English. Flanking him are his dissertation director, O. B. Hardison, and myself as a member of his committee. Within this otherwise unexceptional snapshot there is one detail that seems, by the happiest of accidents, to literalize a metaphor that must have passed through the minds of scores of students in his classes: because of the reflection of the flashbulb in a mirror behind us, a brilliant light seems to emanate from O.B.'s head and shoulders, illuminating the scene.

Anyone who knew O.B. as a teacher will understand and applaud that bit of fortuitous symbolism. His light first shone on me in September 1957. I was a sophomore and a small-town North Carolinian with some vague notions about majoring in American history. In those days of undisintegrated canons, a course in Chaucer, Shakespeare, and Milton was required of all students, and I was randomly assigned to the section listed as "Hardison—MWF, 10 a.m."

Although I was happy enough to take a course that the university so forcefully declared good for me, I was initially a little concerned, along with several of my fellow students, at what seemed to be the extreme youthfulness of the teacher. O.B. was twenty-eight years old at the time but could have passed easily for a rather intense undergraduate among those unaware that he already held a Ph.D. from the University of Wisconsin and was well into the writing of *The Enduring Monument,* his first book. None of us knew about this, or that a collection of his poems had been selected to appear in hardcover in the prestigious "Poets of Today" series edited by John Hall Wheelock, or that he and Marifrancis were well along in the production of what eventually became a family of six children.

I believe, on reflection, that it took about ten minutes of his first class to vaporize my doubts about his claim to authority in the lecture room—along, coincidentally, with any further thoughts about majoring in history. I wish now that I could capture anecdotally what he created in that course and in the three others I was to take with him, but I cannot, because it was a steady process rather than a discrete sequence of ideas and events. But I know that many of us under his tutelage gained convictions that I have never found reason to abandon or revise: that the truths of imaginative literature were among the most important issues on earth; that it was our privilege and obligation to become aware of these truths; and that in seeking to do so we had a guide we could trust with our very souls.

Not that O.B. ever stated things in those terms. His approach to literature was passionate but never theatrical. In lecture and discussion he stayed closely with the texts and let his own example generate the ethical context for students who chose to notice. He was, among many other things, a model of absolute personal and professional responsibility. From the three years I studied with him I don't recall his ever missing a class or even showing up late for one. I assume that he was aware of his own brilliance—he had to have been—but he never let flash or verve or the unanticipated insight substitute for the marvelously detailed and textured preparation evident in his teaching day after day.

O.B. put to rout the old fallacy that research and conscientious teaching were somehow at odds, demonstrating instead the way they complemented each other and letting us see how much the greatness of his own pedagogy derived from his deep involvement with the materials of potential knowledge and in previously unexamined relationships. He held our groups of nineteen- and twenty-year-old undergraduates in rapt attention as he explained how a thirteenth-century ecclesiastic named Herman the German helped shape perceptions of the tragic hero in the drama of the Renaissance. He led us—many of us children of the Bible Belt—to understand how a knowledge of Calvinistic theology helped elucidate the contemporary mystery novel; and then, as though to prove again the relationship between idea and accomplishment, went on to publish (under the name H. O. Bennett), a spy thriller of his own creation. On one memorable day, what started out as a routine survey of Tudor political assumptions turned into a lecture on *King Lear* that I still regard as the most exhilarating classroom experience I have ever had.

O.B. made his students feel that he treated our work with the same respect he accorded Aristotle. He had a martyr's tolerance for undergraduate excess, coupled with a loving parent's ability to correct without damaging our egos more than common sense required. One term paper I wrote, a raveled skein of Chaucer, Freud, and personal confusion, came back rubricated with comments, leaving my argument up against the left-field fence in a dozen ways and at the same time making me feel as though I'd won some kind of prize. O.B. applauded system, method, and orderly procedure, but he also harbored an appreciation for the eccentric, the unconventionally speculative, even the bizarre. He lived in awareness of what he was eventually to write in his spy novel, that "logic is a carpet laid over an abyss."

When I returned to Chapel Hill, after graduate studies in the North, to become O.B.'s office mate and colleague on the English Department faculty, I continued to learn from him about the responsibilities of the academic profession. In the spring of 1966 he appeared on the cover of *Time* magazine as one of the ten-best college teachers in America, and our office began receiving the daily avalanche of mail that inevitably attends that level of distinction. Although he was deeply engaged, as always, with a very large number of writing and research obligations, O.B. resolved to answer each and every letter if it took all summer—as it very nearly did—responding specifically and sincerely to the frequently troubled questions and messages those letters contained.

After he left for the Folger Shakespeare Library and, later, Georgetown University, O.B. kept closely in touch with what he had begun in Chapel Hill, coming back for the final oral exam of every doctoral student whose dissertation was begun under his direction, often staying to lecture to our current students about his ongoing research and to talk with them about their own projects. Even now, as editor of a journal he himself once commanded, I handle essays submitted with occasional notes that their research was encouraged, in its beginnings, by O. B. Hardison.

Fair Allurements to Learning: The Legacy of a Professing Teacher

DAVID A. RICHARDSON

ACTS *of the Imagination* is in fact O. B. Hardison's second *Festschrift*. His first was given to him more than twenty-five years ago:

> *Studies in Spenser*
> *in Honor of*
> *O. B. Hardison, Jr.*
>
> by
> His Students,
>
> Presented
> Chapel Hill, N.C.
> July 27, 1969

This modest typescript of seventy-two pages was a parting gift to O.B. as he left Carolina for the Folger Shakespeare Library. It contained the germs of half a dozen dissertations and reflected his influence as a scholar. It was also a testimonial to O.B. as teacher and mentor, for it sprang from one of his last, best courses at the University of North Carolina.

O.B. later described that course in "Demanding the Impossible" (chapter 6 in *Toward Freedom and Dignity: The Humanities & the Idea of Humanity,* 1972). Curiously, it was a seminar in Spenser, being offered by a professor known most for his love of Milton and criticism and for his provocative lectures in courses that were always oversubscribed. But a Spenserian ether was in the air at Carolina in the 1960s. Landmark books had recently been published by Paul Alpers, Donald Cheney, A. C. Hamilton, A. Kent Hieatt, Thomas P. Roche, Jr., and Kathleen Williams. Alastair Fowler came to Chapel Hill to lecture on numerology and Harry Berger visited for a bombshell seminar. Graduate students were delighting in "our sage and serious poet"—and so was O.B. Having just finished a commentary on Aristotle's *Poetics,* he found the time ripe to study his great poet's great progenitor, so Hardison the Miltonist offered a course on Edmund Spenser.

The subject was nothing new for a Renaissance man, but the method was. And it shows decisively how a successful teacher does not rest on his laurels or old notes. O.B. decided not to make it a traditional lecture course, because "any time you say the same thing more than two or three times it begins to sound like a cliché." He also opted against the question/discussion format: "a question can be important or trivial, off the point or on it. . . . the chances of real communication . . . are low." He scrapped the Socratic method as coercive and intellectually hypocritical, as an exercise in vanity in which the teacher is "the star of the show, the arbiter of truth . . . behind his façade of humility." He also wanted to prevent the traditional fallback of even conscientious students: borrowed notes and catch-up cramming when someone else is "performing." In short, he rejected the old ways of the classroom as "antipedagogy" based on unacceptable assumptions, manipulative methods, and unfortunate outcomes.

Instead he decided that "my basic objective was to beguile my students into reading all of Edmund Spenser." And to achieve this student-centered outcome, he threw full responsibility on them after a few introductory lectures:

> . . .Instead of relying on me, the class would be taught by a series of two-man teams. Student A would offer a presentation of some aspect of the assigned reading that he considered important. . . . There would be only two rules. The subject should be of genuine interest to the speaker. . . . And the presentation could not last more than twenty minutes [to allow] thirty minutes for discussion.
>
> At the end of the presentation, student B would take over. He could comment if he wished for no more than five minutes on the presentation. Then he had to open the floor for discussion and preside, wherever the discussion might lead, until the end of the class period.

The first team presentations were predictable: "I can confess now that they were wretched," O.B. acknowledged, ". . .tangential, awkward, and topheavy with regurgitated scholarship." Even the open discussions parodied Socratic method by throwing in others' ideas unexercised and unbreathed, without the dust and heat of vigorous exchange. Half of the students dropped out; others muttered about paying to take courses from other graduate students. The prospects were bleak: dead scholarship, dead class, dead poet. O.B. thought seriously of abandoning the teaching experiment and taking control himself with a semester of solid, predictable lectures.

But his deep faith in teaching and in the students was soon rewarded. A beginning graduate student tackled Spenser's text on his own—without footnotes or any scholarly apparatus beyond his own curiosity to run with the poem and see where it might take him. When he was done, the class rallied to the text and joined him—not as adversaries or authorities, but as fellow wrestlers with a part of *The Faerie Queene*. Adrenalin surged. The discussion was animated. Ideas flew about the room. After a few more sessions, class meetings couldn't be contained in fifty minutes. Dropouts began returning. Even library scholarship became vital as the dusty stacks yielded up evidence that was relevant to the students' own initiatives in class.

Most important, O.B. noted, "everyone began having fun . . . *through* involvement in Spenser rather than in spite of him." The class achieved his goal of beguiling everyone into reading all of the poetry—through their own initiatives. He observed, "The only valid standard in humanistic education is 'How much has this student developed his own interests? How much growth has occurred in this course?'" And, he concluded in the 1972 essay, if the basic measure of success in teaching is the difference between what students bring to a class and what they take away from it, "I consider the Spenser class one of the most successful I have taught. Or the most successful I have not taught."

But obviously he had taught a great deal in that course. He had worked hard to ensure its success by crafting his strategy, selecting material, structuring meetings, identifying higher expectations, and assigning greater responsibility. Only then did he take the risk of freeing students to instruct themselves in the company of fellow learners, including himself. But even if teaching is regarded only as pouring information from a full vessel into an empty one, O.B. masterminded the transfer, making the process autonomous rather than doing the pouring himself. For, by the principles of the course, just as in Spenser's Garden of Adonis, "Ne needs there Gardiner to set, or sow, / To plant or prune: for of their owne accord / All things, as they created were, doe grow." (*FQ* III vi 34). His class, like the garden, could scarcely have been more fruitful.

Behind this self-impelled Spenser class lay O.B.'s Kantian sense of the imagination: "human beings have a natural and inborn desire to learn." He believed that humanistic education, whether in the classroom, carrel, or quiet study, should be a process of removing mental barriers rather than of merely filling a mind with facts. For

all his delight in displaying his own wit and intellect—and he loved
to put on a good show—he had boundless respect for his students:
trust the inquiring mind and students will surprise you with the
range of their abilities. They will also reward themselves with the
tenacity of their efforts and the depth of unpredictable insights.

It was not easy for O.B. to wait for the discoveries and intellectual eruptions of that Spenser class (he confessed later that anxiety
almost made him abandon his pipe for cigarettes). But he knew
from Milton that waiting and openness have their rewards. These
principles are implicit in one of his own habits as a teacher-scholar:
he had an open-door policy so that students could visit his office
without formal appointments. They might have to wait for him to
finish scratching out a paragraph for his latest project, but as soon
as he cleared his desk he was always available to talk about a
textual crux or a career prospect. Like Old Genius at the doors of
Spenser's garden, he was a gatekeeper—"He letteth in, he letteth
out to wend, / All that to come into the world desire" (32)—wel-
coming and nurturing students in his classes, then sending them
out clothed with new degrees and enthusiasms for the poetry he
loved.

Also like Spenser's garden, O.B.'s model in "Demanding the
Impossible" is timeless. And imitable. I know, because for a decade
I've assigned his essay to challenge students of all ages, abilities,
and backgrounds. Some of my classes have been large *Norton
Anthology* surveys; others, surveys of Tudor or Stuart literature.
Recently O.B.'s essay provided the ground rules for a new Renaissance biography course that included attention to classical rhetoric
and women's writing. Student testimony about that course (and
others) shows that O.B.'s ideals are vital and his methods
rewarding:

—What [the behavioralists] lack is what Hardison demands: the acknowledgment and nurturing of a person's natural love of learning. . . . You can't fake the pop you get from putting together some
theory of your own. . . . This class was a far different experience.
All voices were heard here. . . . all saying, "Look how much there
is to know!"

—Hardison does demand the impossible . . . but that is exactly what
needs to be done. . . . Students need to assume a greater . . . authority in their own education.

—. . . the most important element of [Hardison's] approach was the
transformation of the classroom from a teacher-to-student system to

an intellectual community. Students and teacher became colleagues
working together to share, learn, and grow.

—People were somehow exilarated, vitalized by the idea that they
were responsible for their own education. We used more outside
resources than I had even seen in a classroom, because . . . we
simply loved what we were doing, got excited about it, and . . .
learned to use the tools of our trade. . . . We are involved, engaged,
and empowered.

"Involved, engaged, and empowered"—these are the traits O.B.
wanted to cultivate twenty-five years ago in his graduate students
at the University of North Carolina. They resurface in my undergraduates at an urban commuter campus at the end of the century.
I believe that these qualities are potential in every student. And
as implied by his later cultural studies and multimedia work with
"Lycidas," they are traits he wanted to see in every responsible
member of a free society.

O.B.'s career was informed by a broad social vision that included
more than his many contributions to scholarship, more than his
Herculean service to the profession at a major research institution.
It included an abiding commitment to his own students throughout
his life and to the dialogue of the classroom, to which he returned
after leaving the Folger. I am confident that if his career had not
been interrupted in its prime, O.B. would also have taken his teaching methods beyond literature and the classroom to the computer
technology that so intrigued him, to other practical instruction,
and to students of all ages turned off by traditional lectures.

These broader applications are enormously significant, because
O.B.'s method is more than just the stuff of dreams in an academic
ivory tower. A graphic example from the sciences can stand for
the whole: the joint chemistry curriculum for undergraduate non-
science majors at Princeton, at Indiana—and at Columbia College
of Chicago (Keith Henderson, "Teaching Science to the 'Unteach-
able,'" *Christian Science Monitor,* 16 May 1994, 15).

It's also immediately relevant to the practical needs of
America—to Apple, Intel, Hewlett Packard, Xerox, and other
high-tech corporations. Witness Alan Nowakowski, director of
training at Andersen Consulting's education center in St. Charles,
Illinois: "We're working to re-engineer the entire learning process. . . . taking control out of the hands of instructors and putting
it into the hands of the learner. . . . We want active, not passive,
learners who learn in a context as close to the real work environment as possible. . . . We want people to be able to perform work

processes well, as judged by their peers." Also Marc Rosenberg, learning strategist for AT&T: instead of seeing classrooms as places for "dumping knowledge," he sees them as "places for teams to work together on solving problems" (Nowakowski and Rosenberg are quoted in Lewis J. Perelman, "Kanban to Kanbrain," *Forbes ASAP,* 6 June 1994, 84–95, 94). The goals of these pragmatists are simply permutations of O.B.'s goals for his classes. O.B.'s experience and mine suggests that what's good for the academy may be very good indeed for the marketplace and for our culture at large.

Among "lookers-on in the cockpit of learning," O. B. Hardison's legacy as scholar and administrator is apparent to all who visit the Folger Shakespeare Library, to all who read about classical poetics, medieval drama and criticism, Renaissance prosody, and modern cultural dynamics. His legacy in the classroom is less conspicuous. In the ephemeral press, it includes a *Time* magazine cover honoring him as one of the nation's top ten teachers. Among his students, a truer image is O.B. in a rumpled seersucker suit and a cloud of chalk dust, with Poppo wagging a shaggy tail at his feet.

His true gift to teaching, however, is intangible. I can epitomize it as a succinct reply to the King of Brobdingnag, who asked Gulliver "what methods were used to cultivate the minds and bodies of our young nobility, and in what kind of business they commonly spent the first and teachable part of their lives" (*Gulliver's Travels,* pt. 2, chap. 6). O.B.'s answer surely would have repeated the imperative that marked his last, best course at Carolina: "Demand the impossible."

O. B. Hardison, Jr.: 21 October 1993

MYRA SKLAREW

A year ago, when I thought to say a few words about O. B. Hardison, of his presence among us and all that he stood for, I did not know how hard it would be. The truth is that we miss him because he was a shining light, an inspiration, one of the rare ones who achieved knowledge through play, who possessed—in Henry Taylor's words—an intellectual restlessness. Just as he strode through the halls of the Folger quoting Milton or Spenser or Shakespeare or reciting the lyrics of country and western songs, sometimes in a suit of chain mail at Folger parties—so he loped across centuries in probing exploration. He was as much at home in the Renaissance and in the medieval world as he was in the future. He relished examining possibility and change. He would be the first to be fascinated by the 1993 choice of Nobel scientists, the way the fields of atomic physics, chemistry, and molecular biology inform one another. O.B. understood the necessity to break down artificial barriers, to use all the tools of knowledge no matter where they came from. O.B. recommended interrupting poetry with a bit of plaster patching and believed that the commonplace experiences of everyday life could be seen in ways that gave them a radical new significance. Once, as a youngster, he thought to be an astronomer. He wrote books about Christian rite and drama in the Middle Ages. He saw the history of science as inseparable from the history of the humanities. During his tenure as director of the Folger Shakespeare Library from 1969 to 1983, he founded the Folger Theater, turned the place into a literary salon, brought together a consortium of universities as the Folger Institute, gathered scholars, poets, political leaders, youngsters under its roof and turned the place into a living institution.

How can we speak for O.B.'s life? How characterize his journey? Once years ago I had to take my ninety-four-year-old grandmother to be buried in New England. Along the way her casket was lost, as in a tale by William Faulkner. When we found her again and stood in the cemetery in a raging snowstorm, when the rabbi began to crank up his eulogy—one with the impersonal ring of dozens of others he had given for previous customers over the years, my grandmother's sister could bear it no longer. She grabbed the rabbi's gesticulating arm and stilled it: "Rabbi," she said, "you didn't know my sister. Now I will do the talking." And then she told us stories about our grandmother and as we stood there in the cold cemetery, my grandmother's life and presence flared up in the words of her sister. For O.B. we need neither our rabbi nor my grandmother's sister, but only his words:

"Listen to the music," he wrote in *Pro Musica Antiqua*.

> Listen to the sound of the krummhorn, the rebec,
> The vielle, the virginal, the viola da gamba,
> The scraping and twanging celebration of order.
>
> .   .   .   .
> Throw away the dictionary.
> Live where you are.
> If the sackbut palls,
> Bang on a pianoforte.
> Limber up drums,
> Unleash saxophones,
>
> .   .   .   .   .   .
> This is the way it should be. Your house should be music.
> Welcome it, hold on to it,
>
> .   .   .   .
> When you let go, you will snore in C major.

From his poem "King of the World":

> I have become what I am.
> There is now nothing in me that is not what I am.
> All my roads lead to me.
> I did not expect this to happen.
>
> If I were an oak tree,
> My leaves would be children,
> Everything I love would be branches,
> My enemies would be caterpillars,
> My roots would be fastened deep in red clay.
> You might then be, say, a bird. Something shining with impossible
>   colors.
> I would hold out my branches for you to roost in.
> I would grow leaves to shade you.
> I would give you my enemies to eat.
> My roots would tremble with your singing.

When O.B. began to have doubts about his teaching, about going
through the old motions, he decided on a new plan by which to
"beguile his students into reading all of Edmund Spenser." He
would provide the first six introductory lectures. After that the
class would be taught by a series of two-person teams: one student
would offer a presentation of some aspect of the assigned reading,
a second student would briefly comment and preside over the discussion. "There would be only two rules," O.B. wrote in *Toward
Freedom & Dignity: The Humanities and the Idea of Humanity:*
"The subject should be of genuine interest to the speaker on the
assumption that if it bored him it could not help boring us." And
the presentation could not last more than twenty minutes. Meanwhile, O.B. took a seat by the window and smoked his pipe. If you
want to know how this experiment turned out, read his chapter
called "Demanding the Impossible."

In *Disappearing Through the Skylight: Culture and Technology
in the Twentieth Century,* O.B. describes three evolutionary ep-
ochs: the first where man was "land-oriented"; the second where
carbon man thought of the planet with its gravitational forces as
home; the third, that of the empty spaces between planets as the
"natural habitat" of silicon devices. "They float in these spaces
like Portuguese men-of-war in a warm sea. Their enormous, silvery
arms, covered with solar cells, collect energy from the limitless
tides that wash through space."

Shall we worry about man disappearing into his machines, the
demise of humanity? Perhaps we have come to that place, O.B.
muses, where "the spirit finally separates itself from an outmoded
vehicle" and "realizes the age-old dream of the mystics of rising
beyond the prison of the flesh to behold a light so brilliant it is a
kind of darkness." Yeats, O.B. reminds us, wrote, "Once out of
Nature, I shall never take / My bodily form from any natural thing, /
But such a form as Grecian goldsmiths make / Of hammered
gold. . . ."

"What will those shining constructs of silicon and gold and arse-
nic and germanium look like as they sail the spaces between
worlds?" O.B. asks at the close of *Disappearing Through the
Skylight.*

They will be invisible, but we can try to imagine them, even as fish
might try to imagine the fishermen on the other side of the mirror that
is the water's surface. . . .

They will communicate in the universal language of 0 and 1, into
which they will translate the languages of the five senses. . . . It was

only the need to survive on a dangerous planet sculpted by gravity, covered with oxygen and nitrogen, and illuminated by a sun that led carbon creatures to grow feet for walking and ears for hearing and eyes for seeing. . . . For silicon beings, 100,000 light-years will be as a day's journey on earth, or . . . as a refreshing sleep from which . . . they will awaken with no sense of passage of time or . . . with visions "Of what is past, or passing, or to come."

Part 2
Poetics

Aristotle and the Future of Tragedy

FLETCHER COLLINS, JR.

Having presented a theory of tragedy that has dominated dramatic criticism ever since, Aristotle's *Poetics* might be expected to have included a few specific comments about the musical element of the classic dramas. While he describes and analyzes the plays' literary contents, he reflects little of the nature of a performance-oriented element, the melodies to which substantial sections of the plays were sung, and of which we have no notational record.

Writing or lecturing at the Lyceum in Athens seventy-some years after the great Greek composers were dead, Aristotle was chiefly concerned with literary, philosophical, and abstract analyses. But this rigorous examination was not only retrospective; it also developed something quite divergent: the introduction of a new art in his time. It is an art that "imitates by words alone . . . and has been nameless up to the present time."[1] Had he been in the service of a modern editor he might have had to accept for the title of his lecture *The New Poetry,* instead of *On the Art of Making.* There had already been proclaimed a "New Music."

Like Plato before him, Aristotle had difficulty accepting music as a serious art rather than a form of entertainment. He admits musical-instrument playing to his list of the performing arts—at least "most forms of flute- [*aulos,* a single-reed woodwind] and lyre-playing," but later in the treatise he curtly dismisses music in the plays, perhaps because it is no longer needed by the New Poetry, which was spoken; or because the musical elements in the decadent performances of his day were sensational and vulgar; or because music was less open to abstraction. On the latter point he means "by diction [verse] the act, itself, of making metrical compositions, and by melody, what is completely obvious." So much for melody!

"The power of tragedy," he says, "is felt even without a dramatic performance and actors." The threat of the populist theater in Athens, acclaim for the vulgar—all the kind of thing Aristotle ab-

31

horred in his ideated, aristocratic society—he could avoid by reading the text of the play, by analyzing and evaluating it as literature.
Later in the treatise he goes so far as to place the seeing and
reading of a play on equal footing: "Tragedy even without action
[or unstaged] achieves its function simply by reading."

There are several undercurrents here. For one, Aristotle differ-
entiates theatrical form and content from those of dramatic literature. For another, he claims that the power of the play can be felt
without the bother of its music, and its production and performance—anytime, anywhere—by just reading it. At a similar moment of theatrical decline millennia later, and probably influenced
by Aristotle, Dr. Samuel Johnson proclaimed, "a play read affects
the mind like a play acted." Charles Lamb, moreover, opted for
preferring to read *King Lear.* Aristotle tops this attitude, which he
apparently originated, by saying that "The . . . length . . . of the
physical viewing of the performance is not a matter related to the
art of poetry." The experience of a play in the theater is social;
the experience of a dramatic poem is bookish, solitary, and retrospective, today as then.

We might excuse Aristotle for this divisive and diminishing attitude by supposing that in his day he rarely went to the amphitheater, it having become sensational and vulgar, and that his
experience of the classic plays of yesteryear was largely bookish,
from manuscripts which had no musical notation. A. Gudeman
calculates that Aristotle had acquaintance with about three hundred plays, but only a fraction of these were in production in his
time, and then in degraded form for the postwar audience.[2]

The effect of this attitude to Greek theater art has been disastrous to our understanding of it. As Stephen Halliwell says, "It is
perhaps . . . the most disappointing fact about the *Poetics* that it
does nothing to enrich for us the significance of lyric poetry in
Greek tragedy, and that it may even obstruct, or distract from,
the difficult effort now needed to recover this significance."[3] As a
consequence there is still in academia, where the great plays may
be revived, a dichotomy between Greek Theater Works and Greek
Dramatic Literature, and between studies of theater of any period
and studies of dramatic literature. "If," as Halliwell continues, "we
read the *Poetics* as a text which belongs to a philosophical system
. . . we should not have any difficulty in seeing the significance of
Aristotle's attempt to turn the poet into an artist who is the maker
not of materials for the theatre . . . but of poetic constructs—
muthoi. . . . This philosophical enterprise . . . accounts for the

strong thrust in the *Poetics* towards a theoretical separation of poetry from performance, drama from the theatre."[4]

The consequences of this schism have streamed down the centuries and pretty much determined how modern students and lovers of theater interpret one of the great bodies of theatrical works. We remain today in relation to the classic Greek plays more passive, academic, and readerly than has been the case with interpreters of Shakespeare's plays. Their performance tradition has continued strong enough to flow through and irrigate the purely literary understandings of such as S. H. Butcher's colleagues, A. C. Bradley and Gilbert Murray and has kept at least one eye on the plays as theater, for which they were composed. Unfortunately for us, and potentially for the Greeks, the recovery of the musical tradition of their dramas is extremely difficult, even archaeological, although not more impossible than many a dig.

Beginning with the *Poetics* and trying to enlarge its view, we have first to look at the musical content of the plays. What do we know for certain about the quality and importance of the melodies to which much of the plays were sung? S. H. Butcher set the pace of twentieth-century answers. Echoing Aristotle, he speaks of "the dependent position which music occupied among the Greeks. It was one of the accessories of poetry, to which it was strictly subordinate, and consisted of comparatively simple strains."[5] Butcher similarly quotes Plato in *Laws,* "When there are no words . . . it is very difficult to recognize the meaning of harmony or rhythm, or to see that any worthy object is imitated by them." Telescoping the eras of play production and dramatic literature, he assumes that Aristotle speaks for the playwrights, who were not philosophers or proponents of the New Poetry, where poetry and philosophy prevailed, but had been practicing poet-composers or music-dramatists.

Aristotle's use of *harmonia* as one of the elements of dramatic song has vexed translators and left their readers with little insight into the classic Greek playwrights' method of composition. Early in chapter 1 Aristotle finds that the auditory performance arts "accomplish imitation through rhythm and speech and harmony [*harmonia*], making use of these elements separately or in combination." Later, in chapter 6, he expands on the musical aspect; in italics I supplement his explanations:

Golden: I mean by "language that has been artistically enhanced,"

Golden: that which is accompanied by rhythm and harmony and song;

Collins: that which is accompanied by rhythm and *harmonia, the three elements combining as* song *(melopoeia)*;

Golden: and by the phrase "each of the kinds of linguistic adornment applied separately in the various parts of the play,"
Collins: As above plus *these parts being those that are sung and those that are spoken.*

Golden: I mean that some parts are accomplished by meter alone,
Collins: I mean that some parts, *those that are spoken, such as narrative and dialogue,* are accomplished by meter alone, *without rhythm or harmonia, which are components of melody (melos),*

Golden: and others, in turn, through song.
Collins: and other *parts of the play—odes et al.—are accomplished not only by meter but also by rhythm and harmonia in order to become* song *(melopoeia).*[6]

To translate *harmonia* as modern English "harmony," as in music, is to fail to search for the Greek meanings of the word, and hence to misread portions of chapters 1 and 6. Clearly *harmonia* does not mean vertical harmony and polyphonic composition, the use of several voices on several pitches simultaneously. The Greeks had no such theory or practice. What *harmonia* means to Aristotle we can begin to see from its root, the verb *harmozo:* to join together pieces as in masonry and carpentry; a linkage.[7] In the making of a melody, this would be the serial connections of its pitches from beginning to end of the projected melody. These intervallics, musicologically speaking, do not by themselves make a complete melody; rhythm must be added, it being as Plato says, "order within movement."[8] Euripides gives us a vivid, nontheoretical impression in his nightingale "weaving her fine-spun *harmonia* in the trees,"[9] the rhythmless sounds being indeed *harmonia.*

The composed (or borrowed) intervallic pattern is unique to the composition, but is meanwhile screened to allow only those pitches that are in the scale of the chosen *mode:* Dorian, Lydian, Phrygian, or whatever. This choice of mode is one which modern melodists have not had to make. Our modes have atrophied to only two, major and minor, and since the Middle Ages have been permitted to alternate within a melody. Anglo-American folk melodies retain the ancient idea of mode and American fiddlers and banjoists their "tunings," the changing of pitch of one or more open strings to permit the proper "lay" of a modal tune.

Also involved in the Greek melodist's making of a melody is the

meter of the words. The profile of the melody, and its agreement
with the mode, must have been basically influenced by the meter.
A fine example of Greek use of modal "tuning" in association with
a traditional meter is given in Aristotle's *Politics:* "The dithyramb,
for example, is acknowledged to be Phrygian, a fact of which the
connoisseurs of music offer many proofs, saying, among other
things, that Philoxenus, having attempted to compose his *Mysians*
as a dithyramb in the Dorian mode, found it impossible, and fell
back by the very nature of things into the more appropriate
Phrygian."[10]

Harmonia may therefore be identified as having two symbiotic
meanings: the unique intervallic profile of pitches on its way to
becoming a melody and the profile of pitches required by the chosen traditional mode. The creative is filtered through the traditional
mode; its control gave it an ethical significance. Aristotle of course
assumed that his readers were aware of this musical convention,
and so used *harmonia* to include both the created pattern and its
screen. He recognized that even at this point in the crafting of a
melody the rhythm was still lacking, hence his listing of *harmonia*
separately from rhythm.

Later in this essay I shall describe the striking correspondence
between this method of making a song and the method used in the
making of the twelfth-century religious music-dramas and the court
songs of the troubadours and trouvères.

I do not find necessary a roll call of translators and commenta-
tors who have bypassed or run aground on Aristotle's *harmonia.*
Their approach being literary and philosophical, they have not had
to face the complexities of classic Greek musical practice. Even
Joseph Halliwell, an ardent champion of the need for inclusion of
music in our attempt to perform the classic tragedies, nowhere
mentions harmony or *harmonia.* Butcher in his translation expresses a qualm by enclosing *harmony* in single quotes, and passes
the ball to Munro. Golden three times writes *harmony* (no quotes).
O. B. Hardison, in his excellent commentary on Golden's translation, comes close in defining *harmonia* as "a relation of tones."
R. P. Winnington-Ingram is likewise half-right in saying of *harmonia* that "this word is probably rightly translated 'modes,' for
the opinion of Munro who equated them with *tonoi* has not won
acceptance."[11]

We might today be able to simulate, even realize or recreate, the
melodies for the plays *if* we could project the intervallic pitches.
We have a comprehension of the modes and which one was appropriate to which verbal meter, and we have the words. (Three sides

of a Euclidean trapezoid may perhaps identify the fourth.) The example of the twelfth-century music-dramas and court songs is encouraging. While notation exists for their pitch profiles—a large plus—in other respects we are no more informed about the medieval than about the Greek. The medieval notation is without indication of rhythm, the measure and something of the rhythm being derived from the meter of the verses. It was medieval practice to compose the verses first—Aristotle would approve—and to align the musical phrases to the lines of verse, the complete melody to the strophe or other verse form. The medieval modes, while less stringent than those of the Greeks, operated in the same fashion to formulate the pitch profile. Altogether, then, the documented positions of music in the two Western representatives of the high art of music-drama have much in common. One might add that their plots *(muthos)* are analogous also, the medieval narratives derived from the *New Testament* and saints' legends. This comprehensive analogy may, I submit, be profitably explored for the illumination of the nature of the Greek drama and for correction of Aristotle's lamentably influential view of it.

It was not until the midtwentieth century that several of us began to learn the means of transcribing the medieval plays into plausible modern notation from the manuscripts, and of staging them in their church settings in the full bloom of their musico-poetic expression and theatrical beauty. The earlier predicament with those plays had been much like those still obtaining with the Greek. Karl Young's monumental *Drama of the Medieval Church* (1933, 1962) contained the literary texts of the medieval music-dramas, without a note of music transcription, just the Latin words in a rich variety of metrical patterns, as in modern editions of the Greek plays.

Although without hard documentary field evidence, I venture to suggest that a possible clue to the recreation of the pitch profiles and mensural rhythms of the Greek melodies might be found in an intensive study of modern Greek folk music. Admittedly the foreign forces of upheaval in that part of the world, in particular the disturbances by Arabian and Turkish folk music, may have modified the folk-music style of the classic Greeks, on which the classic playwrights considerably depended. The encouraging fact is that folk styles in music are held very tenaciously, over many centuries and despite major influences for change. Marius Schneider reminds us that "melodic types migrate only when the people migrate. It is certainly a great error to imagine that wherever some foreign utensil or cultural object has been introduced, the corresponding music must inevitably have been adopted as well."[12] One may also reflect that the work of the best artists from all periods is more like than unlike, the sources of human creativeness being universal and immutable.

In puzzling over the intramensural rhythms of certain melodic phrases in the medieval scores, I have frequently found solutions by reference to my own hoard of Anglo-American folksongs, similar versions having been earlier collected in great quantities by F. J. Child without a note of music.[13] There are formulaic, stock phrases that have been orally transmitted as customary, and Greek musicologists suspect that many of the Greek verses are indeed formulaic.[14] There are musical stock phrases in the medieval repertory of *Alleluias* and without doubt similarly in contemporary Greek folk music, vocal and instrumental. To my knowledge no one has yet systematically investigated this music for its recollections of the old Hellenic style, or has a likeness in lines of verse been sought and related to how it is, and may have been, sung.

Other than in the oral tradition we can expect nothing musically useful to have come down to us from the classic Greek. There is a stony notation for two Delphic hymns dating from the second century B.C., but that is about all. Without notation, orality is all there can be, which is another reason to dig deeply into the shards and middens of modern Greek folksong, now perhaps most authentic on the more remote islands.

An analogous situation has lately developed in efforts to transcribe in retrospect the melodies Ambrose used to set his hymns in the fourth century A.D., from the abundant musical notation of twelfth-century hymnbooks, one of them originating in Ambrose's Milan church. As transcribed by Bruno Stäblein, the notation lacks mensural rhythm in the manner described above; pitch profiles are a *harmonia*.[15] But a hint may be taken from the documented fact that Ambrose created these hymns for his sanctuaried congregation, to sing and march around in the freezing temperatures of Ambrose's stony basilica. A legend adds that Ambrose, himself earlier in the military, borrowed the melodies from the marching songs of Roman legionnaires. Retranscription of Stäblein's unrhythmed notation uncannily falls into marching metrics. Of course Ambrose could have composed the melodies in imitation of the Roman marches, but if the latter were known to him he was probably too busy a leader to invent what he could easily remember and borrow. There are similar adaptations by Luther and Wesley of folk melodies, on the excuse that "it was a pity," as Wesley said, "to let the Devil have all the good tunes."

To return to Aristotle, lecturing in his Lyceum. He was necessarily a product of his time and place, both of them unfavorable to continued performance of the classic repertory. The song culture was giving way to a book culture. Athens did better with spectator sports, with entertainments and increased vulgarities. "Why," Aristotle asks in *Politics,* "should we learn it [music] ourselves instead of enjoying the performance of others? . . . We call professional performers vulgar; no freeman would play or sing unless he were intoxicated or in jest." Yet he admits that "music is one of the pleasantest things, whether with or without song."[16] Aristophanes in the *Clouds* contrasts the postwar style with the earlier classics. "The new music was no longer virile, taut, *entonos*—well-tuned and unwavering; it was marked by flamboyant *kampai* ('bends') and by a formless flexibility of melodic line. . . . The modernist tragedian Agathon appears on the stage [and] when he sings his voice is like the zigzagging of ants."[17]

If this is what music had come to in the amphitheater, Aristotle had reason to take himself and the serious art of poetry out of it, even at the cost of leaving us as yet unfulfilled about the music of the great dramas.

Notes

1. All quotations from the *Poetics* are from the translation of Leon Golden, *Aristotle's Poetics: A Translation and Commentary for Students of Literature,* commentary by O. B. Hardison (Englewood Cliffs, N.J.: Prentice-Hall, 1968).
2. A. Gudeman, *Aristoteles: Poetik* (1934).
3. Stephen Halliwell, *Aristotle's Poetics* (London: Duckworth, 1986), 252.
4. Ibid., 343.
5. S. H. Butcher, *Aristotle's Theory of Poetry and Fine Art* (1894; 4th ed. New York: Dover Publications, 1951), 130.
6. I am grateful to Janet Lembke for enlightening me on the basic nomenclature for "parts of the play."
7. Paraphrased from H. G. Liddell and Robert Scott, *A Greek-English Lexicon,* 9th ed. (Oxford: Clarendon Press, 1940), 244.
8. In Plato's *Nomoi.*
9. I am indebted to Isobel Henderson, "Ancient Greek Music," in *Grove's Dictionary of Music and Musicians,* 9 vols. (New York: St. Martin's Press, 1954), 1:384, for this quotation from fragment 773.
10. *Politics,* translated by Benjamin Jowett in R. McKeon, ed., *The Basic Works of Aristotle* (New York: Random House, 1941), 1316.
11. In Leonard Whibley's *A Companion to Greek Studies,* 4th ed., rev. (Cambridge: Cambridge University Press, 1931), 372.
12. "Primitive Music," in *New Oxford History of Music,* 10 vols. (London: Oxford University Press, 1957), 1:28.
13. The melodies have since been added by B. H. Bronson, *The Traditional*

Tunes of the Child Ballads, 4 vols. (Princeton: Princeton University Press, 1959–72).

14. See Henderson, "Ancient Greek Music," 392–93.

15. Bruno Stäblein, ed., *Monumenta Monodica Medii Aevi* (Kassel: Barenreiter, 1956), vol. 1.

16. McKeon, ed., *Politics,* 1310.

17. Paraphrased by Henderson, "Ancient Greek Music," 393.

Katharsis in the Twentieth Century: The Paradigm Shifts

LEON GOLDEN

In his important edition of the *Poetics* published in 1909, Ingram Bywater included an appendix on the various translations of the term *katharsis* that had appeared from the sixteenth century (the first entry is 1527) to the end of the nineteenth century (the final entry is 1899). Nearly all of these translations, certainly all of the important and influential ones, express one of two views concerning the nature of Aristotelian *katharsis:* (1) that the term represents "medical purgation" or (2) that it signifies "moral purification."

When, in 1979, Donald Keesey wrote an article entitled "On Some Recent Interpretations of Catharsis," he found a very different situation in effect.[1] The orthodox interpretations of "purgation" and "purification" had certainly not disappeared but several new lines of interpretation had opened up, bringing forward new translations of *katharsis.* At least one of these new interpretative directions, the one that viewed *katharsis* as "intellectual clarification," was very much in harmony with the way in which a number of modern critics and scholars who were not classicists or philologists understood the goal and pleasure of tragedy. Keesey points out that these critics and scholars were dissatisfied with the orthodox philological analysis of *katharsis* as "purgation" or "purification" and, in rebellion against views that did not make sense to them, had gone on, independently as they thought of Aristotle, to develop their own theories of tragic effect and pleasure that were essentially cognitive in nature.

Thus John Gassner had argued that "enlightenment" that brings about "an understanding of cause and effect" was a decisive feature of *katharsis.*[2] Other perceptive critics also recognized an important cognitive goal in artistic experience. Francis Fergusson identified "perception" as the climactic stage of the audience's aesthetic experience; James Joyce used the term *epiphany* to describe the point at which an audience discovers the inner coherence of a work of

40

art; and Austin Warren used the phrase "rage for order" to designate the goal of the poet and the aspiration of the reader of poetry.

In 1991 Mathias Luserke edited a series of nineteenth- and twentieth-century interpretative essays on the nature of *katharsis*.[3] His volume reflects the powerful influence of Jakob Bernays, who revived the "purgation" theory of *katharsis* in the nineteenth century and extended its influence widely. The contributions of Schadewaldt, Flashar, and Pohlenz, included in Luserke's work, and which he correctly judges still to be highly influential, operate in the shadow of Bernays' emphatic insistence on the role of medical purgation in the aesthetic response to tragedy. Such highly regarded philological studies demonstrate the still-powerful hold of orthodoxy on current academic approaches to the interpretation of *katharsis*. But Luserke also included in his anthology two studies that argued for *katharsis* as clarification, an interpretation that has emerged only in the twentieth century and that Keesey recognized as both a viable alternative to "purgation" and "purification," one that was far more in harmony with the way contemporary critics and aestheticians were thinking about the nature of tragedy. Thus, while the traditional interpretations of *katharsis* show no signs of disappearing from the scene, it is also evident that both inside and outside philological circles a cognitive view of *katharsis*, unknown before the twentieth century, has begun to take hold.

I shall argue in this essay that what has occurred in twentieth-century scholarship on *katharsis* is analogous to what Thomas Kuhn has called a "paradigm shift" in the natural sciences. Kuhn pointed out that scientific theories maintain their influence so long as their explanatory capabilities remain broad and powerful. Whenever data are discovered that begin to subvert the explanatory power of a theory, and this happens with a certain regularity in the natural sciences, the possibility opens up for new and different theories to supplant the previously orthodox one. We shall see that Kuhn's concept is as relevant to aesthetics as it is to the sciences.

In order to understand the nature of the paradigm shift that I suggest is now at work in the interpretation of *katharsis*, we must first clarify the basis for the two dominant, orthodox interpretations of *katharsis*. Those two interpretations were developed within the relatively closed world of classical philology as it operated in the period from the sixteenth through the beginning of the twentieth century. Classical scholars and others found the term *katharsis* enigmatic in the *Poetics* because no formal definition of the term is given in that work. They then proceeded to search for information in the text of Aristotle's other works that could help

them understand *katharsis,* since they recognized that this term
was critical for their comprehension of Aristotle's theory of tragedy. They found two texts that they could privilege as sources for
interpreting the term. The first such text, and the one on which
Jakob Bernays placed great emphasis in his highly influential work
on the medical purgation theory of *katharsis,* is *Politics* 1342.a.1–16
where Aristotle tells us that

> It is thus apparent that we must make use of all the harmonies but we
> must not use all of them in the same way. Rather, we must use the
> most ethical ones for education and those which arouse and inspire
> emotion for hearing when others are playing (for whatever emotion is
> found in an extreme form in some natures also occurs in all natures,
> although it differs in degree, for example pity and fear, and also reli-
> gious ecstasy). For some people are susceptible of being possessed by
> such emotions and we see that these, whenever they make use of melo-
> dies which excite their spirit to mystic frenzy, are brought into a stable
> condition by the religious melodies, as if they had obtained medical
> treatment and katharsis. It is necessary for the same thing to occur to
> those who experience pity and fear, and those who are, in general,
> emotional in nature, and others to the degree that each of them is
> affected by such emotions. And for all there occurs some kind of ka-
> tharsis and relief which is accompanied by pleasure.

Here Bernays had found another use of *katharsis* in an Aristotelian
text and assumed that it had to have the same meaning in this
passage of the *Politics* as it did in the *Poetics.* Bernays, and those
who follow him in this interpretation, apparently were and are not
troubled by the consequences of their identification of aesthetic
katharsis with medical "purgation." For the acceptance of *katharsis* as medical "purgation" requires us, as we shall soon see, to
consider the audience for tragedy to be in a state of psychological
or somatic illness. Yet it has never (to my knowledge) been alleged,
and certainly never demonstrated, that the audiences for Greek
tragedy, or any other audiences, have been in a state of mental,
emotional, or somatic illness at the time when they have sought
out the experience of witnessing tragedy.

Other philologists, before the twentieth century, perhaps because they found the "purgation" explanation unconvincing,
looked elsewhere for help and they discovered it in the *Nicomachean Ethics* 1106.b.16–23, where Aristotle says the following:

> And I mean moral virtue for this is concerned with feelings and actions
> and in these there exists the possibility of excess, deficiency and the

proper mean. For example it is possible to be frightened, to be daring, to desire, to be angry, to pity, and, in general, to feel pleasure and pain either more or less than one should and in both cases in an improper way. But to experience these feelings at those times and occasions when they are appropriate and toward those objects and on those grounds and in those manners which are appropriate is both what is best and represents the mean which is the sign of virtue.

Scholars who were impressed by the mention of "pity" in this passage argued that *katharsis* (even though that term does not appear in this text) must be the process of attuning emotions like pity to be in accord with the proper mean discussed by Aristotle here. An important consequence of their reasoning was to make aesthetic experience a function of moral training and education since it would operate, under the conditions set forth in the *Nicomachean Ethics,* to make an audience truly virtuous by training it to experience the proper mean of all emotions. Holders of this view have never explained how works of art in general are capable of accomplishing such a task or even why such a task is an appropriate function of aesthetic activity. Unconvinced by "purgation," these philologists searched for help in other Aristotelian texts and found a passage in the *Nicomachean Ethics* that gave them an interpretation which they preferred to the medical one. Their view, however, has found very little favor with critics, scholars, and aestheticians, who refuse to identify aesthetics with ethics. Nevertheless, the idea continues to appear from time to time in philological discussions and one recent analysis argues for *katharsis* as a hybrid form of "purification" and "purgation."

In the twentieth century another way of looking at the problem of *katharsis* has come to the fore. It emphasizes two principles: that the proper way of understanding Aristotle's real meaning in regard to *katharsis* must arise from a careful analysis of the text itself; and that insights derived from experts on the way in which words influence the human mind are highly relevant to an understanding of how the words of Greek poets influenced the minds of Greek audiences. We must credit the work of Gerald Else for opening up the first of these two lines of interpretation. Richard McKeon had already argued that the first principles of individual works of both Plato and Aristotle could be significantly different and thus that each work had to be interpreted within its own context rather than by comparison to other texts by the same authors. Else strongly asserted this principle in regard to the *Poetics* when he argued that the work must be interpreted, primarily and essentially, on the basis of its own internal argument. Even more important was his confrontation with the "purgation" theory of *katharsis*. In his edition of the *Poetics* Else writes (440):[4]

> . . . there is another objection to Bernays' interpretation, which would long since have been recognized as fatal if the authority of the *Politics* passage had not been accepted as beyond dispute. His interpretation, no matter how adapted or refined, is inherently and indefeasibly *therapeutic*. It presupposes that we come to the tragic drama (unconsciously, if you will) as patients to be cured, relieved, restored to psychic health. But there is not a word to support this in the *Poetics,* not a hint that the end of the drama is to cure or alleviate pathological states. On the contrary it is evident in every line of the work that Aristotle is presupposing *normal* auditors, normal states of mind and feeling, normal emotional and aesthetic experience.

By explicitly asserting the fact that there is no evidence in the *Poetics* to support the "purgation" theory of *katharsis,* Else emancipated philologists (or at least some of them) from the dead weight of a rather improbable tradition. Moreover, one could easily apply his reasoning to the "purification" theory to show that no evidence in the *Poetics* supports that view as well. Else's work made it respectable to look elsewhere than "purgation" and "purification" for assistance in understanding *katharsis,* and thus it is no surprise that Keesey's survey, unlike Bywater's, contained a number of new attempts to define this important term.

Else proceeded to develop a new interpretation of *katharsis* that saw the term as representing "the purification of the tragic act by the demonstration that its motive was not *miaron* [morally polluted]." This view has not developed a large following and cannot be said to have displaced the older theories of "purgation" and "purification." Yet Else, who strongly resisted recognizing *katharsis* as a cognitive act, still did take an important step in that direction in his own definition of *katharsis*. For how else could we judge that the tragic act was not morally polluted except by an act of intellectual analysis that would trigger a moral judgment?

Else was a skilled philologist and a rebel against orthodoxy but neither his skill nor his rebellion extricated him from the consequences of recognizing only two interpretative possibilities for the Greek term *katharsis:* "purgation" or "purification." Nor in the period when he was forming his views of *katharsis* did he have the benefit of two important studies of the way in which words impact on human beings in aesthetic and medical contexts. Four important steps had to be taken before Else's effective challenge to an unper-

suasive orthodoxy could be supplemented by a radically new interpretation of *katharsis* that was free of the fatal charge of irrelevance
to the actual text of the *Poetics*.

The first task was a philological one: to determine if, in reality,
"purgation" and "purification" were the only viable options for
translating *katharsis*. This problem was solved with no more effort
than that involved in opening an unabridged Greek lexicon, for
katharsis is attested not only in the orthodox meanings of "purgation" and "purification" but also as a philosophical term signifying
"intellectual clarification." Moreover, Plato's statement at
Theaetetus 230. D-E that *elenchos*, the Socratic process of pursuing ultimate truth through a technique of cross-examination, is "the
greatest and most authoritative of all forms of *katharsis*," is clear
evidence that *katharsis* bore an intellectual meaning in the philosophical milieu that Aristotle inhabited. The obvious next step was
to see if *katharsis* in this intellectual sense effectively addressed
the question of relevance to the text of the *Poetics*, the all-
important test that both "purgation" and "purification" failed. It
turned out to be extremely easy to demonstrate this point, for
Aristotle argues in chapter 4 of the *Poetics* that the essential pleasure and final cause of artistic activity is the pleasure of "learning
and inference" and that this pleasure is rooted in our human nature
and one in which we all share in various degrees. Only if *katharsis*
is understood as "intellectual clarification" does the essential information about the ultimate pleasure and final cause of tragedy become a part of Aristotle's definition of tragedy in chapter 6 of the
Poetics, which he explicitly states is a summation of what he has
said up to that point.[5]

The final two advances in establishing "intellectual clarification"
as a potent rival to "purgation" and "purification" were made outside the field of philology. P. Laín Entralgo, a specialist in the
history of medicine who investigated the early development of psy-
chotherapy in Greek culture, showed how words were used in
Greek medicine to evoke a positive psychological effect that could
enhance the healing of somatic disorders. He emphasized the fact
that the "agent of tragic catharsis is not a material purgative, nor
even a melody, but rather that airy, invisible, material and immate-
rial reality that we call the 'word.'"[6] Thus Laín Entralgo argued
that *katharsis* must be understood as a psychological phenomenon
rather than a somatic one. And then Bennett Simon, a practicing
psychiatrist and classical scholar, made it abundantly clear that
words in an aesthetic context and words in a psychotherapeutic

context, while serving different purposes, have one important quality in common:

> Finally, tragedy should bring some altered and new sense of what one is and who he is in relation to those around him. The tragic figures in the plays struggle with their relationships and obligations to those in their past, present, and, future. The audience acquires a new sense of the possibilities in being human and in coming to terms with forces that are more powerful than any one individual. In therapy we also expect an enlarged view of the possibilities that are open in relationships to the self and to others. Thus good therapy and good theater have in common a set of inner processes. Theater is not, and was not for the Greeks, primarily intended to be therapy for especially disturbed or distressed people. It was expected to provide a certain form of pleasure, even in Greek culture, and was an integral part of the *paideia* (education in the broadest sense) of each Athenian.[7]

With these four steps taken, the older, orthodox interpretations of *katharsis* find themselves increasingly under challenge, under stress. If "intellectual clarification" continues to find favor as a viable option for our understanding of *katharsis* because it is a more powerful and satisfying explanation of what we actually experience in tragedy, the challenge to "purgation" and "purification" will become overwhelming and the stress intolerable. Then the paradigm will have shifted and a new interpretative orthodoxy will influence the way we think about *katharsis* as a key aesthetic concept.

Notes

1. Donald Keesey, "On Some Recent Interpretations of Catharsis," *Classical World* 72 (1979): 193–205.

2. Ibid., 197.

3. Mathias Luserke, *Die Aristotelische Katharsis* (Hildesheim: Georg Olm, 1991).

4. *Aristotle's Poetics: The Argument* (Cambridge: Harvard University Press, 1957).

5. For detailed arguments relating to this issue see L. Golden and O. B. Hardison, Jr., *Aristotle's Poetics: A Translation and Commentary for Students of Literature* (Tallahassee: Florida State University Press, 1981): L. Golden, "Catharsis," *Transactions of the American Philological Association* 93 (1962): 51–60; and L. Golden, "The Clarification Theory of *Katharsis*" *Hermes* 104 (1976): 437–52.

6. See *The Therapy of the Word in Classical Antiquity* (New Haven: Yale University Press, 1970), 27.

7. See *Mind and Madness in Ancient Greece* (Ithaca: Cornell University Press, 1978), 144.

Poetry and Epistemology: How "Words, after speech, reach / Into the silence. . . ."

T. V. F. BROGAN

In 1941 Wallace Stevens gave a lecture at Princeton called "The Noble Rider and the Sound of Words"; the rider, is, from the *Phaedrus*, the soul, and the horses are two, noble and base: Stevens is interested, in this lecture as everywhere else, in the imagination and in how the sound of words, in poetry, affects the imagination, i.e., the soul. In the middle of the lecture Stevens makes a remark that, so far as I know, has never been noticed since, despite the fact that critical interest in Stevens's work and theory of poetry is more intense now than at any other time in history. The remark is disarmingly simple: Stevens says, "a poet's words are of things that do not exist without the words." In what follows I hope to make this remark open up to show us something fundamental about the nature of poetry, and about what in philosophy would be called the ontological status of art objects, about the nature and effect of repetition, and hence finally about the nature of knowledge itself, and what knowledge has to do with words. My aim throughout is to show that the close analysis of poetry—disparaged in the nineteenth century as "technical," hence unfaithful to the spirit of art (as if art [Gr. *techne*] were anything *but* technique), and disparaged again in the later twentieth century as formalist—is not only related to "theory," i.e. to more fundamental epistemological issues, but in fact entails them. Put succinctly, textual analysis itself, as methodology, always already entails a metaphysics. That metaphysics is based on the nature of words and on how words are deployed in poetry. But for the present I merely want to repeat Stevens's line and to ask you to hold it in abeyance: "a poet's words are of things that do not exist without the words." We want to know how that can be.

Heterometric Donne

As Polonius says, we must by indirections find directions out, and so I begin with John Donne, great English poet sacred and

profane, Catholic turned Anglican on account of persecution, later
Dean of St. Paul's. In the early part of his life Donne was something
of a rake; later he married for love, a disastrous move politically
for which he suffered nearly ten years; thereafter, his recovered
influence with the King got him what amounted to a bishopric. Out
of this latter period of his life come what most would see as a good
half dozen of the greatest religious poems in the language. But the
poetry of Donne's early period, the *Songs and Sonets* as they were
called when published posthumously, is equally good, though very
different: its theme is love in all its vicissitudes—affection playful
and serious, inconstancy actual or feared, desire mental and physical, jealousy, anguish, and anger—all the usual emotions. But
Donne's poems cut much deeper than merely the vicissitudes of
the life of the emotions: they explore, through that, the nature of
what it means to have a body *and* a mind *and* a soul, especially
when these are not entirely on speaking terms with each other.

As an artist, however, Donne is important because he is more
inventive than perhaps any other poet of the seventeenth century
(the closest competitor is George Herbert) in terms of trying the
largest number of different forms. The *Holy Sonnets* are of course
regular, but the early lyrics of the *Songs and Sonets* are extraordinarily diverse. In fact, the only thing that one can say about all of
them is that they all are set in stanzas. Beyond that, the stanzas
are not the same size, shape, or length, not only from one poem
to the next, but even within one poem itself. This is amazing and
demands some sort ot taxonomy to help us categorize the varieties
of form; what is more amazing still is that no such systematic
taxonomy of stanzaic structures has ever been given for English
poetry. Let us map out the main lines of what one would look like.

The norm in English poetry, as in every other poetry I know, is
that a poet who chooses to write a stanzaic poem (that is, a poem
of more than one stanza) chooses a pattern—say, a quatrain of
four lines in iambic tetrameter having the rhyme scheme *abba*.
The poet does this for the first stanza of the poem, and every other
stanza thereafter follows the same pattern. After the first stanza
the particular rhymes change, of course, but the *abba* rhyme pattern does not. This is what I call *isostrophic* verse: subsequent
stanzas all conform to the first—in classical metrics they are said
to be in *responsion*. Further, it is the norm in English poetry, as
in every other poetry, that the lines of the first stanza, and so every
stanza in the poem, are also of equal length: this is what I call
isometric verse. This too is the norm in all English poetry, whether
stanzaic or not; probably 99 percent of English verse is isometric.
But the poem might not be isostrophic or not isometric or neither.

So we have four possibilities: either the pattern of the first stanza of the poem is followed identically thereafter or it is not; and either the lines of that stanza are all the same length or they are not— thus, isostrophic, heterostrophic, isometric, heterometric.

It is simple fact that most of the poems written in English from Chaucer to Tennyson and Browning are isometric: not only all the poems that are in stanzas, but also all the poems that are in running nonstanzaic verse such as blank verse and the couplet, for example, both written in iambic pentameters and estimated to amount to about three-quarters of all English poetry. But it is from heterometric verse—verse forms that are not normative, but marginal, written at the edges of the convention—that we can learn the most about how poetry really works.

Donne, most of the time, is isostrophic but heterometric: that is, he is interested in writing stanzas whose lines are not all of the same length and in uncovering what effects such structures can achieve. This is in fact rare in English poetry, but not at all ineffective. Quite the contrary: most readers have found Donne's poems extremely powerful. There is a good article waiting to be written about heterometric Donne, and indeed about heterometric verse in general, all of which is uncharted territory.

Heterometric verse comes in several varieties. The one that comes to mind first is the Pindaric ode, popular in the eighteenth century and instanced importantly in Wordsworth's Intimations Ode, but this kind of verse is not metrical nor rhymed in the same sense as Donne's poem: it is in a different category. Closer are the Sapphic in Greek, the elegiac distich in Latin, what is called tail rhyme in French and English, and the Middle English bob and wheel: these are stanzas of long lines closed by one or two short ones. Stanzas of shorter lines closed by a longer one or ones include the Spenserian stanza, where eight lines of ten syllables are followed by a ninth line of twelve syllables. Stanzas that alternate longer and shorter lines include particularly ballad meter, which has form of most of the popular verse written in English since the thirteenth century: stanzas of four lines, each line having 4 or 3 stresses in certain specific patterns: 4-3-4-3 and 3-3-4-3. One might think that 3-4-3-4 and 4-4-4-4 and 3-3-3-3 and half a dozen other patterns would work, too, but they do not, and nobody has yet explained why.

Close Rhyme

Donne's poems explore the possibilities and limits of heterometric verse. His most spectacular exhibition is in the early "Song":

Go and catch a falling star,
  Get with child a mandrake root,
Tell me where all past years are,
  Or who cleft the Devil's foot,
Teach me to hear mermaids singing,
  Or to keep off envy's stinging,
        And find
        What wind
Serves to advance an honest mind.

If thou be'st born to strange sights,
  Things invisible to see,
Ride ten thousand days and nights,
  Till age snow white hairs on thee,
Thou, when thou return'st, wilt tell me,
  All strange wonders that befell thee,
        And swear
        Nowhere
Lives a woman true, and fair.

If thou findst one, let me know,
  Such a pilgrimage were sweet.
Yet do not; I would not go,
  Though at next door we might meet;
Though she were true, when you met her,
  And last, till you write your letter,
        Yet she
        Will be
False, ere I come, to two, or three.

The theme of the inconstant woman is common in the early Donne, and one of the first issues that arises in discussion of this poem is the relation of gender to tone: we must ask whether or not we ought to take this seriously as a piece of misogyny or treat it as a conceit, a deliberate exaggeration (the first stanza is dense with *adynaton,* the impossibility trope), or even perhaps a drinking song. But what I want to emphasize here is the short seventh and eighth lines of each stanza:

        And find / What wind //
        And swear / Nowhere //
        Yet she / Will be //

Probably the Renaissance pronunciation is "wind" as in "wind the clock," the verbal form: this is almost certainly a good rhyme for Donne, not a visual game: up until the mid-seventeenth century, "poetry" could be pronounced so as to rhyme with "eye" and "die," thus: "poe-try." But what I want to point up is the closeness of the rhymes brought about by the sudden shortness of the lines. This is an interesting phenomenon also never explored, which I call "close rhyme": two words contiguous or very close that rhyme. It is the spatial proximity that is being mapped over the sound proximity. One might think that these would not occur very often in poetry, and on the whole perhaps they do not, but on the other hand they are extremely common in ordinary speech: they are used for idioms, proverbs, catch phrases, and formulaic expressions. Close-rhymed formulae in doublet form are legion: *hobnob, hubbub, humdrum, harum-scarum, hodgepodge, helter-skelter, hurly-burly, ill will, powwow, double trouble, riffraff, true blue, steel wheels.* They also come in trinomials—*fair and square, wear and tear, near and dear, high and dry, make or break, slim and trim.* Slightly longer formulae such as *put the pedal to the metal* almost automatically become metrical (this one a trochaic tetrameter) and thus may form the bridge into poetry itself. It was the philologist Wilhelm Grimm, in the mid-nineteenth century—he of the Brothers Grimm—who suggested that it is from formulas such as these that poetic rhyme itself evolved, by gradually increasing the distances. Perhaps so: there is some evidence for this in a special form of the hexameter in Medieval Latin called *leonine verse.*

In isometric verse the whole point of rhyme is that the sound echo occurs at regular intervals. The rhyme scheme may be elaborate—in the Shakespearean sonnet, for example, the rhyme scheme is *abab cdcd efef gg;* but the intervals between rhymes are regular and even, or else regular multiples, because all the lines are of equal length. But in heterometric verse the rhymes suddenly come closer together—it is axiomatic that heterometric verse is rhymed.

Rhyme is chime, but rhyme is also time. We are accustomed to seeing the lines of poetry on the page, and indeed, Jeremy Bentham has observed that lines are what define poetry to begin with: prose is written in paragraphs, but poetry is in lines. But further thinking about this suggests to me that it is more complicated than that; and the reason is that Bentham's claim takes the word "poetry"— "poetry" is made up of lines—for granted and ignores a number of silent assumptions embedded in it that are not at all certain. This leads us to ask what a poem is, or, better, *where* a poem is: or, in other terms, what is its ontological status, or *situs.* I do not think anyone would want to hold that a poem exists on the page, for if we said that, someone could crumple up the piece of paper and burn it, saying she had destroyed the poem, but we could not

agree with that; there are other copies of the poem. Suppose our
poem-burner then burned all known paper texts of the poem—is
the poem gone? But I have memorized the poem, so it still exists.
Still, I am uncomfortable with saying that poems exist only in our
minds: this verges on Croce's theory that artworks exist in their
creator's mind and the physical manifestation is only a poor sec-
ondhand version of the real artwork the artist imagined. No, we
want to insist that poems and artworks have bodies (like people);
they are not mere ideas. The analogy with music is instructive: I
do not think anybody would say that sheet music is music: music
is what you hear in the concert hall or from a recording: the sheet
music is only marks on paper that by a set of known conventions
are meant as directions for performance. And not everything is
specified in those directions. Even when we hear music from a
recording, the physical material of the recording medium—vinyl
for records, magnetic tape for cassettes—is not the music; it is
only a container. Similarly, the marks on the page are not the poem:
they constitute a set of (incomplete) performance directions for
articulating the poem aloud. The poem won't exist until we speak
it. Poetry, in short, is sound.

I am not sure anybody really takes this seriously, for if they did,
much of what is usually said in the handbooks about the nature of
poetry would have to be changed. For one thing, if poetry is sound
qua sound, poetry does not come in lines, for poetry as spoken,
in the air, is pure soundstream—one continuous run of contiguous
sounds, only punctuated at various points by pauses (and mark-
ers—see below) of varying durations. This means that the way a
poem is laid out on the page is in part merely a response to the
exigencies of the physical size of the codex page, hence an illusion
and not fundamental to the nature of the poem itself. We can see
something of this in primitive poetry written in runes. The poem
is one long string of characters, and the only reason it is not in
one long line is that the stone was not enough, so the engraver
went back to the lefthand margin. If it had been a papyrus roll,
presumably there would have been one long line, just as an unfor-
matted paragraph in a computer file is actually one continuous
string of characters: this chain is wrapped between margins on-
screen only because that is the way we like to see it, but that
format is transient, not constitutive.

Well, all right, but so what? Let us return to rhyme. We think
rhyme marks the ends of lines, but that is page-thinking. In the
soundstream, rhymes are echoing sounds spaced every so often.
Most of the time the spacings are relatively regular, such as every

ten syllables, and a good reader quickly learns to expect them there. So not only is the soundstream broken up by pauses into segments or chunks that are equivalent in length, but further, the ends of the segments are marked, aurally, so that they can be recognized. If the marking were visual rather than aural, every tenth syllable or character would be red, sort of a little red flag, a gesture that happens every now and again, pretty regularly. Why should it help to mark the ends of the segments? Marking their ends reassures us that we are following correctly. In isometric verse, all the segments ("lines") are spaced equally. That is good, but better still is heterometric verse, which is also close-rhymed verse, because here the spacing of the segments is suddenly irregular (though irregular in a regular way; notice that Donne's second and third stanzas are identical to the first). That is why close rhyme is of use: it shows us something about how we experience poetry at close range, up close.

Rhyme as Sound

What close rhyme, indeed all rhyme, shows us is something about the nature of repetition, for in fact rhyme itself is simply one species of repetition. In the textbook definition, a rhyme is a sound echo: rhyme/chime, love/dove, me/thee. But that is only half the story. It is true that the rhyme echoes a sound or sound pattern, and in this repeats it, but at the same time the rhyme words have meaning, of course, and while from the first word to the second the sound is re-presented as the same, the sense is different, so that if one is paying attention, one is always aware, in a rhyme, of sameness and difference simultaneously. The meaning is what we notice first, because that is what all language use has geared us to do since we first said Mama and Dada (each itself a repetition). Most of the time when we use language, we get only one message: we talk or listen only for the meaning, ignoring the sounds of the words. The sound is wholly transparent—we listen straight through it. And rhyming in prose is universally felt to be a distraction and a blemish because it momentarily distracts us from meaning, thickening the medium, the sound of words, into opacity, so that we notice their surface texture and pattern, so that we notice the words as words more than for what they say. In short, rhyming in, say, a novel momentarily turns transparent language into opaque language, and opaque language is simply poetry: that's what poetry is.

The effect of rhyme is to give this *double* message simultaneously. One word alone does not create a rhyme: it takes two. At
the moment that we encounter the second, and in the instantaneous
recognition that this is an echo of what we heard before, we hear
again the sound, and know that, and know too the meanings are
different, and know that too, and simultaneously and further still,
that this echo of same-sound *affects* their meanings and the meaning of the whole. So rhymes give us "double audition." Our mind
is actively following the poem as it unravels on the level of meaning, but underneath that, the rhymes are organizing and structuring
the temporal experience of reading the poem, which really means
the processing of meaning itself. In short, the process of meaning-
construction itself is given order, shape, and form. And all the
other poetic devices—meter, alliteration—have the same effect,
for all function in the same way, by creating a marker or unit or
pattern and then reiterating it (and we will not know it the first
time until it has appeared twice) though the semantic context is
different every time. So even if a poem speaks of chaos, ruin,
disorder, decay, it does so with a substrate that speaks, however
quietly, order, shape, form. No Form, No Speech.

In short, poetry teaches us that our verbal experience of the
world—i.e., language—is fundamentally double. On one level there
is Meaning, but underneath there is Sound. It was precisely this
fact that Saussure pointed to early in this century in the devastating
critique of Western metaphysics that Derrida uses as the basis for
deconstruction. People live on the level of meaning when they talk.
Underneath there is the level of the sounds of the words, but they
are oblivious to that. And underneath the sounds of the words is
the real world. People assume that words connect (through sounds)
to things. But, as Saussure calmly pointed out, the sound structure
of language is wholly arbitrary and capricious, random and unmoti-
vated, and not connected to things in the world at all. There's an
unbridgeable gap between signifiers and signifieds. True enough,
in language. But poetry teaches us that sound itself has a life of
its own on the level of sound. In poetry, even apart from meaning,
sound is active, purely on the level of sound, doing two things:
first, shading and influencing meaning, and second, organizing the
temporal experience of reading by way of repetition. In what follows, I want to anatomize the phenomenology of repetition on the
micro level, moment by moment, as we experience it, for this is
what order does to the flow. Heraclitus was wrong to talk about
putting your hand in the river: we are *in* the river. And the river
is words: we live in the river of language.

Repetition

What happens, at those moments when the rhyme occurs, is what happens in all repetition: what was, in the past, a present moment, is retrieved, further down the line, further along in time, and reenacted, so that what was a present moment at some point in the past is momentarily made the present moment now, in the present. In ordinary life, without repetition, we experience the present for a brief interval—some say up to seven seconds, some say a half-second—and then it is gone, past, history: we move on to a new, different present, and the old experience is gone forever. You are doing this as you read my words right now. Memory may recall it, but memory is a fickle and creative thing. Repetition functions to reinstantiate the present, every so often. It recreates, precisely, the present-that-was as the present-that-is, now—but with one crucial difference: what-was, now become what-is, is augmented over what-is when it was, then, made fuller and richer, by having added to it our inevitable subconscious recognition that time has passed in the meantime, and that what-is, now, is what-was, then, *but also more*. So repetition functions to re-create, to thwart the linear character of time by reinstantiating.

Let us imagine time as a straight line, the *x* axis of a Cartesian graph, stretching from prehistory on the left to the future on the right, with us moving left to right, and occasionally very much against our will. But we do not move on this line from point to point, as classical mathematics would have it: that way Xeno's Paradox lies. The concept of points may be a useful conceptual tool in mathematics, but it is simply irrelevant to our ordinary experience as sentient beings in the world. In our experience of time we move by frames, little chunks of time that constitute a present—brief glimpse-frames that have no particular temporal span to them, though' in clock-time they may well cover several seconds, presumably even longer in, say, meditation. Repetition functions to pick up a preceding frame in the series, which was not so long ago that we have forgotten it, and re-present it. We are aware, if we are fully aware, (1) that it's now; (2) that it was also a now back then; (3) that this is what that felt like, back then; and that (4) it feels that way now again, too, except more so (or less!) for what has come between, and so changed things, however subtly.

Rhyme does this: indeed rhyme itself instantiates this in its very construction as a device, for to make a rhyme we do not say swear/swear, we say swear/where—two syllables with the same medial vowel, same final consonant, but different initial consonant. Sameness and difference are apprehended by the mind in one indivisible simultaneous act that bridges (ignores) the temporal distance between reading the first word and reading the second by overlaying the second frame on the first and finding them the same. And what rhyme does, close rhyme does even more powerfully, for the distance between the frames is very, very short, so it is as if the present is simply carried on, continued, extended even further and never becomes future. Perhaps that is why T. S. Eliot uses a good half-dozen close rhymes in *Four Quartets,* and why, perhaps, he chooses this particular construction to express how "words, after speech, reach / Into silence." For this is in fact the subject of *Four Quartets:* getting off the timeline, either by achieving moments of intense consciousness through memory or reverie *(Burnt Norton),* by escape from the agony of history by way of detachment and the cycle *(East Coker),* by recognition of the vast, slow, ineffable "ground swell" in all matter *(The Dry Salvages),* and by meditation and prayer *(Little Gidding),* to arrive at a space where time no longer exists, no longer matters, no longer ticks. This is sometimes agony, sometimes ecstasy, "when time stops and time is never ending," because the two become indistinguishable. This is "the still point of the turning world," where the dance goes on—"oh do not call it fixity"—because the mind is active and alert, but we no longer walk the line. And if the line is the *x* axis of the Cartesian graph, then the intense moment is the vertical axis. The English language does not have a word for this vertical dimension; *eternity* is as good as any other. What must be said about it is that no maneuver on the horizontal dimension will get us vertical: all such maneuvers are wrong turns. Further, verticality is available at any instant, any point along the line: eternity is not in front of us in the future, nor even above us right now, but in a *wholly different direction* from these, though still always available at any moment, or every moment. This is what I take Eliot to mean, finally: "Not the intense moment / Isolated, with no before and no after, / But a lifetime burning in every moment." And this, too, insofar as I understand him, is what I take Kierkegaard to mean by "the moment." How is it that "words, after speech, reach / Into the silence"? Just this, according to Eliot: "Only by the form, the pattern, / Can words or music reach / The stillness." The pattern is a pattern because it is repetition, and repetition re-creates the present, holds it in stasis, suspending the sequence. When Stevens says that the poet's words are of things that do not exist without the words, he is saying that words are not secondary to our experience of the world, they are primary. In the Bible we are exhorted to "hold fast to the form of sound words" (2 Tim 1:13). We might think that we could apply this by saying that the poet should choose sound words just as a good carpenter chooses sound lumber. But remembering Stevens and his meditation on the poet and the sound of words, we should say rather that words in poetry *are words,* not because they express meaning but because they *are sound,* because they take their life in sound. It is as sound that they teach us what words are.

John Cage's Dublin, Lyn Hejinian's Leningrad: Poetic Cities as Cyberspaces

MARJORIE PERLOFF

IN chapter 5 ("Lotus Eaters") of *Ulysses,* Leopold Bloom sets out from home to begin his circuitous voyage through Dublin. We read:

> By lorries along Sir John Rogerson's Quay Mr. Bloom walked soberly, past Windmill lane, Leask's the linseed crusher's, the postal telegraph office. Could have given that address too. And past the sailors' home. He turned from the morning noises of the quayside and walked through Lime street. By Brady's cottages a boy for the skins lolled, his bucket of offal linked, smoking a chewed fagbutt. A smaller girl with scars of eczema on her forehead eyed him, listlessly holding her battered caskhoop. Tell him if he smokes he won't grow. O let him! His life isn't such a bed of roses! Waiting outside pubs to bring da home. Come home to ma, da, Slack hour: won't be many there. He crossed Townsend street, passed the frowning face of Bethel. El, yes: house of: Aleph, Beth. And past Nichols' the undertaker's. At eleven it is. Time enough. Daresay Corny Kelleher bagged that job at O'Neill's. Singing with his eyes shut. Corny. Met her once in the park. In the dark. What a lark. Police tout. Her name and address she then told with my tooraloom tooraloom tay. O, surely he begged it. Bury him cheap in a whatyoumaycall. With my tooraloom, tooraloom, tooraloom, tooraloom.[1]

Here is a classic modernist treatment of the city. At one level, Joyce's fictional mode is one of scrupulous documentary realism: we know exactly *where* Bloom walks and what shops and buildings he passes; these are, moreover, actual sites, whose existence in 1904, the time of the novel, can be verified. Indeed, the map of Dublin provides Joyce with a basic geometric grid: the central area, approximately two square miles, is encircled by the canal and divided neatly into quarters. The river Liffey, running from west to east, bisects the city, and Sackville Street, running north and south, crosses the Liffey at O'Connell Bridge. "Lotus Eaters" is set in the southeast quadrant (from Westland Row and past Trinity College to the baths); the northeast quadrant contains the slum and dock areas ("Circe," "Eumaeus"); the southwest is the business district centering around the castle ("Wandering Rocks"), and the northwest features the Ormond Hotel ("Sirens") and Kiernan's pub ("Cyclops"). The center of town, from Nelson's Pillar down Sackville Street, across O'Connell Bridge, and through the shopping district, can be traced almost step by step in "Lestrygonians," when Bloom wanders the streets on the way to lunch. And in the "Hades" chapter, the funeral carriage makes it way from the southeast, through the city center, and on to the northern outskirts.[2]

It is well known that Joyce mapped out his characters' movements through the city with a slide rule and compass. At the same time, Dublin functions as symbolic locale: 16 June at 10 A.M., a hot sultry day in Dublin, is emblematic of the narcotic state of the Lotus Eaters, whose tale provides the mythic analogue for Joyce's chapter. At this "slack hour," the boy in front of Brady's cottages "lolls" and smokes a "chewed fagbutt." The "smaller girl" "eye[s] Bloom listlessly"; in the next paragraph, Bloom stops in front of the Oriental Tea Company and daydreams about the exotic East. And further: Joyce has planted any number of metonymic images that prefigure what is to come: the "postal telegraph office" looks ahead to the Westland Street post office where Bloom picks up, under the pseudonym Henry Flower (again a lotus reference), the secret letter from his pen pal Martha Clifford. The "sailors' home" points toward the garrulous old mariner of "Eumaeus"; "Lime street" is appropriately named for a chapter that centers on the longing for the Orient; "Bethel" points to Bloom's Jewish heritage; "Nichols' the undertaker" reminds him that at eleven he is going to Paddy Dignam's funeral, where the undertaker will be Corny Kelleher.

But Joyce—and this is again characteristic of modernism—uses his symbolist urban setting as a stimulus that prompts Bloom's very private stream of consciousness. "Tell him if he smokes he won't grow," he thinks watching the boy with his "chewed fagbutt," and then, being a nonjudgmental, kindly type, he thinks better of this reprimand: "O let him! His life isn't such a bed of roses! Waiting outside pubs to bring da home. Come home to ma, da." And that thought, in turn, foreshadows the image of young Dingham's memory of his "da" in the Hades chapter. Toward the end of the paragraph, linguistic play begins to take over. "Met her once in the park. In the dark. What a lark." And then, thinking of Corny Kelleher, the undertaker, Bloom declares playfully: "Bury him cheap in a whatyoumaycall. With my tooraloom, tooraloom, tooraloom, tooraloom."

Joyce's Dublin, Eliot's London, Proust's Paris, Thomas Mann's Venice—these modernist cities are revealed to us through their architecture. Their materiality is palpable, the settings being startlingly real if not surreal (for example, Eliot's "A crowd flowed over London Bridge, so many / I had not thought death had undone so many. . . ."), their value is densely symbolic (Dublin as image of urban paralysis and loneliness, Proust's Paris as locus of class conflict and social climbing, Mann's Venice as the exotic Other); they elicit a new language that is polyglot, sophisticated, intricate—and determined to Make It New. In architectural terms, the modernist city is the *metropolis,* as Georg Simmel characterized it in 1903:

> A man does not end with the boundaries of his body or the vicinity that he immediately fills with his activity, but only with the sum of effects that extend from him in time and space: so too a city consists first in the totality of its effects that extend beyond its immediacy.[3]

The city thus shapes human behavior: indeed, in *Ulysses,* the individual psyche becomes an extension of a very specific urban geography. It is, for example, on *Townsend* Street that Bloom becomes aware of "Nichols' the undertaker's"—a reminder of Dignam's impending funeral but also of his own mortality, his precarious existence.

The modernist city, in short, is characterized by its density (both real and symbolic), its specificity and depth. Even in *Finnegans Wake,* where space and time become much more fluid and indeterminate, the *point de repère* is metropolitan Dublin, that "Irish capitol city . . . of two syllables and six letters, with a deltic origin and a nuinous end," which can boast of having "the most expansive peopling thoroughfare in the world"; Dublin, with its "blightblack workingstacks at twelvepins a dozen and the noobibusses sleighding along Safetyfirst Street and the derryjellybies snooping around Tell-No-Tailors' Corner and the fumes and the hopes and the strupithump of his ville's indigenous romekeepers, homesweepers, domecreepers . . . and all the uproor from all the aufroofs."[4]

But what happens to this "uproor from all the aufroofs" in the elaborately condensed "writing through" of *Finnegans Wake* produced by John Cage as a radio drama *(Hörspiel)* called *Roaratorio: An Irish Circus on "Finnegans Wake"*? Is Dublin still felt as a presence in this postmodern performance piece or is the urban code displaced by a new emphasis on what has been called liquid architecture? These are the questions I wish to address here.

The title *Roaratorio,* as Cage tells Klaus Schöning, who produced the radio piece for IRCAM in Paris in 1979, comes from the *Wake* itself, in a passage where the subjects of King Saint Finnerty the Festive prepare for "this longawaited Messiagh of roaratorios" (*FW* 41). Cage calls it a "circus" because "there is not one center but . . . life itself is a plurality of centers."[5] *Roaratorio* is designed to be "free of melody and free of harmony and free of counterpoint: free of musical theory." Again, if an oratorio "is like a church-opera, in which the people don't act, they simply stand there and sing . . . a 'roaratorio' is . . .out in the world. It's not in the church." (*R* 89). And so "roaring" is par for the course.

But what kind of "roaring"? An entry into this curious homage to Joyce's Dublin may be found in a comment made by Schöning in the course of working with Cage:

> A fugue is a more complicated genre; but it can be broken up by a single sound, say from a fire engine" (from *Silence*)
> Paraphrase: *Roaratorio* is a more complicated genre; it cannot be broken up by a single sound, say from a fire engine. (*R* 19)

Another way of putting this is to say that Cage has dematerialized his chosen city and replaced it with what we now call cyberspace, "a parallel universe," in Michael Benedikt's words, "created and sustained by the world's computers and communication lines," whose "corridors form wherever electricity runs with intelligence."[6] In the realm of cyberspace, writes Marcos Novak, "The notions of city, square, temple, institution, home, infrastructure are permanently extended. The city, traditionally the continuous city of physical proximity, becomes the discontinuous city of cultural and intellectual community. Architecture, normally understood in the context of the first, conventional city, shifts to the structure of relationships, connections and associations that are webbed over and around the simple world of appearance and accommodations of commonplace functions."[7]

The "structure of relationships, connections and associations" of Cage's "discontinuous city" is characterized by its elaborate layering. To begin, the verbal text was produced, as I have shown more fully in *Radical Artifice: Writing Poetry in the Age of Media,*[8] by submitting *Finnegans Wake* to a series of chance-generated operations (derived from the *I-Ching* but adapted for the computer on a program called *Mesolist*), that yielded a forty-one-page mesostic text, using the string JAMES JOYCE. As Cage explains it:

> A mesostic is like an acrostic; I used the name of JAMES JOYCE. And had I written acrostics the name would have gone down the margin, the left handside. But a mesostic is a road down the middle. So I would look for a word with *J* in it that didn't have an *A* because the *A* belongs on the second line of JAMES. And then a word with *A* that didn't have an *M*, and an *M* that didn't have an *E*, and an *E* that didn't have an *S* and in this way I made a path through the entire book. . . . [And further] I made the rule of not repeating a syllable that had already been used to express the *J* of James. So I kept an index, a card index . . . [and reduced Joyce's 626-page text to] 41 pages. (*R* 75)

Thus, to take just one example, the first page of the *Wake* (see figure 1) yields no more than the two short mesostics that open *Roaratorio:*

```
wroth with twoone nathandJoe
               A
               M
             jhEm
             Shen


          pftJschute
          sOlid man
that the humptYhillhead of humself
       is at the knoCk out
          in thEpark
```

                                                        (*R* 29)

The "knoCk out / in thE park" in those last two lines is a reference to Castle Knock, in the cemetery near the west gate of Phoenix Park in Dublin. But whereas in the *Wake,* Phoenix Park can be said to symbolize the Garden of Eden—the setting of H. C. Earwicker's innocent youth as well as his "fall" (he was caught peeping at or exhibiting himself to a couple of girls), in *Roaratorio* such locales function neither realistically nor symbolically; rather Dublin becomes a kind of informational city, a dematerialized space that nevertheless—and this is the paradox—is always identifiable as a city that is not New York, not London, not Paris, not Istanbul or Delhi or Tokyo, but quite clearly Dublin.

Let me explain. When Cage was invited to provide "musical accompaniment" for his *Writing through Finnegans Wake,* he used the following procedure. The forty-one-page text became a ruler

I

wroth with twone nathandJoe 3
A
Malt
JhEm
Shen

pftJschute
sOlid man
that the humptYillhead of humself
is at the knoCk out
in thE park

Jiccup 4
the fAther
Most
hEaven
Skysign

Judges
Or
deuteronomY
watsCh
futurE

pentschanJeuchy
chAp
Mighty
cEment
and edificeS

the Jebel and the 5
crOpherb
flYday
and she allCasually
ansars hElpers

Die vertikale Zahlenreihe gibt die Seiten des *Finnegans Wake* von James Joyce an. Die über die Textseiten verstreuten Interpunktionszeichen wurden aus dem Originaltext herausgelöst.
The margin numbers indicate the pages of *Finnegans Wake* by James Joyce. The scattered punctuation marks were extracted from the original text.

Fig. 1

for the one-hour *Hörspiel.* Now, as Cage explains, "places mentioned in the *Wake* are identified in Louis Mink's book *A Finnegans
Wake Gazetteer* . . . by page and line. And so a sound coming from
Nagasaki, or from Canberra in Australia, or from a town in Ireland
or a street in Dublin—could be identified by page and line and
then put into this hour, where it belonged in relation to the page
and line of *Finnegans Wake*" (*R* 89).The number of places mentioned (2,462) was reduced by chance operations to 626, a number
arbitrarily chosen so as to match the 626 pages of the *Wake* in the
Viking edition (*R* 95). About half of these were in Ireland and half
of the Irish places in Dublin.

But how can "place" be represented in terms of sound on
multitrack tape? Cage's method was to go to the places in question
(or send friends and colleagues to those he could not reach himself)
and then record the sounds actually heard onsite. Here are his
instructions to his fellow collectors:

> The recordings should be at least thirty seconds long and not longer
> than a few minutes. The sounds do not have to be chosen. Simply go
> to the place indicated, e.g., Düsseldorf, anywhere in it, and make a
> recording of whatever sound is there when you arrive.
> As I mentioned, I need a recording of ambient sound from your part
> of the world from———. It will be used in a piece of music I'm making
> to be called *Roaratorio,* based on James Joyce's *Finnegans Wake.* It
> will be what could be called an *Irish Circus.* If you could send me a tape
> or cassette, preferably ¼″ tape, stereo recording (any length between 30
> seconds and five or ten minutes) made in ———, I would be very
> grateful. . . . You can simply accept the sounds which are in the place
> you go to when you make the recording. If there is some question
> about where you should go, you could answer it by some chance opera-
> tion, such as dropping a coin on a map. (*R* 119; first two ellipses are
> Cage's)

It sounds, at first, like some sort of joke. What difference can it
make, the reader may well ask, whether a baby's cry or church
bell or the bark of a dog or running water is recorded in Dublin
or in Kansas City? When Klaus Schöning recalls that "Trieste,"
mentioned in the *Wake,* enters the sound track in the course of a
recording "seven thousand metres above Trieste and the Berlitz
School of James Joyce," made "on the flight from Lyon to Bel-
grade" (*R* 13), isn't he pulling our leg? Obviously, whatever sound
is recorded on such a flight can have nothing to do with Trieste.
Again, when Cage explains to Schöning that collecting sounds in
Ireland "meant getting up early in the morning and driving some-

times as late as ten o'clock in the evening. . . . We would go say 200 miles and record a sound say in Skibbereen and it would be say just a dog barking or a chicken crowing, whatever happened to be there when we arrived" (*R* 95), we may well wonder whether the one-minute recording made in Skibbereen was worth the effort.

Let us suspend our disbelief for a moment and see how the sounds in question were placed on the "ruler." Not only does the hour-long performance contain 626 sounds based on the places mentioned in the *Wake,* but simultaneous programs were made from the actual sounds mentioned in Joyce's book, as well as from "appropriate" music. First, a listing of the sounds cited in the *Wake* was made and again condensed by means of chance operations (see Cage's list, *R* 132, reproduced here). These sounds were then classified into categories (such as thunderclaps, farts, musical instruments, bells, clocks, chimes, guns, animals and birds, water: see list, *R* 147, also reproduced here), and again transferred from their spatial position to a temporal one: for example, the reference to the "with what strong voice of false jiccup!" (*FW* 4, lines 10–11) means that we hear a hiccup at the corresponding point in time (ca. one minute) on the hour-long tape. But note—and this is very important—that at the point where we hear the hiccup, the spoken mesostic text has reached the point of "and she allCasually / ansars hElpers" (*R* 29), which has nothing to do with "Jiccup." The information coming through the channel is thus multiform and layered: there is no dominant sound, no center.

And further: Cage has incorporated a variety of Irish musics into the piece. A friend told him that he should enlist the voice of Joe Heaney, "the king of Irish singers and one hundred per cent the real McCoy." Cage took a special trip to England, where Heaney was performing, and the latter instructed him in the kinds of Irish music to include: "the flute, the fiddle, the bodhran [a sheepskin drum] . . . and the Uillean pipes," as played by Seamus Ennis. Again, recordings of songs and melodies (in performances by soloists or composed variations of such solos) were superimposed on a multitrack tape to make a "circus of relevant musics" (*R* 175). The "score" includes familiar Irish songs like "Dark is the colour of my true love's hair" and "Little red fox," but also various hornpipes, reels, bodhran duets, and improvised pieces.

All these sounds were then superimposed on one another by a series of mathematical operations, the collection of sixteen multitrack tapes being combined into one. "The material," says Cage, "is then a plurality of forms"; it has "what Joyce called 'soundsense'" (*R* 103). But doesn't it matter, Schöning asks Cage,

Listing through *Finnegans Wake* (chapter 1)
The numbers show the page and line from the original edition by James Joyce.

03.04	*violer d'amores*
.09	*avoice from afire bellowsed mishe mishe*
.15–17	*(bababadalgharaghtakamminarronnkonn-bronntonnerronntuonnthunntrovarrhoun-awnskawntoohoohoordenenthurnuk!)*
	christian minstrelsy
04.02–03	*Brékkek Kékkek Kékkek Kékkek! Kóax Kóax Kóax! Ualu Ualu Ualu! Quaouauh!*
.07	*apeal*
.08	*a toll, a toll*
.10–11	*with what strawng voice of false jiccup!*
05.03	*larrons o'toolers clittering up*
.03–04	*tombles a'buckets clottering down*
.09	*Hohohoho*
.11	*Hahahaha*
.15	*thunder of his arafatas*
.16	*that shebby choruysh of unkalified muzzlenimiissilehims*
.31	*fargobawlers*
.32–33	*megaphoggs*
06.06	*all the uproor from all the aufroofs*
.11	*lute*
.16–17	*duodisimally profusive plethora of ululation*
.18–19	*And the all gianed in with the shout-most shoviality*
.21	*Some in kinkin corass, more, kankan keening*
.22	*Belling him up*
.24–25	*E'erawhere in this whorl would ye hear sich a din again?*
.25–26	*With their deepbrow fundigs and the dusty fidelios*
.28	*Tee the tootal of the fluid hang the twoddle of the fuddled, O!*
.29	*Hurrah*
.36	*baywinds' oboboes shall wail him*

From *Roaratorio* by John Cage, ed. Klaus Schöning (Athanaeum, 1985).

Categories and Number of All Sounds Used in *Roaratorio*

A. LISTING THROUGH *FINNEGANS WAKE:*

	Part I	Part II
Thunderclaps	6	4
Thunder rumbles and earthquake sounds	29	27
Laughing and Crying (Laughtears)	64	100
Loud voice sounds (shouts, etc.)	31	22
Farts	5	5
Musical instruments (short)	66	96
Bells, clocks, chimes	28	42
Guns, explosions	32	36
Wails	7	11
Animals and particular birds	56	113
Music (instrumental and singing)	57	145
Water	34	24
Birds (in general)	16	18
Singing	64	72
	495	715
		495
B. PLACES		1,210
		1,083
	Grand Total	2,293

From *Roaratorio* by John Cage, ed. Klaus Schöning (Athanaeum, 1985).

that the sound track often drowns out the reciter's voice so that the words cannot be understood? From Cage's perspective this is no problem, for "this is our experience in life every day. Wherever we are a larger amount of what we have to experience is being destroyed every instant. If for instance . . . you go to a museum where you would think that you have . . . peace and quiet as you are looking at the Mona Lisa someone passes in front of you or bumps into you from behind" (*R* 101–3). In keeping with the circus format, the sounds never coalesce or merge; they retain their individual identities. Nor can the sounds heard in any sense "accompany" the words or provide a musical setting. The separate strata remain separate.

To what extent is *Roaratorio* what Cage calls an "Irish Circus"? Does its locale continue to be Joyce's Dublin or is the new urban

architecture amorphous? On the one hand, Cage wants to empha-
size the work's internationalism: he tells Schöning that "Ciaran
McMathoona, the chief in radio of the traditional music for the
Irish folklore and a charming man," was "delighted that *Finnegans
Wake* an Irish work—that a *hörspiel* on it should be commissioned
by a German radio station . . . and that it should be made by an
American with John Fullemann who is Swiss and his wife, who is
Swedish" (*R* 93). Schöning adds that "it's a production of WDR
Köln with KRO Hilversum and SDR Stuttgart"; and further, it was
done in a French research studio. "The whole thing is interna-
tional," Cage explains. "It's all the world" (*R* 93). On the other
hand—and this is a characteristically Cagean paradox—there can
be no doubt that the finished multitrack piece is designed to signify
Irishness, even what we might call Dublinicity.

The sounds in question were recorded in such places as Bally-
hooly (town in County Cork), Swords (North of County Dublin),
Kish Lightship (east of Dublin Bay), and Enniskerry (County
Wicklow); sounds made in Ireland predominate (about three to
one), but recordings were also made in places as far afield as Da-
mascus, Prague, Baghdad, Madras, Sydney, and Lima. In the first
few minutes of the "roaratorio" proper (3:10 to 4:10 on the tape),
I distinguish the following sounds:

water poured into a bucket	laughter
fiddle music	gunshot
car braking	whistle
bird song	tram screeching to a halt
church bells	fire engine
baby crying	motor boat
cowbells	orchestra
automobile traffic	baby crying
rooster crowing	fire alarm
church choir	motorcycle
soprano singing	waterfall

And all the while, Cage is reading from his Joyce mesostics, the
dominant sound being the repeated *J* of *James Joyce*.[9]

The effect is to make us feel that we are in a particular space:
Dublin, or at least Ireland, even as we can neither visualize that
space nor make an architectural drawing of it, and even as the text
is always opening up to the larger electronic world and admitting
sounds from Buenos Aires or Canberra or Helsinki. In the same
vein, Cage's is a text to be heard that must also be read, for in
reading *Roaratorio,* one comes across many features that are ob-

scured by the oral presentation, beginning with the *Wake*'s punctuation, that Cage has liberally spread around the page. Take the
stanza

> Juxta-
> explanatiOn was put in loo of
> eYes
> lokil Calour and lucal odour
> to havE

The oral performance hides the pun "loo" / "lieu," the phonetic
spelling of lokil Calour" ("local color"), with its play on the Norse
God Loki and the Italian patriot Cavour" and the mesostic embedding of "Yes" in "eYes." Neither speech nor writing has priority
in this nice exemplar of a Derridean system of differences.

It is a system of differences, one might add, that curiously anticipates the "informational city," as Manuel Castells has characterized it.[10] A 1992 *New York Times* architectural column by Herbert
Muschamp describes the offices of the financial trading firm of
D. E. Shaw in midtown Manhattan as tapping into the "interna-
tional network of electronic communications that keeps the global
economy humming. The 'streets' of this city have no potholes.
They are paved not with asphalt but with telephone lines and radio
waves that stretch between cites and leap across national borders."
As for the offices themselves, they are open around the clock
"though for much of that time the firm's windowless hexagonal
trading room is unattended by human hands. Machines hold down
the fort. Silently, with lights flickering, batteries of computers go
about their programmed business. . . . These machines are the
traffic lights of the informational city."[11]

This description of the informational city helps us to make sense
of Cage's project in his *Irish Circus on Finnegans Wake*. Although
the language of *Roaratorio* is entirely Joyce's, that language,
spliced, endowed with capitals where there should be none, and
radically condensed by the process of lineation, is transformed
into an electronic communications network whose "streets" are
telephone lines and radio waves that connect the many parts of the
world where sounds have been collected: Joyce's text, condensed,
minimalized, fractured, fades in and out in what is a floating abstract realm or space flow. At one level, Cage's seems to be the
very model of the dematerialized city, "Dublin" as "realm of pure
information . . . decontaminating the natural and urban land-
scapes, redeeming them, saving them from the chain-dragging bull-

dozers of the paper industry, from the diesel smoke of courier and
post office trucks, from jet fuel fumes and clogged airports, from
billboards . . . pollutions . . . and corruptions attendant to the
process of moving information attached to *things*" (*MB* 3).

But dispersal is only part of the story. In *The Global City,* Saskia
Sassen has forcefully argued that "the territorial dispersal of economic activity at the national and world scale [paradoxically] creates a need for expanded central control and management": the
city becomes the "command point in the organization of the world
economy," the "key location and marketplace for leading indus-
tries." New York, London, Frankfurt, Paris, Hong Kong, Sao
Paolo: in all these "maximum population and resource dispersal"
has led to "new systems of economic order and agglomeration,"
new systems of central control.[12] Just so, Cage's seemingly "open"
and "decentered" *Circus* is governed, whether overtly or not, by
the "command point" of the artist: Cage, after all, is always in
control. If the sounds seem fortuitous, let us remember that they
must be accommodated to precisely the hour format, that they
come at points chosen and charted by Cage himself, who has
planned every single detail. Indeed, if Joyce's geometric grid gives
way to Cage's "cyberspace," that cyberspace has its own superpro-
grammer. The use of chance operations, we should note, does not
mean that anything is left to chance.

Can the art work or poetic composition avoid this degree of
control? The "liquid architecture" of *Roaratorio* may be dematerialized; it may well be an architecture that, in Marcos Novak's
words, "is no longer satisfied with only space and form and light
and all the aspects of the real world . . . an architecture of fluctuat-
ing relations between abstract elements" (*MBC* 251), but this is not
to say that dematerialization ushers in a new kind of freedom.
Cage's Dublin may have "transcended" the boundaries of Joyce's
four-square grid, but that transcendence is, after all, produced by
the individual figure of the poet, controlling the multitrack tape
performance from behind the scenes.

I do not mean to imply that such artistic authority is a bad thing.
Poetry is, after all, with rare exceptions like the Japanese *renga,*
a form of individual production, and however much the author of
the *Roaratorio* may have wanted to get rid of the ego, his stylistic
signature remains highly individual, indeed uniquely Cagean. To
take another, later example of this tension between the dematerialization of space and the specification of the poet's language, I want
to look at a long poem published in 1991: Lyn Hejinian's three-

hundred-page *Oxota,* subtitled *A Short Russian Novel.*[13] This lyric novel is written in the fourteen-line rhyming stanza of Pushkin's *Evgeny Onegin* and its "story" consistently but very indirectly alludes to the love intrigues, social events, and nature descriptions of Pushkin's great poem. His Petersburg becomes her Leningrad, the Leningrad visited over a two- or three-year period by a poet whose familiarity with the Russian language is only sketchy and who is totally captivated by Russia even as she finds she cannot understand it.

The title *Oxota* (Russian for "hunt"), refers, I think, to the poet's hunt for meaning. Whereas Pushkin's Tatyana is "hunted by love's anguish" (book 3, xx), Hejinian's "describer-perceiver" hunts among words and sentences for clues and connections. But what Hejinian calls a "glass prose" (a transparency model, a window on reality) is no longer adequate. Narrative, in these circumstances, becomes a language game: as Hejinian put it in an essay called "The Rejection of Closure," "The very idea of reference is spatial: over here is word, over there is thing at which the word is shooting amiable love-arrows," and thus "the struggle between language and that which it claims to depict or express" is what determines the very shape narrative takes. "Language discovers what one might know, which in turn is always less than what language might say."[14]

From *Writing is an Aid to Memory* (1978) and *My Life* (1980), to her recent long metaphysical poem "The Person," Hejinian has refused all notions of the self as "some core reality at the heart of our sense of being," the still-dominant myth of the "artist's 'own voice,' issuing from an inner, fundamental, sincere, essential, irreducible, consistent self, an identity which is unique and separable from all other human identities." Rather, "The person . . . is a mobile (or mobilized) reference point; or to put it another way, subjectivity is not an entity but a dynamic." "Certainly," Hejinian concedes, "I have an experience of being in position, at a time and place, and of being conscious of this, but this position is temporary, and beyond that, I have no experience of being except in position." Thus "the experience of the self" is perceived "as a relationship rather than an existence."[15]

In this scheme of things psychology means not self-revelation, as in a more traditional poetry, but, in Wallace Stevens's words, "description without place." Consider chapter 1, in which the narrator ("Lyn") arrives in Leningrad to stay (as we know from later poems) with the Russian poet Arkadii Dragomoschenko, whom she is translating.

> This time we are both
> The old thaw is inert, everything set again in snow
> At insomnia, at apathy
> We must learn to endure the insecurity as we read
> The felt need for a love intrigue
> There is no person—he or she was appeased and withdrawn
> There is relationship but it lacks simplicity
> People are very aggressive and every week more so
> The Soviet colonel appearing in such of our stories
> He is sentimental and duckfooted
> He is held fast, he is in his principles
> But here is a small piece of the truth—I am glad to greet you
> There, just with a few simple words it is possible to say the truth
> It is so because often men and women have their sense of honor.
>
> (*O*, 11)

Where does this "scene" take place and what is its information channel? In good epic tradition, the poem opens *in medias res* with "This time," the implication being that "this time" (arriving again in the Soviet Union) will be measured against another time that was somehow different. But "This time we are both" immediately displays Hejinian's deceptive flatness: the language seems totally ordinary and yet it throws out any number of plot lines. Perhaps it means that "We are both here," but then who are "we"? And what is it we both are? Both poets, one American, one Russian, or one woman and one man? Both guests of the Soviet government? Both ready for a relationship? Or if "both" is construed, not as the predicate nominative but as the modifier of the predicative adjective(s), we might read it as "both tired and hungry," "both frightened and elated," and so on.

In any case, something is about to happen "this time." The "thaw" of line 2 may well refer to the brief political respite of the Khrushchev years as well as the actual weather conditions; soon "everything [is] set again in snow." And just as Pushkin's dedicatory stanza describes his poem as the product "of carefree hours, of fun, / of sleeplessness, faint inspirations," Hejinian refers to "insomnia" and "apathy," warning her reader even as she warns herself that "We must learn to endure the insecurity as we read / The felt need for a love intrigue / There is no person—he or she was appeased and withdrawn." The "need for a love intrigue" refers, of course, to the Onegin-Tatyana romance that is Pushkin's "subject";

in our own fractured world, such "love intrigue" seems to have given way to the diminished romance of "relationship," and even then a relationship that "lacks simplicity." Indeed, all sorts of sexual and familial relationships, all more or less complicated, will be presented for our inspection, and part of the fun of reading *Oxota* will be to figure out who is drawn to whom, for how long, and what the sexual and/or political dynamics are.

In the meantime, the stage is set for the unfolding of events: "People are very aggressive and every week more so." The "duckfooted" colonel, who will appear and reappear throughout the narrative, an embodiment of "principles" and "sentimental" old truths, is introduced and then, like a stock character in a cheap thriller, mysteriously disappears again. And now the stanza ends on a turn of phrase that is brilliantly deployed throughout *Oxota,* especially in the early chapters, where the poet records how it feels to be a linguistic alien in a country one wants so badly to understand. "Here is a small piece of the truth—I am glad to greet you" is the poet's rendition of the way "polite" Russian hosts greet their American guests, the excessive formality of phrasing being a function of unfamiliarity rather than good manners.

Many of us have had the experience of meeting foreigners who seem extremely, if not excessively, polite until we realize they are speaking a careful English based on the classroom model or grammar book. Translated into colloquial English, line 12 carries something like the locution "Believe me, I am so glad to meet you." But in bringing "the truth" into speech twice and in concluding that "It is so because often men and women have their sense of honor," we are immediately *in* a language world—and, in Wittgensteinian terms, the limits of my language are the limits of my world—that is largely alien to the American visitor. Accordingly, for the "we" who are "both," assimilation will depend, not on finding out what the words mean, but how they are used, how to read the signs. And, as Hejinian wittily implies throughout, this is no easy matter. When someone says to us "There, just with a few simple words it is possible to say the truth," we surmise the presence of a sensibility that may not be there at all.

But then words like "there" are always suspect in Hejinian's scheme of things, origin and location, whether of speech or event, being all but impossible to define. The line "People are very aggressive and every week more so," for instance, sounds like a snatch of conversation overheard while waiting on line at the butcher shop. But it may also refer to something quoted from the newspaper or, for that matter, it may record Lyn's own appraisal of her surroundings. Even the stilted Russian constructions of the English language cannot always be attributed to X or Y; often, they may be Hejinian's own, as she tries to make herself understood to those who have schoolbook English. They may even be approximations of Russian syntax, as laboriously translated into English by the poet. The pattern is further complicated by the gaps between statements and/or lines, one perception thus failing to lead, as Charles Olson would have it, immediately (or even remotely) to a further perception.

It is important to notice here that, as in the case of Cage's *Roaratorio,* disjunctiveness does not always posit an imagistic or filmlike collage surface, or even the free association of stream-of-consciousness. Language does not represent "thought"; on the contrary, linguistic artifice is emphasized by the embedding of images in a network of abstractions, as in "everything set again in snow," or by the positioning of abstractions in unlikely grammatical constructions, as in the locution "At insomnia, at apathy," on the model of "at school" or "at home." The resulting poem-novel is, as Hejinian puts it in chapter 2, "something neither invented nor constructed but moving through that time as I experienced it unable to take part personally in the hunting." It is as if the text avoids the requisite distance between subject and object and lets "events" unfold so that the reader feels as if she has come in on a conversation whose participants cannot be located.

In cyberspace, Marcos Novak explains, "the identity of objects does not have to be manifested physically; it can be hidden in a small difference in an attribute that is not displayed" (*MBC* 239). And again, "Cyberspace offers the opportunity of maximizing the benefits of separating *data, information,* and *form*" (*MBC* 225). This seems to me nicely applicable to what we might call Hejinian's cyberversion of Leningrad. Forms are no longer symbolic, yielding such and such information and data; rather, everything happens in an unspecifiable space/time realm of "minimal restriction" (*MBC* 234). "Being there," as in the *Roaratorio,* is the special pleasure of this dematerialized universe, but where is "there"?

The "new urbanism," it seems, has penetrated not only the culture of built environments but also the seemingly very different culture of poetic discourse. The question is not just whether Cage's "Dublin" or Hejinian's "Leningrad" can be conventionally located and mapped but whether, in the larger sense, poetry can continue to operate under the old rules of versification, stanza form, justified margins—all attributes, after all, of a confined and recognizable space. Or is it possible that poetic territory is becoming, in Benedikt's description of cyberspace (*MBC* 2), "billowing, glittering, humming, coursing, a Borgesian library, a city; intimate, immense, firm, liquid, recognizable and unrecognizable at once"?

Notes

1. James Joyce, *Ulysses* (New York: Random House, 1961), 70. Subsequently cited in the text as *U.*

2. See Richard M. Kain, *Fabulous Voyager: A Study of James Joyce's "Ulysses."* Rev. ed. (New York: Viking Press, 1958), 37–39.

3. Georg Simmel, "Metropolis and Mental Life," in *The Conflict in Modern Culture and Other Essays,* trans. and ed. K. Peter Etzkorn (New York: Teachers College Press, 1968), 12.

4. James Joyce, *Finnegans Wake* (1939; reprint, New York: Penguin Books, 1967), 140, 6. Subsequently cited as *FW.*

5. John Cage / Klau Schöning, "Laughtears: Conversation on *Roaraortio,*" in John Cage, *Roaratorio: An Irish Circus on Finnegans Wake,*" ed. Klaus Schöning (Köningstein: Athenäum, 1985), 107. This book is subsequently cited as *R.*

6. Michael Benedikt, Introduction to *Cyberspace: First Steps,* ed. Michael Benedikt (Cambridge and London: MIT Press, 1992), 3. This collection is subsequently cited as *MBC.*

7. Marcos Novak, "Liquid Architectures in Cyberspace," in *MBC,* 225–54; 249.

8. Marjorie Perloff, *Radical Artifice: Writing Poetry in the Age of Media* (Chicago and London: University of Chicago Press, 1992), 150–61.

9. The /j/ phoneme is foregrounded, not only by its repetition, but because /j/ is never a silent letter in English as are /y/ and /e/ and, when it appears in a compound like "neAtly," the /a/. The /j/ sound thus dominates: "pftJschute," "Jiccup," "Judges," "Jollybrool," "Jerrybuilding," "Jutę," "Jubilee," "Japijap," and so on.

10. Manuel Castells, *The Informational City: Information Technology, Economic Restructuring, and the Urban-Regional Process* (Oxford: Basil Blackwell, 1989), chap. 3, passim.

11. Herbert Muschamp, *New York Times,* 8 July 1992, Section 2, p. 1.

12. Saskia Sassen, *The Global City* (Princeton: Princeton University Press, 1991), 3–5.

13. Lyn Hejinian, *Oxota: A Short Russian Novel* (Great Barrington, Mass.: The Figures, 1991); subsequently cited as *O.* For a fuller discussion of the poetics of *Oxota,* see my "How Russian Is It: Lyn Hejinian's *Oxota,*" in *Parnassus: Poetry in Review* 17 (Spring 1993); 186–209.

14. *Poetics Journal* 4 (May 1984): 138–39.

15. "The Person and Description," Symposium on "The Poetics of Everyday Life," *Poetics Journal* 9 (1991): 166–67.

Poetics in Practice: "The Gift: A Life of Lorenzo Da Ponte—a Fragment"

DAVID R. SLAVITT

To be picked up and then
put down, discarded,
not only by Amadeus (bad enough)
but by the gods themselves . . .

If New York was real, the grocery store and the job
at Columbia College (teaching Italian), then Mozart
was a dream and their collaboration a dream.
Or, if that was real, then this was all nightmare
from which he might yet rouse to break the surface
like some great sea-beast, streaming tears of terror
and gratitude.

          🙐   🙐   🙐

In Ceneda Emanuele was born to Geremia
and Rachele Conegliano, after whose death
Geremia courted a Christian woman—
girl, really—Orasala Pasqua Paietta.
The laws required conversion before the wedding,
the children's too. They took the name of the local
bishop, da Ponte. The father became at a stroke
Gasparo, and his eldest son, Lorenzo.
And Emanuele?
                  Disappears.
No mention of those first fourteen years;
they slip from his memoirs if not his mind,

From *A Gift* by David R. Slavitt. (Baton Rouge: Louisiana State University Press, 1996).

with the other, earlier name, the other religion.

                                                            ❧   ❧   ❧

A matter of small steps, from the catechism
to further, subtler questions—what a bright lad
deserves and can only get by taking orders,
minor ones first, to go to the seminary,
and then, when the bishop dies
                                        and his father suffers
reverses, priestly vows
so he can continue study at Portogruaro.

He did believe
                         (as much as any Borgia)
in the Church
                     as theater.

                                                            ❧   ❧   ❧

Transport, flight, and then a precipitous fall,
in art as in life.
With women, for instance, in Venice,
those libertine years.
He and Casanova knew each other
and disapproved of each other.
                                         Angiola
Tiepolo was the first, gorgeous, hot tempered—
her elder brother, Girolamo, was bad,
a gambler, almost Angiola's pimp
(some suspected worse).
They were not part of the plan.

To have a plan, however vague,
                                         the sense of a career,
a talent coming into its own was the least
a clever fellow like that would owe himself.

To float, drift, see again and again
the sun dip down and waters of the lagoon
turn to black velvet, glinting with torch-light brilliants,
was to reckon in self-loathing the cost of every
moment of pleasure:

the sin was the waste of time.

&ea;   &ea;   &ea;

From Venice then in flight,
before the arrest warrant of the Council of Ten
could impede him, to safety, across the border—
into Gorizia, and the arms of an innkeeper there,
a gorgeous woman,
                              German, or maybe Slovenian.
He never knew,
spoke neither language, and she had no Italian.
But they made clear enough their instant lust.

The best days of his life, that long wallow,
                                          a paradise.
At length, his money ran out.
She left a purse of gold coins under the pillow,
which he, in pride, refused.

The idyll was over
in any event, a dream more vivid than most
but lacking the disagreeable, credible grit
of impatience or mere inattention.
                                    Love is not
that simple initial soaring.

Those amazing days betrayed—
and were betrayed by—the rest of his life.

&ea;   &ea;   &ea;

Joseph II, now that Maria Theresa,
his mum, was dead, was Emperor and could do
whatever he liked. He chose to be liberal, nice,
and dress like a modest burgher.
(He warned his sister Marie Antoinette
that her showy extravagance was dangerous.)

Waving his hand in the air,
he decreed he no longer liked Singspiel.
Genug!
Let there be Italians again.

Da Ponte arrived at the right moment, parlayed
introductions to reach at last the
      GRAND CHAMBERLAIN'S OFFICE
where, talking fast, he got himself appointed
Burgtheater Poet.
           Confirmed, in course, by Joseph
before whom da Ponte came.

         "How many
plays have you written, signor?" his majesty asks.
"None, sire." (This, in terror.)

         The Emperor
smiles and jokes: "Splendid. A virgin muse."

The virgin learned soon enough the whorey tricks:
Adaptation, translation, theft,
         the politics
of opera houses—managers with their passions
for special effects (bells and birds were in fashion),
the prima donnas, jealous of one another,
the soprano ingenue (not to mention her mother),
and the composer, a collaborator but
at any moment he'll turn on you and cut
the best lines in the whole book, or reverse
their order, and change the meter.
         Your empty purse
won't let you argue back. A *suggeritore,*
it prompts you to agree at once. The story,
a dismal one, was familiar enough to go
with a graceful minor-key continuo.

           ﻬ ﻬ ﻬ

Hack work corrodes the spirit, grinds you down,
destroys your self-respect. Destroys you.
Il ricco d'un giorno (from Bertati's text)
was the dumbest of the three ideas he'd offered:
of course Salieri picked it.

The mad hope
         grows like a mold on bread
that it's not so bad,

                    is better than you think—
but what that means
is only that your judgment is going too,
you can't tell good from bad, are a fraud, impostor,
and sooner or later will be exposed. Why not
quit now?
                Get out
                        with some dignity left . . .
And go where?

So you dip your quill again
into the poisoned inkwell, scrawl more words,
and hope that in the general disaster
no one will notice which shortcomings were yours.

                        ❧ ❧ ❧

A castrophe: shuffling feet and laughter,
catcalls even. Salieri's music was wretched
("stolen from everywhere!"—so Zinzendorf),
and the singing none too good. No one excused
the libretto either.

                They did it again, and again,
six times in all, each performance a torture
for everyone.

Salieri walked away
swearing never to work with da Ponte again.
The Emperor, nevertheless, demanded another,
if only to keep the appointment from going to Casti,
whom Casanova called "buffoon and pimp."
(The Emperor didn't like Casanova either.)
"You must pluck up your courage again," he told da Ponte,
"and give us another."
                A blessing, was it, or curse?

                        ❧ ❧ ❧

Meanwhile, the teeth, the pain of teeth, the griefs
of dentistry . . . A love triangle also,
with a girl who loved da Ponte, while another,
Doriguti, a fellow lodger, fellow

Italian, loved the girl.
                                   And in his pain,
da Ponte, with an abscess, was willing to try
the cure Doriguti offered—engraver's acid,
which nearly killed him.
                                   All his teeth fell out.
For two years he could hardly keep down the little
he'd managed to gum and, without gagging, swallow
in pain
humiliation,
wretchedness.

                        ❧   ❧   ❧

But then a change in fortune—nothing to bank on,
except that misfortune is not reliable either.
If we assume intention somewhere, the relenting
may only be to keep our hopes alive
that they may torment us further, as torturers do,
who learn how far they can go and still bring back
from oblivion's lip their broken quivering subjects.

That, too, is misleading:
there's no plan to it,
no sense.

Martín y Soler,
just arrived in Vienna, needed a book.
Protégé of the Spanish ambassador's wife,
he got himself introduced to Emperor Joseph,
who passed him on to da Ponte with prompt result—
The Good-Hearted Grouch.
                                   It was Goldoni's play
cut down, done up, reworked.
                                   He was luckier now,
or maybe he'd picked up the knack from reading,
going to hear performances, paying attention:
reduction and embellishment,
reshaping prose into singable verse . . .
A witchy business,
you never know, until the composer sets it,
how well or badly you've done.
                                   (You still can't say

for sure, knowing he could have taken good
work and words and wrecked them, ruined them all.)

But rousing applause
from start to finish—even for recitatives.
A success, or at least enough so that offers of work
came in from several composers, including one
who'd enjoyed, four years before, a degree of success
with a piece in German on Turkish harems—
Mozzart
(which is how da Ponte spelled it all his life).

         ⁊ ⁊ ⁊

A genius, but they all claim that.
                 A boor,
as if to defy the world to recognize
beneath the boorishness his real refinement.
And a fondness for crude jokes.

What can one say of such a passage?
Da Ponte claimed and believed
his poetry was the door through which that music came,
the emotions and wit of his librettos
gave rise to those of the music.

But look at that last
Masonic nonsense, incoherent, almost
insane . . .
         Die Zauberflöte.
As if to deny da Ponte any credit.

The start was awkward
and their first meeting inauspicious.
Mozart explained his distaste (one tried to smile)
for rhymes
as well as his fondness for farce,
                 even slapstick.
Da Ponte put the best face on it he could,
needing the work.
           He gets no credit for that.

He was, as if on a child's whim, first picked up

and then dropped,
ignored, and left to disappear
                              beneath a chair
servants ought to be cleaning under but don't.

&a.   &a.   &a.

Their theme, at first and all along: forgiveness,
a relenting that da Ponte had all but despaired of and yet
had sometimes imagined coming down from heaven,
an angel's gift—
                    the angel looked like his mother,
or else that woman he'd known at the inn,
or some conflation, confection of all the others
who'd shown him teasing glimpses
of what the world
                    ought to have been.

Tormented as we are,
we suppose we have deserved it—and therefore pray
as Almaviva does at the end,
"Perdono!"
kneeling down before the contessa,
"Perdono!"

With Mozart, that odd, coarse, brilliant fellow,
he found at least for a while,
the relenting of which he'd dreamed.

&a.   &a.   &a.

At the time, it was nothing, another job of work,
another composer to please. It seemed to go well,
but they never had the success da Ponte expected.

But did they know how good they were? Did they realize,
themselves, and could they believe in what they felt,
at least sometimes?

Da Ponte was never sure what Mozart thought.

For himself . . . ?
                    Not really.

No.

◌ ◌ ◌

Rhymes, at times like chimes: their ringing
into his head was a way of bringing
the balance of honor back toward level.
Let Mozart hate them and go to the devil.
Ed in vece del fandango
Una marcia per il fango,
Per montagne, per valloni,
Colle nevi e i sollioni,
Al concerto de trombone . . .

Da Ponte held his ground; let him chew on that,
and Mozart did; and out of Figaro's mouth
came music one would die to hear in heaven.

◌ ◌ ◌

And then, in Prague,
Domenico Guardasoni, the impresario there, made them a decent
offer: they had a success with Bertati's libretto
for Gazzaniga's opera, *réchauffé*.

What da Ponte remembers: how they all behaved
as if he'd written their parts, scribbling fast
and laughing to himself.

At the Duscheks' house,
Casanova is there (now reduced
to librarian and pet of Count Waldstein),
the singers, of course,
                    and Mozart,
who says he is going to town, horrifying them all.
The overture, he was sworn, is in his head,
but musicians are not psychics,
                              require a score,
all the parts copied out.
                    They contrive therefore
a plot:
        Signora Bondini asks the composer
to fetch the gloves she has left on the harpsichord.

When Mozart goes in to get them, they lock him in
and tell him he can't leave
                                    until he's produced
the music.

He asks for candles, paper, pens,
cakes, and wine, and these the company brings him,
hoisting them up to the windowsill with poles
from the grape arbor.
                            Da Ponte passes up
a pot,
        and the maestro, laughing, calls down not
his thanks but regrets that he can't fill it
                                        and pour it
down
        on da Ponte's
                    despicable
                            head.
Laughter. Blackout.
                    A grand success
for the opening then in Prague of *Il dissoluto
punito; o sia, Il don Giovanni.*
                            Da Ponte,
called back to Vienna,
                    misses his moment.

As if he were Masetto, and God, the Don
who's decided he is a churl and doesn't deserve
even a brief taste of such a sweetness.

             🙦   🙦   🙦

In Vienna, however, a consolation—the singer,
La Ferrarese, or Adriana Gabrieli.
Nancy Storace had gone away to London,
and singing her roles
                    was this one,
with a huge range from alto to coloratura.
Stocky, really, and not an accomplished actress,
but with fire there in the eyes,
the heart,
        the voice,
                she struck

fire in a listener.
In him.

They set up another complicated business—
he, La Ferrarese, and her husband,
one del Bene, with whom, for a change, da Ponte
was on good terms.

And where are the rules for these things set down,
how should men behave? Or women?

At the theater, trouble,
their patron, the Emperor, worried about the costs
of his entertainments. Also—some said—ailing,
but at any rate less smitten by Celestina
Coltellini, the soprano,
                              his mistress
whose tiresome tirades he could avoid
by shutting down the theater.

They could all go away and leave him in peace . . .

Da Ponte begged permission to carry on,
to find the money somehow, from the Viennese
bon ton.
             Weary, Joseph scribbled his name
to the piece of paper.

With all this, *Così fan tutte,* to show
how funny it is, precarious, grotesque,
and yet one can contrive to behave with style,
as the women do at the end, in their curious triumph
where it's never clear which one winds up with Guglielmo
and which with Ferrando.
Still, the music plays,
cheerily, heartily, heartlessly on.

Mozart and he had hoped to share those zecchini
the gentlemen on stage so prized,
but five performances only . . .
                                        Then the theater
closed
for the Emperor's death.

His brother, Leopold, came from Tuscany
to take in hand the affairs of a somewhat disordered
state.
      Everywhere, spies,
                informers,
                        agents provocateurs.

Even the theater,
              especially there.
The Ferrarese's contract was running out.
Da Ponte could tell how the wind was blowing.
                        Letters,
frantic letters—to St. Petersburg,
where his friend Martin y Soler might work him
an appointment
              as court poet of Russia . . . ?
Or maybe London,
where he and Mozart might find some job together?
(Mozart had that bizarre Masonic pageant
and couldn't think of leaving—not for months.)

                  ε&   ε&   ε&

Under that pressure, the truth comes out,
his belief that he is a fraud
                  will be found out,
impostor, apostate,
mountebank . . .

His plots
depended always on such devices
with actors changing their costumes
and acting at one remove,
acting at acting:
Susanna and Rosina in Almaviva's garden,
or the Don and Leporello
under Elvira's window—
for the thrill of it,
              the desperation of it,
or merely the knowledge that whatever it is
cannot long continue:
mortality but concentrated,
life.

Then in *Così* that insane Albanian business.
In grotesque getups the callow fellows
find true selves and true loves . . .

And then lose them?
It is not clear.

Da Ponte is waiting to see
what will happen, hoping, and yet too shrewd
to support it can go on much longer.

Like a mother,
a run of good luck will sicken, die,
and leave you
                    orphaned,
renamed,
            unselfed,
                    undone.

Part 3
The English Renaissance

Justice and Renaissance Poetics

PAUL RAMSEY

> I inwardly did nothing!
> O Iscariotlike crime!
> Beauty is everlasting,
> And dust is for a time.
> —Marianne Moore, *In Distrust of Merits*

THE protagonist of a delightful short story by Carolyn Osborn, remembering, with less than entire delight, childhood Christmas presents, says, "Louisa May Alcott's books I rather liked except for their pervasive air of dutifulness which made me wary."[1] Osborn's wit is instructive and has its morals.

Suspicion of moral instruction in literature is widespread and has its causes, including the desire of audiences to escape moral and social restrictions through the play of art. Pauline Kael entitled a book about the movies *Kiss Kiss Bang Bang*.

Or, to put it another way: what is literature for? To be enjoyed. And yet, what do we enjoy most? What we can take seriously. For, as John Dryden says, "though the fancy may be great and the words flowing, yet the soul is but half satisfied when there is not truth in the foundation."[2] Those truths, not really deniable, constitute an essential part of Renaissance poetics, a poetics this essay shall support and illustrate.

Poetry is thus for delight as well as for instruction and for instruction as well as delight (and instruction in order to delight), and literature offers many and complex relatings between delight and instruction,[3] between art and truth, art as a *"just and lively image"*[4] of truth. Renaissance poetics and poetry understood that very well, as did Aristotle, Horace, Longinus, and others. Boccaccio writes, "Poetry comes from God; . . . its zeal is exalted; it drives the mind to a great longing for utterance; it invents . . . and orders . . . and adorns; and thus it covers truth with a fair and fitting veil of fiction."[5]

91

Such a tradition knew that Homer speaks to our hearts; it knew also, in Homeric phrase, that the heart is "dark-all-round,"[6] capable of being stirred to rage and deepened tears, and yet capable also of seeking what needs to be known. John Dryden writes, with a subtle and summing precision, "Poesy must resemble natural truth, but it must *be* ethical."[7] Poetry represents our experience: the representation is (or is not) ethically sound. Poems are artifacts; poems speak; poems judge.

One way that literature judges is by representing people toward whom it inevitably takes attitudes. Renaissance theorists, responding to the charge that poetry was immoral, urged that poetry teaches by offering us examples of virtue, which we may consequently emulate, and examples of vices to avoid.[8] The Renaissance concept of decorum, not to be validly dismissed as socially frivolous or politically hierarchical, and its relation to metrical practice, is crucial to our understanding of English Renaissance poetics and poetry, or, for that matter, of any other poetry.[9] Montgomery Belgion has argued that fiction is argument by example, and adds that a chief method of so arguing is "by enlisting the reader's sympathy for one character and rousing his antipathy against another,"[10] which puts him very much in line with a long tradition. Boccaccio writes in the fourteenth century, "Literature is exemplification or proof in fictitious form,"[11] and J. W. Binns sums the tradition by quoting Alberi Gentili, writing in the sixteenth century, "poetry falls under that area of logic which is engaged in the construction of examples."[12] That is not all that fiction, poetry, and drama are,[13] but it is importantly one of the things that they are, and the moral force of that truth should be plain enough. For fiction, poetry, and drama present characters and topics and offer attitudes towards those characters and topics, and to persuade us of attitudes is to engage, necessarily, logically, and inextricably, in moral suasion.

Nor can a literary artifact avoid such attitudes, for instance by being wholly neutral. For neutrality is an attitude, with distinct moral and evaluative implications depending on the context. Our lives and characters are complex and complexly chosen and derived, and a single piece of literature is not apt to do much to change them. At the same time one should not underrate the power of literature to affect action and belief.

Literature, then, offers examples and attitudes towards those examples, and people respond to such suasion. That is one way in which literature is moral judgment, moral truth (or error).

Another way in which literature is moral judgment is by statement, directly or by implication. The Elizabethan love for "gnomes," aphorism, and commonplaces speaks here, as does our experience. We like to hear truth well said.

Do we disagree about what is truth? Yes, we do, some of us, some of the time. We disagree and advance reasons for our disagreements, both activities implying a commitment to truth and to the possibility of discussing it intelligibly. Modern versions of skepticism, deconstruction, or reader's interpretation set readers "free" at unbearable cost, including the loss of all freedom to arrive at any genuineness or truth, and inevitably lunge them along in involved self-inconsistency neither masterable nor utterly disavowable. Hence the writhing rhetoric of the failure-to-evade.[14] And various denials of the possibility of intelligible meaning take the form of aphorism or commonplace, statements that exemplify what is denied—a poem should not mean but be;[15] no ideas but in things;[16] the poem of [the act of] the mind in the act of finding the individual thing.[17] Or Wallace Stevens, denying in strong poetry the possibility of just poetry, "That elemental parent, the green night, / Teaching a fusky alphabet."[18] We like to hear, well said, what we believe, even if that belief undercuts belief and the possibility of saying well.

Yet poetry does not merely say. Philip Sidney tells us that "Now, for the Poet, he nothing affirmes, and therefore neuer lyeth"[19] and Allen Tate writes of a stanza of Keats: "The stanza is neither true nor false; it is an object that exists."[20]

Surely Sidney and Tate are in some sense right. Sidney is right, since an author does not speak as such in his or her own person; the (more-or-less) invented narrator or character does the speaking, hence the author cannot be said to "affirm" (assert) each sentence in the work to be true. Yet the author still holds a responsibility for what is said, for instance by encouraging the audience to agree or disagree with the narrator or character, and hence does not really avoid all the responsibility for what is done and said in the work. And Sidney is also very much a defender of the high estate of poetry, its moral and religious strength. And Tate is right in asserting that the work is an artifact, not only a statement. A work of literary art is a statement *and* an artifact. The critic's job is to discriminate and to accord.

Sidney elsewhere in the *Apologie* shows that poetry teaches moral truth by example: "you see *Vlisses* in a storme, and in other hard plights . . . they are but exercises in patience and magnanimitie."[21] He also writes that "Poesie . . . should be *Eikastike,* which some learned haue defined, figuring foorth good things."[22] That is, Sidney believes that poetry was eikastic, based upon probabilities

and related to dialectic, rather than phantastic and related to so-
phistic and falsehood.[23] To figure forth good things is to teach virtue; to be related to probability is to be capable of, concordant
with, and reaching toward truth.

Allen Tate writes, nobly and relevantly, that the poet "is responsible . . . for the mastery of a disciplined language which will not
shun the full report of the reality conveyed to him by his awareness:
he must hold, in Yeats's great phrase, 'reality and justice in single
thought.'"[24] To report reality is to tell truth and to evaluate it
justly—that is, truly. Justice is founded on truth and is true.

At times Plato denied, for instance in the tenth book of the *Republic,* that the mimesis, the image of poetry, was valid, but Platonic and Neoplatonic fervor can see poetry as transcendent
toward the Divine Beauty[25] while also achieving a true and essential image of moral truth in action. Elstred, in Thomas Lodge's
The Complaint of Elstred, says, "Behold in me the tragedy of life, /
The true *Idea* of this worldly woe."[26] Note the combining of transcendence, the Platonic form, and moral and psychological understanding, a major Renaissance power of poetry.

Samuel Daniel's *The Complaint of Rosamond* deserves that
commendation and definition even more than Elstred, though the
poem of Elstred has its interest and power: that the Renaissance
writers so believed tells much of the accommodation of the classics
and of the power and beauty of all genuine poetry, which lifts our
hearts and helps define the nature of human action.[27]

These relations tangle deepeningly yet clearly in Shakespeare.
Sonnet 116 ends, "If this be error and upon me prov'd, / I never
writ, and no man ever lov'd."[28] The assertion is moral and ontological argument in a valid form of the hypothetical argument: if A,
then B; if not B, therefore not A. The couplet is the first premise
("if A, then B"). The rest of the argument is implicit and valid.
Since the poem is being written as he writes it, the statement "I
never writ, and no man ever lov'd" is and is thus proven false,
then the first statement "If this be error and upon me prov'd" is
consequently proven false. Thus the statement of the ideality of
love that is the poem is proven true. A critic of Shakespeare could
point out that Shakespeare, though he has proven the conclusion
true within the argument, has not proven that the first premise, the
couplet itself, is true. Shakespeare, knowing this, has faithfully
asserted the truth of what he says, and subtly and tauntingly has
shifted the burden of proof to the critic. "If this be error and upon
me prov'd" is a sort of logical dare. The logic of truth is troth, and
firm belief.

Richard III offers a bitter counterstatement and involution.

An[ne].	I would I knew thy heart.
Rich[ard].	'Tis figur'd in my tongue.
An.	I feare me, both are false.
Rich.	Then neuer Man was true.[29]

If (A) Richard's heart and tongue are false, then (b) never Man was true. So if any man was ever true, then it is false that Richard's heart and tongue are both false and that consequently his heart or tongue must be true. Like the couplet of Sonnet 116, Richard's argument justifies him within the argument. But he is lying, so the premise is false, and he is consequently and knowingly implying that all men are as false as he, a brutal and cynical piece of cynicism. "All men are bad, and in their badness reign" (as the speaker in Shakespeare's Sonnet 120 asserts in trying, not very convincingly, to deny).[30] Since the capital of the Folio's "Man" also suggests the class, the universal, Richard is attacking the very nature of mankind, which is blasphemy as well as cynicism. Christ, the only man who is also the class (*Man* Incarnate), is being denied. As Richmond later says in the play, Richard is "One that hath euer beene Gods Enemy."[31]

To be God's enemy is to lie and in the very process to deny the possibility of truth, to be unjust in the very center of one's intellect, bound to the Father of Lies.[32] Justice is profoundly involved with statement, with truth, with the possibility of statements stating truth, of being just to reality. To be just is to be true, and telling truth is implicit in Sidney's concept of the *eikastic* and in Tate's concept of responsibility. It means being true to the richness and complexity and plainness of one's experience and knowledge.

Can one be rhetorical and be true? Yes, by propriety, by decorum. Is that answer a simple answer? No. Rhetoric's relationships to decorum are not just opposition or compliance or irrelevance or separation. The use and abuse of persuasive eloquence; the sense of propriety to genre, style, audience, intent; the distinctions of style are much present in Renaissance education and poetry and encouraged poets to simultaneous and not always consistent love of plainness and love of richly manifested art.

Tensions and irresolutions are there, as there are between delight and instruction, but their presence does not necessarily mean failure or energizing antipoetics or perpetually and self-instructive-and-destructive self-reference, as much modern criticism would have it. The results are rich art and understanding worthy of our

praise, analysis, understanding, and emulation. Nor are the problems as desperate or intercounterfused as it sometimes seems or
is claimed.

Let us look a little at what was typically said by the Renaissance
critics and rhetoricians. The key word is *decorum*.

Thomas Wilson in *The Arte of Rhetorique* teaches that good
discourse should be plain. The poet or orator should "vtter his
mind in plain wordes, suche as are vsually receiued . . . without
goyng aboute the busshe. . . . For what manne can be delited or
yet be perswaded, with the onely hearyng of those thynges, which
he knoweth not what thei meane."[33]

Proper English does not consist of elaborate, allusive, and obscure literary showing-off. That is, there is improper decoration.
The poet or orator justifies plainness by propriety (decorum),
proper for good and normative English, proper to the audience (a
justly learned, unpedantic, unpretentious audience), and proper for
persuasion. "Elocution, is an appliying of apte wordes and sentences to the matter, founde out to confirme the cause," Wilson
writes.[34] He also teaches that discourse should have a style "apt
and mete,"[35] appropriate to the subject, properly consistent
throughout the discourse. The concept of unity is justified by the
concept of propriety. The concept does not outlaw shifts of tone,
catachreses, irony, or mock-epic. The total unity may well be complex; the unity needs to be achieved.

Having achieved such skills, the poet or orator should then seek
"exornacion," which "is a gorgiousse beautifiynge of the tongue
with borowed wordes, and chaung of sentence or speache, with
muche varietie."[36] Tropes are "vsed to beautifie the sentence, as
precious stones are sette in a ryng, to commende the golde."[37]

The tension between plainness and exornation (ornament, decoration) is easily perceived, a tension felt (very fruitfully at the best,
and with proper fruit) by Renaissance poets as well as by modern
critics and theorists. Hamlet has fun with Polonius's pompous criticism of the art of the theater; Hamlet achieves his own varied
exornation as well. Yet one connection with decorum is immediately apparent: the ornament should be fit, the precious stones
commend the gold, the pearl necklace be appropriate to the beauty
of the wearer, the beauty of both being enhanced by the ornament.

The temptation of exornation is to the insincere, the showily or
obscurely elaborate. The temptation of plainness is toward dull-
ness. J. V. Cunningham plainly writes, with the eloquence of wit:
"The difficulty with the flat style, of course, is that it is flat."[38] The
best Renaissance poetry achieves accommodation, richness, and

seriousness, the plain heartfelt and hungered for with a desire for the Golden Age, when "simple Truth did rayne, and was of all admyred,"[39] and the plain richly justified by context, delight, and instruction made one. And since such poetry happened, the relevant problems cannot be theoretically impossible of resolution: what happens is possible.

What happens is just evaluation appropriately within genre, a just evaluation that requires irreplaceable and singular individual judgment and valid concepts of what is just. In Spenser's Cave of Astraea, Astraea, the Goddess of Justice, teaches Artegal:

> There she him taught to weigh both right and wrong
> In equall ballance with due recompence,
> And equitie to measure out along,
> According to the line of conscience,
> When so it needs with rigour to dispence.[40]

The parable works for the critic and poet as well as for the judge or statesman or philosopher. Learning to judge well requires teaching and practice (not the automatic application of precepts) in, first, choosing what weights to use and making sure the balance and weights are appropriately and accurately ordered, and then knowing when to make equitable adjustments according to the singular instance. For a weight to be just it must be precisely and measurably well made. William Smith, in "A Breeff Description of the Famous Cittie of London," 1588, writes of "waightes & measures" that "if they [those testing the weights and measures] ffynd them not just: they break them in peeces."[41] Yet having just weights is not all there is to accurate weighing. The process is possible, difficult, intelligible and mysterious, and needs doing.

One of the chief ways in which English Renaissance poets learned to evaluate justly was by precision of rhythm within a metrical system that had great precision and great possibility of variation, the variations being significantly felt as meaning. The orator has the many tonalities of voice; the poet has rhythm perfected by meter. Wilson says of a speaker that his "deliueraunce" should have "grace, as the sound of a lute, or any suche instrument doeth geue."[42] The English Renaissance poets sought to tune their instruments variously, and justly, a justice that accords with "sentencies . . . well framed, and . . . words aptly vsed."[43] Not only is such justice artistic and moving: it *judges,* in judgment that can be just, which account in no small part for the Psalms' enduring power. That the greatest English translation of the Psalms was the King

James Psalms, in the period of the English Renaissance, is relevant
and heartening to the theses of this essay.

Sir Thomas Wyatt's sonnet "My galy charged with forgetful-
ness," a great translation of a great sonnet, Petrarch's Rime 189
(Sonnet 156), translates Petrarch's phrase "per aspro mare"
[through the harsh (or sharp) sea] "Thorrough sharpe sees."[44] The
Petrarchan phrase is harsh; the Wyatt translation catches perturba-
tion of crowded motion and the sharpness of the recurrent seas. Its
decorum is manifest and powerful, sound-locking-to-sense, without
being exhibitionistic.

Richard Barnfield writes of rabbits: "Some speckled here and
there with daintie spots."[45] Yes, they are, "spots" spotty, the
"speckled" somehow speckled, the line "dainty." And the playfulness is appropriate to the topic and treatment as it also is when
Barnfield protests against Artifice, praising a glove for being "Not
quaintly over-wrought with curious knots."[46] Sir Edward Dyer (or
someone—the attribution is uncertain)[47] writes of a timepiece:
"The Diall stirres, yet none perceiues it moouve."[48] The line focuses on "Diall," stirs strongly yet hesitantly with "stirres," moves
forward with only a quiet perception of its motion. Shakespeare
heard the power, the haunting paradoxicality of time, which much
obsessed him, and caught it, emulatively, powerfully, transform-
ingly, in Sonnet 104, lines 9–12.

> Ah yet doth Beauty, like a dial hand,
> Steal from his figure, and no pace perceiv'd;
> So your sweet hue, which methinks still doth stand,
> Hath motion, and mine eye may be deceiv'd.

Thomas Campion writes, translating a line of Catullus: "My
sweetest Lesbia, let us live and love."[49] The dignified convention
sets a basic tone of lyric strength, and the metrical and grammatical parallelism of "Les-," "live," and "love," figured into related
prominence by sound, meter, and alliteration, states the meaning
of the poem: the identity of true life and true love.

Chidiock Tichborne writes, before his execution:

> My glasse is full, and now my glass is runne;
> And now I liue, and now my life is done.[50]

"Glasse" and "life" are presented and repeated, then hasten
away, the motion and brevity signifying what is said.

Edward de Vere, earl of Oxford, writes, in mature and troubled fatigue:

> And weare I ded, no thought should me torment
> Nor wordes, nor wronges, nor loves, nor hopes, nor fears.[51]

Torment struggles; the "wordes" and "wronges" and "loves" and "hopes" and "fears," which constitute a mighty summation, with the dignity of the general, of what actually troubles human life, are strongly stressed and paralleled in their meaning, which is pain and meaningless struggle, in the troubled mind and feelings of the speaker.

Thomas Lodge writes:

> Hart vnstable, light as feathers.
> Tongue vntrustie, subtil sighted,
> Wanton will, with change delighted[52]

We believe him because he sounds what he says, in ways partially analyzable, singularly and truly present.

An anonymous inscription in St. Mary Magdalene, Milk Street, London, told us:

> Grasse of levitie,
> Span in brevitie,
> Flowers felicitie,
> Fire of miserie,
> Windes stabilitie
> is mortalitie.[53]

That sadly and strangely brief? Yes. How do we know? The inscription says it so. The church acted out the poem's truth of fire and wind: it was destroyed in the Great Fire of London.[54]

Examples abound in poetry, all our good poetry, because such workings are substantial to poetry; yet it may be fair to say (the statistics cannot be had) that English Renaissance poetry offers peculiarly many and effective examples of such effects, because a sound poetic and practice had been achieved, responsive to tradition, to genre, to subtle and varied decorums, to good models of learning from Italy and the classics and earlier English poets, the individual talent enlivened by sound and continuing and subtly changing tradition.

Nor is the tradition all joy and faith, ease, and clarity and genres neatly fulfilled. Not whatsoever. Think of Lear, of Timon, of much powerfully and desperately conveyed. Style can be appropriate and revelatory of doubt and pain: uncertainty, breakdown, violence can be caught in the strengths and mixings of genre and in the struggle against form. *Samson Agonistes* is a great example of the struggle within metrical form,[55] and Longinus offers some examples, brilliantly minute in rhetoric, grand in meaning, of how disorders succeed.[56]

Power, moral understanding, good rhetoric, propriety, the delight in form—all are constitutive in the English Renaissance's best understanding of what poetry is and does, but disorder is there too—shadows of night are on the page, as in a greatly strange moment in one of Ben Jonson's most beautiful and moving lyrics, which I shall discuss as a conclusion to this essay.

On My First Sonne.

FArewell, thou child of my right hand, and ioy;
My sinne was too much hope of thee, lou'd boy,
Seuen yeeres tho'wert lent to me, and I thee pay,
Exacted by the fate, on the iust day.
 O, could I loose all father, now. For why
 Will man lament the state he should enuie?
 To haue so soone scap'd worlds, and fleshes rage,
And, if no other miserie, yet age?
Rest in soft peace, and, ask'd, say here doth lye
Ben. Ionson his best piece of *poetrie.*
For whose sake, hence-forth, all his vowes be such
As what he loues may neuer like too much.[57]

"Exacted by the fate, on the iust day" is an exactingly just line. It implies that the child died on his birthday, its birthday then its death [fate] day, a return that to the father is just, even "fiscally." He must return what he was loaned and pay at the precisely appropriate time, as justice exacts. Jonson also alludes to the Mosaic law, stated in Deuteronomy 15:1–2, that at the end of seven years there shall be a release of debt.[58]

The cry becomes even more strange: "O, could I loose all father now." The idiom halts, in pain. The *lose-loose* pun (or word—the two words are intricately and historically connected) works more than one way: could lose, set loose, be loosed from what? fatherhood? my father? God's fatherhood? The noun *father,* without even an article to singularize it, violates and conjures language: thus all three—fatherhood, my father, God's fatherhood—reach towards being meant, in a pained brokenness of idiom. Not to have to be a father; not to have a father and thus not to be born; not to have a heavenly father who exacts justice. We love in Jonson his precision and exactitude of formal and emotional empowering within his controlled genre; here syntax and feeling fracture under stress, and yet withstand.

Notes

1. Carolyn Osborn, "A Christmas Survival Kit," from *A Texas Christmas*, ed. John Edward Weems. (Dallas: Pressworks, 1983), 111–22, 117.

2. John Dryden, "A Defence of an Essay of Dramatic Poesy," *Of Dramatic Poesy*, ed. George Watson, 2 vols. (New York: Dutton, 1962), 1:121.

3. See Paul Ramsey, *The Lively and the Just* (Tuscaloosa: University of Alabama Press), 11–16.

4. John Dryden, "An Essay of Dramatic Poesy," *Of Dramatic Poesy*, 1:25, italics original.

5. Boccaccio, *In Defence of Poetry*, ed. Jeremiah Reedy (Toronto: Centre of Medieval Studies by the Pontifical Institute of Mediaeval Studies, 1978); *Geneaologiae Deorum Gentilium, Liber XIV*, chap. 7, p. 34, trans. mine. "Poesis . . . est . . . ex sinu dei procedens. . . . Huius enim feruoris sunt sublimes effectus . . . puta mentem in desiderium dicendi compellere . . . inuenciones excogitare, meditatas ordine certo componere, ornare . . . uelamento fabuloso atque decenti ueritatem contegere" (34). See Charles S. Osgood, *Boccaccio on Poetry*, 2d ed. (New York: Liberal Arts Press, 1956), xxv–xxxvi for comment and 39 for his translation of the larger passage and context.

6. Homer *Iliad* 1.103 and elsewhere. Dr. Esther Hansen pointed out that the phrase is literally true as well as true in deep metaphor. We cannot normally see into the rib cage of a living person.

7. Dryden, "A Defence of an Essay," *Of Dramatic Poesy*, 1:121, italics original.

8. See O. B. Hardison, introduction, to *English Literary Criticism: The Renaissance*, ed. O. B. Hardison (New York: Meredith, 1963), 8.

9. See Rosemond Tuve, *Elizabethan and Metaphysical Imagery* (Chicago: University of Chicago Press, 1947), esp. chap. 9, for a wise and complex view of such matters. Also see Arthur F. Kinney, *Humanist Poetics* (Amherst: University of Massachusetts Press, 1986), esp. "Sir Philip Sidney, the Arcadia, and the Poetic Uses of Philosophy," esp. 285–91; and Heinrich F. Plett, "Style in Renaissance Poetics," *Renaissance Eloquence*, ed. James J. Murphy (Berkeley and Los Angeles: University of California Press, 1983), esp. 366–67 and ref.

10. Montgomery Belgion, "The Irresponsible Propagandist," *The Human Parrot and Other Essays* (1931; reprint, Freeport, N.Y.: Books for Libraries Press, 1967), 93.

11. Boccaccio, *In Defence of Poetry*, ed. Reedy, 41 (chap. 9 of book 14), 41, "fabula est exemplificari seu demonstratiua sub figmento loquutio." The translation is mine.

12. J. W. Binns, *Intellectual Culture in Elizabethan and Jacobean England: The Latin Writings of the Age* (Leeds: Francis Cairnes, 1990), 144. See also, for discussion of some of the variety of application of exempla, John Steadman's *The*

Lamb and the Elephant (San Marino, Calif.: Huntington Library, 1974), esp. 128–30.

13. For some further modes of poetry's use of logic and structure, see J. V. Cunningham, *Tradition and Poetic Structure* (Denver: Alan Swallow, 1960), esp. "Logic and Lyric," 40–58, and "The Logic of Structure," in *The Fickle Glass,* ed. Paul Ramsey, (New York: AMS Press, 1979), 117–234. For some relationships between such structures in various arts, see Steadman, *Lamb and Elephant,* 180–92.

14. Contemporary criticism offers, in Wallace Stevens's phrase, "pages of illustration." For some, and I would like to hope crucial, discussion, see Paul Ramsey, *The Truth of Value* (Atlantic Highlands, N.J.: Humanities Press, 1985), perhaps esp. 35, and the long accompanying note 9 on 115–16; and Ramsey, *Lively and Just,* esp. 103–17. For a defense of Stevens's procedures, a defense I respect aesthetically very much, see Harold Bloom, *Wallace Stevens: The Poems of Our Climate* (Ithaca and London: Cornell University Press, 1977), throughout. Yes, such procedures can make for strong and moving poetry if a strong and moving poet adopts them or desperately and hopelessly has them adopt him. Bloom finds, 2–3, that Stevens goes through crises, or Crossings, as "the Crossing of Election in 1915" (realizing that he was a poet of power) and "The Crossing of Solipsism (the fear that poetry is merely subjective and worthless [Bloom might paraphrase his notion elegantly otherwise, but I think my paraphrase just] . . . its crux . . . in 1921–22, and . . . not resolved until 1934–36. . . . The final crossing, that of Identification [the achievement of unity and great poetic strength, the Mirror and the Lamp well placed] took place in 1942." A happy ending? Hardly. Bloom goes on in the next sentence to say "it would be absurd to say that his remaining years were without poetic crises," since crisis-poems keep happening. At the book's end, Bloom writes, "Against the unifying interplay of the steps that tropes constitute in the dance of meaning, there is always a disjunctive or intertropical [and inter-arctic-al and inter-Antarctic-al?], which is a missing element in our understanding of the reading process" (406). That is, Stevens, reading, and criticism never get anywhere: I prefer, and not only prefer but think true, a poetics such as Renaissance poetics that can get somewhere.

15. Archibald MacLeish, "Ars Poetica," *Poems, 1924–1933* (Boston: Houghton Mifflin, 1933), 123.

16. William Carlos Williams, "A Sort of a Song," *The Collected Later Poems of William Carlos Williams,* rev. ed. (New York: New Directions, 1963), 7.

17. Wallace Stevens, "Of Modern Poetry," *The Collected Poems of Wallace Stevens* (New York: Alfred A. Knopf, 1954), 239–40, esp. the first and last lines of the poem.

18. Stevens, *Collected Poems,* "Phosphor Reading by His Own Light," 267.

19. Sir Philip Sidney, *An Apologie for Poetrie* (London, 1595), sig. G4v. Facsimile edition, no. 413 of the English Experience (Amsterdam and New York: Da Capo Press, 1971).

20. Allen Tate, "Three Types of Poetry," *On the Limits of Poetry* (New York: Swallow Press and William Morrow, 1948), 112 and context.

21. Sidney, *Apologie,* sig. E2v.

22. Ibid., sig. H2.

23. See Hardison, *English Literary Criticism,* 129, n. 23, and idem, *The Enduring Monument* (Chapel Hill: University of North Carolina Press), 56, for a discussion of eikastic poetry. See also Kathy Eden's excellent discussion of Sidney's theory in "The Logic and Psychology of Renaissance Fiction: Sidney's *Apology*

for Poetry," sect. 4 of "Image and Imitation," in *Poetic and Legal Fiction in the Aristotelian Tradition,* in Kathy Eden (Princeton: Princeton University Press, 1986), 157–75.

24. Allen Tate, "To Whom Is the Poet Responsible?", *The Forlorn Demon* (Chicago: Regnery, 1953), 29. See William Butler Yeats, *A Vision* (reissue with the author's final revisions) (New York: Macmillan, 1956), 25.

25. See John Vyvyan, *Shakespeare and Platonic Beauty* (New York: Barnes and Noble, 1961), esp. 15–60 and appendices.

26. Thomas Lodge, *Phillis . . . and Elstred* (London: John Busbie, 1593), sig. H4. See Hardison, *Enduring Monument,* 56–58, for a discussion of *idea* and related notions, including *pictura* and *eidolon,* in Renaissance criticism.

27. For a discussion of Kenneth Burke's similar theory, see Walter A. Davis, *The Act of Interpretation: A Critique of Literary Reason* (Chicago and London: University of Chicago Press, 1978), esp. 35, and George Knox, *Critical Moments: Kenneth Burke's Categories and Critiques* (Seattle: University of Washington Press, 1957), esp. 4, where he says Burke's theory involves "levels" and "hier-archy" and "dancing of an attitude." That does not sound much like Renaissance poetics, but, on reflection (my reflection, anyway), it is very close. (So is very much criticism close to Renaissance poetics, especially insofar as the criticism and Renaissance poetics are true.) See also the discussion of Burke in "Symbolic Action" and its references in the third edition of *Princeton Encyclopedia of Poetry and Poetics,* ed. Alex Preminger and T. V. J. Brogan, assoc. ed. O. B. Hardison, et al. (Princeton: Princeton University Press, 1993.)

28. Quotations from Shakespeare's Sonnets are from my not-yet-published edition.

29. Quoted from the Norton facsimile, *The First Folio of Shakespeare,* ed. Charlton Hinman (New York: W. W. Norton, 1968), 530, through-lines 387–90 (1.2.192–95 [by line numeration of *The Riverside Shakespeare,* ed. G. Blakemore Evans et al. (Boston: Houghton Mifflin, 1974), 716]).

30. See the discussion in Ramsey, *Glass,* 146–48.

31. Norton facsimile, 557, line 3718 (5.3.252, Riverside ed.).

32. See Saint Anselm, "De Veritate," in *Opera Omnia,* 5 vols. (Edinburgh: Thomas Nelson, 1940–51, 1946 for vol. 1), 180–81.

33. Thomas Wilson, *The Arte of Rhetorique.* (London: Ihon Kingston, 1553), sig. M4v. Facsimile edition, no. 206 of the English Experience (Amsterdam and New York: Da Capo Press, 1971), sig. a.i., fol. 1.

34. Ibid., sig. a.iv, fol. 4.

35. Ibid., sig. y.iv, fol. 88.

36. Ibid., sig. z.ii, fol. 90.

37. Ibid., sig. y.iv., fol. 88.

38. J. V. Cunningham, "Lyric Style in the 1590's," in *The Problem of Style,* ed. J. V. Cunningham (Greenwich, Conn.: Fawcett Publications), 168.

39. Edmund Spenser, *The Second Part of the Faerie Queene* (London, 1596), book 5, prologue, stanza 3, line 9, sig. M4v, 184.

40. Ibid., canto 1, sig. M7, 189.

41. British Library, Harleian manuscript 6363, fol. 13.

42. Wilson, *Rhetorique,* sig. a.ii., fol. 2.

43. Ibid.

44. Quoted from Francesco Petrarcha, *Le Rime* (Florence: Salani, 1965), 227, Sonet 156, line 2; *The Collected Poems of Sir Thomas Wyatt,* ed. Kenneth Muir (Cambridge: Harvard University Press, 1949), 28, line 2.

45. Richard Barnfield, "The Affecionate Shepherd," stanza 32, line 5, in *The Poems of Richard Barnfield,* intro. Montague Summers (London: Fortune Press, [1936]), 7.

46. Richard Barnfield, *Cynthia* (London, 1595), Sonnet 14, verse 2, sig. C4v.

47. See Hyder Edward Rollins, ed., and Frances Davison, comp., *A Poetical Rhapsody 1602–1621* (Cambridge: Harvard University Press, 1931), 2:165. The poem is anonymous in the anthology.

48. Quoted from "The lowest Trees have tops," in ibid., 1:186, no. 128 for text, and 2:164–71 for commentary.

49. Thomas Campion, from *A Booke of Ayres* (1601), poem no. 1 in *The Works of Thomas Campion,* ed. Walter R. Davis (London: Faber and Faber, 1969), 18. See footnotes to 18 for discussion of Catullus.

50. *Certaine English Verses, Presented vnto the Queenes Most Excellent Maiestie* . . . (London: Henrie Haslop, 1586), sig. Aiiv.

51. Quoted from British Library, Add. MS 22583, fol. 95v. See *The Poems of Edward de Vere . . . and Essex,* ed. Steve W. May, *Studies in Philology,* no. 5 (Early Winter 1980): 37.

52. Thomas Lodge, "An Ode," in *Phillis* (London: John Busbie, 1593), sig. H3v.

53. Quoted from John Stow, *The Survay of London,* revised by Anthony Munday (London, 1618), 531, sig. Mm2. The poem appeared on the monument of Sir William Stone, d. 14 September 1607.

54. See Charles Knight, *London,* rev. E. Walford, 6 vols. (London: Virtue, [1851 and later]), 5:164.

55. See Yvor Winters, *In Defense of Reason* (London: Routledge and Kegan Paul, 1960), 147.

56. Longinus, *On the Sublime,* trans. Nicholas Boileau Despreaux (1674) and William Smith (1729) (Delmar, N.Y.: Scholars Facsimiles and Reprints, 1975), 57. Cf. Boileau, 50.

57. Epigram no. 45, in *The Workes of Beniamin Jonson* (London, 1616), 780–81, sigs. [Ttt6v]–Vuu [1]. Jonson calls his epigrams the ripest of his studies (767, sig. [Sss6]).

58. See Kathryn Walls, "The 'Just Day' in Jonson's 'On My First Sonne,'" *Notes and Queries* 222 (1977): 136.

Spenser's Farewell to Dido: The Public Turn

RONALD HORTON

NOVEMBER in Spenser's *The Shepheardes Calender* has been from the first one of the most admired and most mysterious of the twelve eclogues, if we may credit the observations of Spenser's equally mysterious though less generally admired annotator, E. K. The eclogue has seemed questionably placed and curiously addressed. Its zodiacal sign is wrong (line 16; the fish belongs to February), and "Dido," the eulogized deceased, has so far proved unidentifiable. Dido's identity, says E. K., is "unknowen and closely buried in the Authors conceit."[1] The mystery is all the more tantalizing in that Dido was not a standard pastoral name; its provenance is heroic, not bucolic. And yet, as S. K. Heninger remarks, "The interpretative crux of *November* rests with the identity of Dido," which is thus far undiscerned.[2] I wish to address this question; but before doing so I will need to consider the preceding one, the position of *November* in the *Calender* itself. Situating *November* in the scheme of the *Calender* will provide some groundwork for my conclusions concerning Dido.

The *Calender*, of course, arranges its twelve pastoral pieces by month and by season, from *January* to *December*, maintaining general correlation between the settings, activities, and moods of the eclogues and the time of the year. *January* and *December* are closely associated in setting, mood, and verse form, providing cyclical continuity as the old year yields to the new. Isabel MacCaffrey speaks for most critics of her time and since in citing W. W. Greg's account of the *Calender's* structure as "still the most comprehensive and objective":

> The architectonic basis of Spenser's design consists of the three Colin eclogues standing respectively at the beginning, in the middle, and at close of the year. These are symmetrically arranged . . . [and supported] by two subsidiary eclogues, those of April and August, in both of which another shepherd sings one of Colin's lays.[3]

105

John D. Bernard sees *June* also as the thematic center of the *Calender,* reflecting the balancing point "between pastoral alienation and pastoral contentment."[4] This analysis has the advantage of associating the primary structural contour with the story of Colin Clout, the central figure. It does not account for the position of *November,* the one other eclogue in which Colin appears and the only one in which he sings his own formal lay.

The four eclogues with Colin—*January, June, November, and December*—are designated "Plaintive" in E. K.'s three-way classification: the three that halve the year plus *November. February, May, July, September,* and *October* are "Moral," and the others, "which conceive matter of love, or commendation of special personages," are "recreative." Guided by this scheme, which E. K. acknowledges to be somewhat rough, impaired by his ignorance of the "special purpose and meaning" of "a fewe," we may refine our sense of the poem's contours. *January* through *June* forms a chiasmic sequence (plaintive-moral-recreative-recreative-moral-plaintive). A central panel, *April* through *August,* shows simple bilateral symmetry (recreative-moral-plaintive-moral-recreative). *May* through *September* exhibits antithetical bilateral symmetry (moral-plaintive-moral-recreative-moral). *September* through *December* is binary *(moral-moral-plaintive-plaintive).* Within the encompassing circularity of the *Calender* the symmetry of the groupings gradually relaxes, from the envelope structure of eclogues 1–6 to the bilateral symmetry of 4–8, the antithetical bilateralism of 5–9, and the binary association of 9–12. The structure uncoils as counterrelational stasis yields to linearity.

If we accept the implications of this analysis and regard the plaintive eclogues as the spine of the structure and therefore formally normative in the *Calender,* it seems natural to see the recreative and moral modes as thematic opposites associated with the seasons. We may notice in the first six eclogues a recreative loop but also, beginning as early as *May* and extending through *October,* a tendency toward arrangement along a moral axis. A brightening and darkening of tone, of course, suit the spring and autumn seasons, but the correlation is not precise, the latter beginning before midsummer. There seem instead to be lines of development toward moral seriousness, a seriousness that assimilates and transforms the recreative, investing it with moral purpose. In the latter half of the *Calender,* the recreative assimilates to the moral and both to the plaintive, a process culminating in the final quarter of the poem and centering on *November.*

This analysis of the framework's dynamics has, of course, been conducted on a high level of abstraction and may seem unconvincing without a closer look at the conduct of the eclogues. Immediately after *January,* which presents the character of Colin and his situation, is the first moral eclogue. *February,* however, is more than just an exemplar of satirical moralism; it is clearly paradigmatic. The dyspeptic, pompous old shepherd Thenot and the jeering youth Cuddie are confrontational spokesmen for the moral and recreative modes, which seem here irreconcilable. Both express views of love that are unrealistic and extreme. Cuddie confidently advocates the pursuit of love that has bound Colin:

> But *Phyllis* is myne for many dayes:
> I wonne her with a gyrdle of gelt,
> Embost with buegle about the belt.
>
> (64–66)

Thenot replies,

> Thou art a fon, of thy love to boste,
> All that is lent to love, wyll be lost.
>
> (69–70)

In the recreative *April,* however, it is Thenot who calls for a song of Colin from Hobbinol, who sings of "fayre *Elisa.*" (34). Conversely, in recreative *August,* Cuddie, after judging the singing match, sings a plaintive lay of Colin on the sorrows of love, taking a line similar to Thenot's in *February.* In *October* a still more serious Cuddie moralizes, if in a self-regarding way, on the decay of poetry due to the decline of patronage and material reward. Thenot and Cuddie thus connect through Colin and in the course of their careers in the *Calender* participate in one another's modes.

The moral-ecclesiastical series *May, July,* and *September* presents deadlocked debate between good and bad pastors in *May* and *July* (*May* repeating the dialogue-and-fable format of *February* but with animals rather than plants discoursing). Up through *July,* moral dialogue in the *Calender* ends in impasse, although some common ground emerges at the end of *July* in shared admiration for Algrind. *September* is in the form of an interview rather than a conflictus. Hobbinol, who in *April* spoke for Arcadian *otium,* here questions Diggon Davie concerning what he has learned of church corruption. Diggon, like Cuddie in *October,* is a reconstructed libertine, no longer a self-seeking scorner of strictness. Summer's end shows secular amoralists engaged in moral discourse with softened moral antipathies.

March, which begins the recreative series, is pure *jeu d'esprit.*
Thomalin's account to Willye of his misencounter with the love
god is entirely comical. *April,* incorporating Colin's song in honor
of Elisa, raises the recreative to the sublime, showing that delight
need be no less for being serious. In *August,* the third and last
recreative eclogue, Willye reappears in a singing match, which ends
with a lover's lament by Colin sung by Cuddie. The recreative
momentarily takes on moral high seriousness in *April,* and finally
in *August* flows into the plaintive. There does seem to be a soften-
ing of generic boundaries as we approach the last quarter of the
year.

In moral *October* the moral-satirical merges with the plaintive,
as poetry is discussed in a social context. Piers, whose moralism
has earlier been directed against religious wrong, corrects the aesthetic values of Cuddie, who with Hobbinol ranks next to Colin in
singing. Poetry, Piers insists, is a moral vocation whose chief end
is the improvement of its auditors. He urges Cuddie to redirect his
ambition toward a nobler career goal than that which is the cause
of his frustration: material reward. The pattern has been laid down
in Vergil. But all that Cuddie can get from Piers's admonition is
the lack of a patron such as Vergil's Maecenas. Wine and wealth,
to Cuddie, are adequate inspiration and reward. He has no ear, no
heart, for Piers's intangibles:

> *Cuddie,* the prayse is better, then the price,
> The glory eke much greater than the gayne:
> O what an honor is it, to restraine
> The lust of lawlesse youth with good advice:
> Or pricke them forth with pleasaunce of thy vaine,
> Whereto thou list their trayned willes entice.
>
> (19–24)

Cuddie should turn from "the base and viler clowne" (37), the
matter of popular verse, "And sing of bloody Mars, of wars, of
giusts" (39), the matter of heroic poetry after the example of Vergil.
But he is too demoralized to consider the attempt: "For *Colin* fittes
such famous flight to scanne" (88).

The viewpoint of *October* articulates with all three modes—
moral, recreative, and plaintive—pointing toward a synthesis of
moral purpose and aesthetic pleasure in higher subject matter and
style. The moral Piers discourses with the champion singer of the
lighter lay, Cuddie, and both agree on the sad state of poetry.
Cuddie is no remedy, however, because of his earthbound perspec-

tive. What is needed is a poet with Piers's high-mindedness and Cuddie's skill. Enter Colin Clout in the *November* eclogue.

October thus sets the stage for the climactic appearance of Colin Clout in *November*. It establishes an ethical context for his performance, delineating the role and career path of the poet, and identifies Colin as possessing the skills necessary for success in that role and career. *November* will show Colin, in a minor poetic mode, willingly putting these skills to noble use. In *October* the plaintive, moral, and recreative modes are loosely associated in the characters, tone, and subject matter. In *November* they will triumphantly converge.

November, a plaintive eclogue, exhibits the dialogue-song format of the recreative eclogues *April* and *August*. The quintessential moralist Thenot urges Colin to sing a song "of some jouissance" (2) as in earlier days—of "thy loved lasse" (7) or of Pan—something that Colin can be remembered by. Though Thenot deplores the effect on Colin of "love's misgovernaunce" (4), he evidently is not now opposed to shepherds' love on principle. Colin replies that such songs are out of season but agrees to improvise a song on a subject suggested by Thenot: the death of Dido. Oddly, the shepherd's embodiment of stern moralism requests a song in the recreative mode and is satisfied by a lament. The lament, it turns out, will nevertheless yield doctrine and delight of the highest order. In the course of the lament we hear that Dido's death has been instructive:

> Now have I learnd (a lesson derely bought)
> That nys on earth assuraunce to be sought.
>
> (156–57)

Soon, however, the "careful verse" (162) becomes a "joyfull verse" (172):

> Why wayle we then? why weary we the Gods with playnts,
> As if some evill were to her betight?
> She raignes a goddesse now emong the saints;
> That whilome was the saynt of shepheardes light.
>
> (173–77)

No critical concept was more widely known and assumed by Renaissance literary theorists and practitioners than Horace's observation that the best poetry gives both profit and pleasure. To succeed with the young, poetry must delight; to succeed with the old, it must teach; to succeed with both old and young, it must

combine these didactic and recreative functions. Poetry, argues
Philip Sidney in the *Defense of Poesy,* is better than history to
teach and than philosophy to move with delight, combining the
strengths without the weaknesses of these honored disciplines. Poetry indeed delights *in order* to teach. This central tenet of Renaissance criticism, reflected in Piers's admonition, is theoretical
grounding for the converging of the moral and recreative modes in
the *Calender.* First shown dissevered, they gradually connect and
coalesce, the moral becoming more articulate and winsome and
the recreative more questioning and serious. Whereas in the absence of Colin the other shepherds address national evils in their
earnest, quaint, often fumbling ways or spend their hours idling,
in Colin's interaction with Thenot and subsequent performance in
November the instructive and pleasurable become one. The Hora-
tian ideal is formalized in the action of the poem.

Now if we give the dial of the *Calendar* a two-month turn
counter-clockwise so that the year begins in March, as in the older
reckoning, certain symmetries highlight Colin's increasing participation in the pastoral life, in person or by proxy. *June* and *November,* the two eclogues other than *January* and *December* in which
Colin is heard in his own voice, are positioned symmetrically in
the twelve months. *April, August,* and *November,* which incorporate songs of Colin, sung by Hobbinol in *April* and Cuddie in *August* and by Colin himself in *November,* are also proportionally
placed. *August* is the year's turning point, like *June* in the published order. *April* and *November* appear one month after the beginning of the natural year and one month before the conclusion
of the Christian year. They incorporate encomia idealizing Elisa
and Dido-Elissa,[5] set pieces intended to dazzle as prime advertise-
ments of poetic skill. Their effect is apotheosis: pagan deification
of the "Queene of shepheardes all" (34) in *April,* Christian canon-
ization of the "saynt of shepheards light" (176) in *November.*

A Vergilian context is suggested by Thenot's and Hobbinol's
emblems appended to *April.* Together they repeat the words spoken by Aeneas when after having been cast ashore near Carthage
he encounters his mother, Venus, disguised as a virgin huntress.

O quam te memorum Virgo? [By what name, Maiden, may I know
    you?]
O dea certe. [Surely a goddess.]

They obviously reinforce the association of Colin's Elisa with England's virgin queen and both with the virgin goddess Diana, whose

shape Venus has assumed. But the Vergilian allusion also associates *April* with *November,* whose celebree, another powerful female force in Aeneas's life, has died. Venus has come to explain to her son where he has landed and where he must go. She directs him towards the palace of Dido. Venus's words to her bewildered son on his arrival on the coast of North Africa and Dido's furious reproaches and subsequent suicide on his departure demarcate the experience of Aeneas in the first four books of Vergil's epic: a period of subjection to passion, which will end, after the summons of Mercury, with Aeneas's leaving Carthage in obedience to the will of the gods. And this brings us to the second of the questions surrounding *November* noted at the beginning: the identity of Dido.

Spenser's age inherited two Didos from literary tradition. The Ovidian Dido is a victim of faithlessness in love, abandoned by Aeneas despite his vows. This is the Dido of Jean de Meun, of the twelfth-century *Roman d'Enéas,* and of late-medieval love complaints modeled on the *Heroides.* She is one of Cupid's saints in Chaucer's *Legend of Good Women,* provoked to suicide by her treacherous lover, who "swore so depe to hire to be trewe, / For wel or wo, and chaunge hire for no newe."[6] The Vergilian Dido, constructed by a thousand years of allegorical interpretation from Fulgentius to Landino, is a subverter of high purpose, a Circe figure detaining Aeneas from his heaven-inspired mission and threatening to stunt his moral growth. She images the pull of the passions against moral duty and mission.[7] Aeneas's sojourn in Carthage is, at best, emotional immaturity. Prolonged, it becomes censurable moral truancy. The values of Renaissance humanists naturally favored Aeneas over Dido.[8]

The mourned and enskied Dido of the *November* eclogue evokes the martyred saint of the *Legend of Good Women* lamented by Colin's master, the English Tityrus. The tone is appropriately melancholy, before it turns to joy (163), and is favorable to Dido throughout. But it is clear from the prefatory *Letter to Sir Walter Raleigh,* appended by Spenser to the first edition of *The Faerie Queene,* that his Aeneas was that of the Romish Tityrus, Vergil (*October,* 55). The Vergilian epic hero was for Spenser as for Tasso morally normative, combining the moral excellencies of the "good governour" and "vertuous man" imaged separately by Homer in Agamemnon and Ulysses.

This double status of Dido, psychologically positive but morally negative, is provided for in Vergil's account and seems to have influenced Spenser's choice of Dido as the heroine of *November.*

Her death, while a joyous celebration, serves, like her namesake's, as a corrective of Colin's behavior in the *Calender.* And yet Dido is to be envied and honored. In lines 178–79 Colin sees his Dido, as Aeneas his abandoned queen, walking "in *Elisian* fieldes so free." Dido has died to be resurrected and installed in a much worthier and more consequential position than that of a "saynt of shepherds light." She is a genial spirit able to affect life in Arcadia more significantly than before. Love of the Vergilian Dido is the enemy of achievement and growth, what Thenot had in mind when he insisted to Cuddie, "All that is lent to love, wyll be lost" (*February,* 70). Another love, urged on Cuddie by Piers, the sensible moralist of *October,* can lift one "out of the loathsome myre" (92) and "rayse ones mynd above the starry skie" (94). Love is the cure for love. Vergil's Carthaginian Dido can be translated into Spenser's Dido-Elissa. Dido occupies two rungs on Spenser's ladder of love.

The allegorical reading of Vergil's narrative took hold partly because, as E. M. W. Tillyard observed, it was really to an extent warranted in the text.[9] There is an inwardness to the career of Aeneas as Vergil devised it, especially in the first, or "Odyssean," half of the epic. Brooks Otis, one of Vergil's most astute critics, gives convincing support to this reading, in language suggestive of the Colin story and of Spenser's self-projection in Colin's plight. In book 4 of the *Aeneid,* Aeneas "is caught and temporarily lost in the tempestuous passion of Dido and in his own passion for her. . . . We see the true vulnerability of the man, the real consequence of the loss of Anchises, his unreadiness for a destiny that required initiative of the most resolute kind. In short, the problem posed by Book 4 is precisely Aeneas' eclipse, his passivity and weakness. . . . He fails to be what he has to be if he is really to lay claim to either heroism or *pietas.*"[10]

Philip Sidney understood from his own experience the conflicting moral claims on Aeneas and the difficulty of negotiating them honorably. Like Spenser, he found in the Vergilian Aeneas an example of proper self-rule:

> Only let *Aeneas* be worne in the tablet of your memory; how he governeth himselfe in the ruine of his Country; in the preserving his old Father, and carrying away his religious ceremonies; in obeying the Gods commandement to leave *Dido,* though not onely all passionate kindness, but even the humane consideration of vertuous gratefulness, would have craved other of him; how in storms; howe in warre; howe in peace; how a fugitive; how victorious; how besiedged; how besiedg-

ing; howe to strangers; howe to allyes; how to enemies; howe to his owne: lastly, how in his inward selfe, and how in his outward government. And I thinke, in a minde not preiudiced with a preiudicating humor, hee will be found in excellencie fruitfull.[11]

Despite the moral ambiguity of Aeneas's decision to leave Dido, it is clear to Sidney that a conviction of duty must override all emotional reluctance and hesitation. Venus must yield to Mercury. Dido is to be pitied but is no less to be refused.

What I am proposing is a reading of the *November* eclogue in keeping with the implied Vergilian allegorical context. The Odyssean *Aeneid* is shadowed in *The Shepheardes Calender,* as are both the Odyssean and the Iliadic halves in *The Faerie Queene,* especially the Book of Holiness. Accordingly, Colin's *November* dirge is Spenser's farewell to Dido, formalizing the traditional turn from the poetry that centers on self and serves the self-absorbed to public discourse directed toward public recognition and reward. It is not the renunciation of earthly for ideal love of Petrarch's *Canzoniere* and its imitators; for ideal love in Spenser is typically revealed in moral and social impact rather than in spiritual exaltation. Spenser's great work, like that of Aeneas, is of this world and lies ahead. Like Aeneas, he is committed to a mission that will try the limit of his skill and wisdom. The raising of Troynovant will cost him much that is worthy as well as unworthy in his time-bound pursuits. But Dido's death, for Spenser as for Aeneas, is essential and augurs better days. Thenot's pronouncement, "For dead is Dido, dead alas and drent" (37), is a key unlocking an obsessive egocentric prison, releasing creative forces that can benefit humanity. Her voluntary death is necessary to her rebirth in poetry of oracular power and moral vision.

It seems then that Spenser expected the *Calender* to be read against the full spread of Vergil's work as a poet. But what of Colin's adieu to love and happiness and life in *December?* The twelfth eclogue is conspicuously anticlimactic, and seems so for reasons other than just the cycle of months, the necessity of its connecting with *January.* Colin's description of his condition to Hobbinol in the pivotal *June* alludes to the opening lines of the *Aeneid,* associating Colin with Vergil's frustrated questing hero: "But I unhappy man, whom cruell fate, / And angry Gods pursue from coste to coste, / Can nowhere fynd, to shroude my luckless pate" (14–16). Colin at the end of the *Calender* has aged in the Odyssean phase of Aeneas's career. He is stuck in Carthage, though having witnessed momentarily in vision the distant shores.

This is not Spenser's case. As the logic of the calendar asserts itself in the physical decline of the character Colin as an inhabitant of Arcadia, we recognize that he has never been more than a hypothetical persona for the author. Spenser is announcing his own departure for Troynovant, which he must help to build. Dido being dead, his pastoral world must die with her. In *December* Colin recapitulates his wasted life and Spenser signals the dying of his own youth. As Colin hangs his pipe upon the tree, Spenser certifies the passing of the infatuations and poetic subject matters and modes that suited their season but that, if continued, will distract and detain him, as surely as a Calypso or Circe or Dido, from his nation-building mission. The enfeebling of Colin in *December,* like the weakening of Hobbinol in *October,* is the dying of the author's youth into maturity, an event to be celebrated, then left in the past. In *December* Spenser reprises his farewell to Dido in a farewell to Colin. Arcadia, Sidney notwithstanding, furnishes few subjects for a heroic poem.

This movement from private preoccupation to public performance, I have argued, in a study directed years ago by the honoree of this volume, is a powerful organizational principle of *The Faerie Queene.*[12] The movement is staged as a vocational crisis in *The Shepheardes Calender,* the resolution of which requires a willed redirection of the poetic imagination. Colin's story defines the true poet's relation to the specious Petrarchism that Spenser associated with unmanly introversion and psychological confusion. It encumbers Colin from the beginning (its fullest expression is in *January*) and is with him at the end. Courtly eroticism is deceitful, a dead end that mocks the ambitious poet, unworthy of his abilities and devotion. Moralizing pessimism, on the other side, is also a trap. We must not take as normative Thenot's earlier cynicism toward love. The viewpoints of Thenot and Cuddie in *February,* then, do not constitute the whole of Spenser's imaginary world. Reading *The Shepheardes Calender* in our post-Blakean era, we tend to divide the eclogues between Innocence and Experience, fitting them to our prevailing world view. We fail to see that they are dissociated and distorted in Spenser's Arcadia for lack of a participating Colin. What we are presented with instead is the age-old tragedy of inarticulate wisdom.[13] Colin is so entirely wrapped up in himself he cannot serve the world to which he is given. The world awaits his *melior ego* at the end.

Notes

1. *The Yale Edition of the Shorter Poems of Edmund Spenser,* ed. William A. Oram et al. (New Haven: Yale University Press, 1989), 196. All quotations from *The Shepheardes Calender* will refer to this edition.

2. "The Shepheardes Calender," *The Spenser Encyclopedia*, ed. A. C. Hamilton (Toronto: University of Toronto Press, 1990), 650.

3. "From Allegory to Pastoral in *The Shepheardes* Calender," *ELH* 36 (1969): 92–93; W. W. Greg, *Pastoral Poetry and Pastoral Drama* (London: Sidgwick, 1906), 90.

4. "'June' and the Structure of Spenser's *Shepheardes Calender*," *Philological Quarterly* 60 (1981): 316.

5. Elissa is Vergil's other name for Dido, perhaps reflected in *"Elisian* fields" (179).

6. F. N. Robinson, ed., *The Works of Geoffrey Chaucer,* 2d ed. (Boston: Houghton Mifflin, 1957), 503.

7. Merritt Hughes, *Virgil and Spenser* (1929; reprint, Port Washington, N.Y.: Kennikat, 1969), 336–37. Gilbert Highet points out that Shakespeare modeled Cleopatra on the Ovidian Dido and cites lines directly quoted from her reproach of Aeneas in the *Heroides* (*The Classical Tradition* [1949; reprint, New York: Galaxy, 1957], 205–6, 621). See D. C. Allen, *Mysteriously Meant: The Rediscovery of Pagan Symbolism and Allegorical Interpretation in the Renaissance* (Baltimore: Johns Hopkins University Press, 1970), 135–62, for a detailed account of medieval allegorical interpretation of the *Aeneid.* Leslie T. Whipp's "Weep for Dido: Spenser's November Eclogue," in *Spenser Studies: A Renaissance Poetry Annual* 11 (1990), New York: AMS Press, 1994, pages 17–30, applies this background to the Dido of *November* in an argument that has some parallels with my discussion but became known to me too late to be made use of.

8. Hughes, *Virgil and Spenser,* 336–37.

9. *The English Epic and Its Background* (1954; reprint, New York: Oxford University Press, 1966), 137.

10. *Virgil: A Study in Civilized Poetry* (Oxford: Clarendon Press, 1963), 266.

11. *An Apology for Poetry,* ed. Geoffrey Shepherd (London: Nelson, 1965), 119–20.

12. *The Unity of "The Faerie Queene"* (Athens: University of Georgia Press, 1979).

13. Cf. the inept aged "goodly Oake" of Thenot's fable in *February,* who "cast him to replie / Welle as he couth" (189–90), and the simple curate Sir John mentioned by Palinode in *May,* for whose preaching he would borrow Piers's tale: "For well he meanes, but little can say" (311).

Sidney, Shakespeare, and the Fallen Poet

ROBERT L. MONTGOMERY

SHAKESPEARE'S Sonnet 84, one of a cluster of metapoetic sonnets ranging from 76 through 86, celebrates the young man by arguing that any poet writing of him perhaps does best "if he can tell, / That you are you" (7–8), and Shakespeare's speaker adds the imperative, "Let him but copy what in you is writ" (9). This last phrase clearly quotes Sidney's Astrophil, who concludes the third sonnet, "then all my deed / But copying is, what in her Nature writes" (*Astrophil and Stella*, 13–14).[1] Shakespeare's borrowing marries his work to one of the more persistent features of Petrarchan love poetry, the problem of how to praise well but without artifice; and that in turn calls up a related issue but one of greater range and significance, the status of the poet and the nature of his efforts, a preoccupation in the sequences of Sidney and Shakespeare both and as such a consciously designed part of their fictional worlds.[2]

As Germaine Warkentin has remarked, one of the distinctive features of the late medieval and Renaissance poetic sequence is that the poet, as well as his mistress, is the subject of the verse.[3] Astrophil's consciousness of his role as poet and ultimately his frustration as poet and lover both are grounded in his unblushing effort at seductive persuasion. At first Astrophil offers up a series of caustic and sarcastic comments on kinds of poetic artifice and indirection as a contrast to his own full-frontal sincerity. This is the burden of Sonnet 3, which will do duty for 6 and 15 as well.

> Let dainty wits cry on the sisters nine,
> That bravely masked, their fancies may be told:
> Or Pindar's apes, flaunt they in phrases fine,
> Enam'lling with pied flowers their thoughts of gold:
>   Or else let them in statlier glory shine,
> Ennobling new-found tropes with problems old:
> Or with strange similes enrich each line,
> Of herbs or beasts, which Ind or Afric hold.
>   For me, in sooth, no muse but one I know;
>   Phrases and problems from my reach do grow,

116

And strange things grow too dear for my poor sprites.
How then? Even thus: in Stella's face I read
What love and beauty be; then all my deed
But copying is, what in her nature writes.

In addition to the pose of genuine feeling, there is the claim of
exclusivity, the notion that as poet he has but one subject and one
source of inspiration and that they are the same. The consequence,
in exaggerated terms, is the nearly automatic imitation of the object
of affection, though curiously Astrophil offers little explicit or detailed notion of the style he would use to describe Stella's face,
except that it would not resemble the styles and procedures he has
just so caustically itemized. And as most readers are aware, the
poems of this kind are sufficiently conventional, sufficiently "Pe-
trarchist" to belie his claims. We should keep in mind also that the
first sonnet in *Astrophil and Stella* announces Astrophil's intention
to persuade Stella not simply to return his affection but to yield
to him. Sincerity and exclusivity are thus both instruments bent
to Astrophil's purpose and so should be understood as weapons
in his rhetorical armory.[4]

The speaker in Shakespeare's Sonnet 84 echoes Sidney only up
to a point: persuasion is his motive only as a kind of masked but
anxious pleading. Astrophil in Sonnet 1 proclaims an exclusive
inspiration in Stella to gain "pity" and "grace," the two most important stages in female sexual surrender; Shakespeare's speaker
has begun to mull over the difficulties, both moral and rhetorical,
of exclusive and singular praise, even as it dominates his verse.
Shakespeare, I would argue, wants to acknowledge the problem
Sidney has opened up, and he wants as well to give it a different
setting and a different reading. Nevertheless, as Anne Ferry has
demonstrated, there is a good deal of common ground between
the two,[5] with Shakespeare seeking his own direction by adapting
Astrophil's mode of compliment to a very different persona.

Here is Shakespeare's Sonnet 84:

Who is it that says most which can say more
Than this rich praise—that you alone are you,
In whose confine immurèd is the store
Which should example where your equal grew?
Lean penury within that pen doth dwell
That to his subject lends not some small glory,
But he that writes to you, if he can tell
That you are you, so dignifies his story;
Let him but copy what in you is writ,

> Not making worse what nature made so clear,
> And such a counterpart shall fame his wit,
> Making his style admirèd everywhere.
> You to your beauteous blessings add a curse,
> Being fond on praise, which makes your praises worse.

The awkward first quatrain, more a puzzle to be solved than a graceful compliment, is usefully paraphrased by Stephen Booth: "Not even those who say most (in quantity and/or quality) can say anything more in your praise than that only you have the distinction of being you. No one has it in him to think of something with which you can be compared (because the qualities your equal would have to possess are possessed only by you)."[6] Incomparability is normally considered high praise,[7] but we should at least glance a different possible reading. It might go as follows: what is being said is true of every individual. We are all incomparable. Only you are you. Only I am I. Each human has a separate and distinct identity. This flatfooted meaning is of course not that pursued in lines 7–9, which quote Sidney's much less equivocal tribute to uniqueness, but the hint of a less hyperbolic, more literal (and hence as Booth points out, nonsensical) interpretation at least helps qualify the conceit as compliment.

Perhaps the most immediate issue in the poem is the speaker's discovery of the impossibility of a transparent imitation of the object of praise, of simple presentation, or representation without the contamination of the authorial presence or artistry that not only alters the portrait but also shifts attention from the object of praise to the praiser. Shakespeare's Sonnet 59, which echoes Sidney's childbirth conceit for the poet's process of creation (as in *Astrophil and Stella* 1 and 37), explores the difficulties involved in the effort of praising, as it partly changes focus from the young man to the admiring poet, and in Sonnet 84 the very act of copying "shall fame [the poet's] wit, / Making his style admirèd everywhere," a discovery like that of Astrophil's "It is a praise to praise, when thou art praised" (35.14). But Shakespeare's speaker has turned the poem more decisively away from its role of praising to deal with copying as an element in the poet's reputation, an issue posed more candidly by Astrophil's conclusion to Sonnet 15:

> But if (both for your love and skill) your name
> You seek to nurse at fullest breasts of fame,
> Stella behold, and then begin to endite.

In contrast to Astrophil's confident tones, Shakespeare's speaker seems hesitant, even self-contradictory. On the one hand the praising poet who simply registers the singularity of the young man "so dignifies his story," and at least avoids "making worse what nature made so clear," but on the other hand the poet who adds nothing to his subject is starved, a condition Shakespeare's speaker attributes to himself in Sonnet 85, "My tongue-tied Muse in manners holds her still." However, the reading of Sonnet 84 is made equivocal by the placing of the negative in line 6, "That to his subject lends not some small glory." If "not" belongs to the verb "lends," then the line reads, "That does not lend some small glory to his subject." In other words, the poet who adds nothing of his own is starved or penurious indeed. But if "not" belongs to "small," lines 4 and 5 should be rendered to mean that the penurious poet is (paradoxically) the one who tries to embellish his subject, to lend it a great glory.[8] The crucial quotation of Sidney, "Let him but copy what in you is writ," appears a simple command, but it is not simple at all in the Renaissance understanding of the imitative and rhetorical process it evokes.

That process is the tradition of rhetorical exercise of *copia,* sometimes anglicized to "copy," that carries the sense of "reproduce" within the context of rhetoric as well as generally and at large. It also gathers in the meaning of abundance, which is another name for rhetorical variation, the exercise of attempting to say something in as many different ways as possible. Erasmus's *De utraque verborum ac rerum copia* (1512) is the standard Renaissance book of explanation and instruction in the art of varying and in its opening paragraph sets down distinctions pertinent to the interests and problems of Shakespeare's speaker, and probably deliberately recalled in his utterance. Erasmus perceives a situation in which *copia,* pursued randomly, produces verbal obscurity and overabundance, betraying paradoxically a kind of emptiness:

Whence we see it befalls not a few mortals that they strive for this divine excellence [abundant eloquence] diligently, indeed but unsuccessfully, and fall into a kind of futile and amorphous loquacity, as with a multitude of inane thoughts and words thrown together without discrimination, they alike obscure the subject and burden the ears of their wretched hearers. To such a degree is this true that a number of writers, having gone so far as to deliver precepts concerning this very thing . . . seem to have accomplished nothing else than, having professed copia [abundance] to have betrayed their poverty.[9]

Erasmus's term for poverty is *iopiam*,[10] where Shakespeare employs the more vivid "lean penury" to label the poet who cannot in some way enhance his subject or, if the second meaning is preferred, carries embellishment too far. Terence Cave points to another and related matter in discussing appropriate *copia* as suiting *verba* to *res:* "It is no accident that the discussion [that of Erasmus] of *copia rerum* culminates in a method for 'imitation' *(ratio colligendi exempla)* where it is not reality that is imitated but other writers, not ideas, but texts."[11] This is precisely the form of imitation Astrophil dismisses in Sonnets 1 and 3, and in part he is echoed, as we have seen, by Shakespeare's speaker, but perhaps with the addition of a glancing reference to the Erasmian understanding of *copia* as both imitation and eloquence.

To recapitulate, Sonnet 84 appears to be saying that normally the mark of a capable poet is his ability to add something to the subject but that the young man's excellence is so distinctive that the poet able to render him as he is will burnish his reputation by that achievement rather than by his skill at embellishment. The poem, as with several others of its type, expresses an aspect of the problem of praising, even as it praises the young man for his singularity. Sonnet 103, "Alack, what poverty my Muse brings forth," repeats the conceit in 84, and keeps the allusion to Erasmus and the habit of *copia* alive, but makes the point more sharply that the speaker's poetic invention is impoverished by the very being of the young man. Yet the two sonnets taken together are an example of the central general feature of *copia,* saying the same thing variously, and hence not exhibiting creative penury even as they confess it. But this neat clash of motive and achievement is undone by the sudden and entirely unprepared-for final couplet of 84, which will be discussed later.

For the moment, what concerns me is the sonnet's concentration on the issue of reputation. First of all, poetic praise is not meant for the eyes and ears of the young man alone. Devotion may be exclusive, but the language of devotion is to be public. The praising poet has a strong personal, even careerist interest in the object of devotion and the act of praising. Such is the burden of the several poems promising the young man immortality—for example, Sonnets 17, 18, 19, 54, 55, 60, 63, 65, 74, 77, and 81. There are sonnets in which the speaker (71 and 72, chiefly) expresses the wish for anonymity, but the metapoetic sonnets generally assume not only that others will read the speaker's poems but also that poetic tributes to the young man by the speaker and the rival poet, and perhaps others, are an open and known phenomenon. On the whole, reputation for the epideictic poet is conventionally a positive value,[12] but for Shakespeare's speaker, like Sidney's Astrophil, there is the price of dependency to be paid, and that price is both emotional and professional. Indeed, a poem like Sonnet 103, nominally a self-deprecating compliment to the young man—"The argument all bare is of more worth / Than when it hath my added praise beside" (3–4)—verges on complaint. But this is an undertone. By far the greater penalty is that the speaker, as a poet, is in thrall to his subject, even though the tone of lines acknowledging dependence is often positive, as in Sonnet 76:

> Why is my verse so barren of new pride,
> So far from variation or quick change?
> Why with the time do I not glance aside
> To new-found methods and to compounds strange?
> Why write I still all one, ever the same,
> And keep invention in a noted weed,
> That every word doth almost tell my name,
> Showing their birth and where they did proceed?
> O, know, sweet love, I always write of you,
> And you and love are still my argument;
> So all my best is dressing old words new,
> Spending again what is already spent:
>   For as the sun is daily new and old,
>   So is my love still telling what is told.

The opening line is a genuinely ambiguous question. Barrenness bears a negative weight, and new pride, new attire, novelty, can either be negative or positive, though in this poem the speaker, like Astrophil, is rather pleased to avoid newfangleness and says so repeatedly so as to practice *copia,* the variation from which he claims exemption. The poem repeats itself: the question "why" is asked three times in the octave, and the query is never answered at all. Line 9, which structurally should at least begin an answer, instead restates the proposition in another grammatical form and is followed by two metaphors, "dressing" and "spending," and a simile, "For as the sun is daily new and old," a transparent paradox that allows the speaker to accommodate some of the variety he says he avoids. The entirety of the poem, nevertheless, is a demonstration of the redundant poetics it asserts but does nothing to explain. Then we must consider "spending what is already spent" (12) and "telling what is told," both phrases suggesting an exhausting or exhaustive repetition,[13] and suggesting also a kind of futility in the restriction to one subject and one style. It is characteristic of the sonnets to combine positive utterances with phrases or grammatical constructions that suggest the possibility of a different and negative sense, or, as Booth describes it, "Shakespeare's fascination with actions that are their own counteractions,"[14] as, notoriously, in 116, "Let me not to the marriage of true minds," a poem anxiously and worriedly urging a positive conviction almost entirely in negative terms, or in 105:

> Therefore my verse, to constancy confined,
> One thing expressing, leaves out difference.
>
> (7–8)

"Confined" strongly suggests the possibility, even the desire, for a larger poetic scope and represents a version of Astrophil's acknowledgment in Sonnet 2 of a kind of bondage for poet and lover both. He is, he suggests in Sonnet 50, helpless to control the process of begetting poetry and helpless as well to make his verses adequate to their subject. These children are allowed to survive only because "their forefront bare sweet Stella's name" (14). Astrophil and Shakespeare's speaker insist on the singularity of their poetic subject and the exclusivity of their attention and devotion, and they insist as well on self-deprecation almost to the point of abandoning any initiative or control as poet. Astrophil makes a whole string of such pronouncements: ". . . the all my deed / But copying is what in her nature writes" (3.13–14); ". . . all the map of my state I display, / When trembling voice brings forth that I do Stella love" (6.13–14); "Stella behold, and then begin to endite" (15.14); "My very ink turns straight to Stella's name" (19.6); ". . . the race / Of all my thoughts hath neither stop nor start / But only Stella's eyes and Stella's heart" (23.12–14); "Love only reading unto me this art" (28.14); "For let me but name her, whom I do love, / So sweet sounds straight mine ear and heart do hit / That I well find no eloquence like it" (55.12–14); "My lips are sweet, inspired with Stella's kiss" (74.14); and finally, "For all my words thy beauty doth endite, / And love doth hold my hand and make me write" (90.13–14). Taken together, these passages—all but one of them concluding the sonnets in which they appear—reiterate the case without entirely demonstrating it. They are all part of the process of praise and taken at face value at odds with the rhetoric of seduction and yet seriously implicated in that effort. Astrophil claims a dependence on Stella as subject and inspiration, indeed as almost dictating his lines, that would, if we believed it, deny him another aspect of the poet's role in the Petrarchan convention, that of witty inventor. But it is a commonplace of Sidney criticism that the very poems disclaiming artistic ingenuity are themselves ingenious.

Shakespeare's speaker's language of dependence and poetic allegiance points to an even more complex division of poetic roles and a far more troubled self-deprecation, partly because as poet he must view himself enviously in comparison to the rival poet and partly because his sense of social and emotional inferiority to the young man is complicated by the awareness of the young man's moral weaknesses. The appetite for flattery, "Being fond on praise" (84.14), has already been mentioned. Like a communicable disease it infects the poet, "it makes your praises worse,"[15] so the young man, whoever praises him, and the praising verse are all blighted at once.

The other complication is involved in the conventions of rhetoric and praise that preoccupy Astrophil and Shakespeare's speaker as in Sonnet 76 quoted above. These are familiar issues: they include what Astrophil considers the excesses of verbal adornment, amplification, the masks of allegory, well-worn conceits, and over ingenuity, as well as their opposites in plain-speaking and, above all, the assertion that the poet's language stems from his own situation, not from the imitation of other writers.

Shakespeare's speaker lacks Astrophil's extended list of stylistic sins, but his posture is similar in that he sets the virtue of a transparent style exactly imitating his subject against the additions and fullness of a vague set of others, as well as the rival poet. Here too the claim to simplicity is contradicted by the ingenuity and conceitedness of the poems and by the way in which repetition is seen as a virtue, as a token of emotional constancy, and yet becomes a mode of elegant varying and hence as much a symptom of the speaker's wit as of sincerity. The poet, even the kind of poet Shakespeare's speaker sometimes claims to be—humble, self-effacing, riveted to a single subject, unwilling to add anything different to the process by which the young man is allowed to dominate and limit the verse that celebrates him—is nevertheless involved in self-publicity:

> I never saw that you did painting need,
> And therefore to your fair no painting set;
> I found, or thought I found, you did exceed
> The barren tender of a poet's debt;
> And therefore have I slept in your report,
> That you yourself, being extant, well might show

How far a modern quill doth come too short,
Speaking of worth, what worth in you doth grow.
This silence for my sin you did impute,
Which shall be most my glory being dumb;
For I impair not beauty being mute,
When others would give life and bring a tomb.
    There lives more life in one of your fair eyes
    Than both your poets can in praise devise.

(83)

Parenthetically, I should add that the hint that the young man in some fashion just possibly might not exceed the poet's capacity to render him justly, that there might be some flaw in his imputed perfection, anticipates the open accusation in 84 that he is "fond on praise" (14). More curiously, Sonnet 83 is a poem about abstaining from poetry, claiming that poetry, at least the rival's poetry, impairs beauty and kills what it would give life to. Again, by separating himself from other poets the speaker manages his own praise by flourishing his restraint.

This reflexivity extends to the theme that repetition is the appropriate stylistic mode for praising the young man, a theme that finds, paradoxically, its most elaborate expression in Sonnet 105:

Let not my love be called idolatry,
Nor my belovèd as an idol show,
Since all alike my songs and praises be
To one, of one, still such, and ever so.
Kind is my love today, tomorrow kind,
Still constant in a wondrous excellence;
Therefore my verse, to constance confined,
One thing expressing, leaves out difference.
"Fair, kind, and true" is all my argument,
"Fair, kind, and true," varying to other words;
And in this change is my invention spent,
Three themes in one, which wondrous scope affords.
    Fair, kind, and true have often lived alone,
    Which three till now never kept seat in one.

The pose here is that the speaker's repetitious language renders his exclusive devotion, that its reductive reiteration of the same three adjectives or variations upon them exhaust his inventive powers, and that such an apparently minimal effort—attesting to the union of the three virtues—bespeaks a miracle akin to the doctrine of the trinity. Like Sonnet 83, the speaker's humility is of the kind that announces itself, and of course the structure of the poem links it indelibly to the sort of amplification taught by Erasmus and noticeable in the stylistic habits of the sequence as a whole.[16] Yet at the same time the commitment to repetition could be understood as a serious stylistic fault, as in Quintilian:

> A worse fault [than *tautology*] is *homoeideia*, or sameness, a term applied to a style which has no variety to relieve its tedium, and which presents a uniform monotony of hue. This is one of the surest signs of lack of art *[arte oratio]*, and produces a uniquely unpleasing effect, not merely on the mind, but on the ear, on account of its sameness of thought, the uniformity of its figures, and the monotony of its structure.[17]

Apropos of 105.10 Booth remarks that there is a "trivial and insignificant, but also undeniable, conflict between constancy and variation of any kind,"[18] but in the context of rhetorical convention the conflict is not trivial or insignificant: at one extreme variation alone is the vice of chaotic syle; at the other, endless repetition is tiresome monotony, so that one might view the speaker, when he intones "To one, of one, still such, and ever so"(105.4), as indeed impoverished and yet at the very least trying bravely to make the best of it. The poem is deployed wittily to offer a solution of the problem, but that solution is evasive, at least insofar as it appears to reconcile high praise and the unadorned, transparent rendering of the young man's quality. We should register the harsh alternative between idolatry and monotony as the poet's dilemma in the young man sonnets, the situation in which the only way to claim a humble simplicity lies within the pathways of witty amplification—that is, within the conventions the speaker seems bent on avoiding.

Astrophil too encounters such a dilemma, though it emerges in different circumstances and with different trappings. His condition as poet is that his poetry defeats his sexual purpose: in Sonnet 45 he finds Stella more affected by a fable than his own frustration, so he concludes,

> Then think, my dear, that you in me do read
> Of lover's ruin some sad tragedy:
> I am not I, pity the tale of me.

The last line is both semifacetious and coarse, and it sums up as well Astrophil's discovery that what he construes as his genuine suffering and its poetic expression is unpersuasive. This discovery suggests that what he had accepted as the poet-lover's code, that the rhetoric of authentic feeling would elicit responsive feeling in the person addressed, does not work. And, as the last two sonnets in *Astrophil and Stella* testify, there seems to be no exit from convention for lover or poet.

Shakespeare's metapoetic sonnets demonstrate rhetorical convention by their very form even as they assert a distance from it, as if his speaker had half-consciously discovered that the only space for distinctive personal expression is within established practice. And the convention of praise exacts another penalty that is at once personal and artistic. The young man's fall from perfection as being "too fond on praise" has already been discussed. He has other weaknesses, his "shame" and "sensual fault" introduced in Sonnets 34 and 35, his "lascivious grace" in 40, and "pretty wrongs" in 41 and 42, both indicating he has trafficked with the speaker's mistress. (The triangular situation is, of course, spelled out in Sonnet 144.) There are moments when the speaker totally ignores the moral imperfections in his friend, as in Sonnet 37, "So I, made lame by Fortune's dearest spite, / Take all my comfort of they worth and truth" (3–4), or 38 and 39. But these are immediately followed by 40, 41, and 42 and preceded by 35 and 36, so that they seem to be an effort on the speaker's part to convince himself of a more attractive truth.

Truth is a word that reverberates through the Sonnets and underscores the moral problem that erupts continually in the speaker's effort to work out his status as poet. To return to Sonnet 105, the three-times repeated phrase "Fair, kind, and true" offers at least two meanings of "true," the most obvious and prominent being "faithful" or "constant." Kerrigan suggests "natural integrity, spontaneous honesty, constancy, true rather than feigned beauty." He notes also the excessive protesting of the speaker beginning with the disavowal of idolatry that seeks to compensate for a weak argument.[19] Moreover, the assertions of the speaker's devotion and constancy, both their repetition and the attempt to make a virtue of repetitiousness, tend to encourage the perception that something like idolatry is indeed the matter, and this would be other than "truth."[20] Therefore, not only are the speaker's style and invention severely limited by repetition, but they are implicated in a serious impiety.

Just as ironic is Sonnet 21, another echoing of Astrophil's contemptuous dismissal of other poets and other styles:

> So is it not with me as with that Muse,
> Stirred by a painted beauty to his verse,
> Who heaven itself for ornament doth use,

And every fair with his fair doth rehearse,
Making a couplement of proud compare
With sun and moon, with earth and sea's rich gems,
With April's first-born flowers, and all things rare
That heaven's air in this huge rondure hems.
O, let me, true in love, but truly write,
And then believe me, my love is as fair
As any mother's child, though not so bright
As those gold candles fixed in heaven's air.
  Let them say more that like of hearsay well;
  I will not praise that purpose not to sell.

The poem is simultaneously an echo of Sidney's first sonnet, "Loving in truth, and fain in verse my love to show," as well as the third, and a glancing mockery of Astrophil's comparison of Stella to the sun in several places, as well as an ironic reminder that in both Sonnets 18 and 130 Shakespeare's speaker invokes the very terms of comparison he tries to set at a distance.

So far I have presented Shakespeare's speaker's effort to define a minimalist poetic style as equivocal and almost self-defeating. I would add to this perception the point that the verses I have quoted are less a series of comments on the proper language of praise than they are an expression of the ways in which the speaker exemplifies a moral dimension in a particular poetic convention. We have already seen that the phrase "to constancy confined" has both positive and negative implications, and to elaborate on the negative it can be remarked that confinement may lead to a willful excusing of the young man's weaknesses. One form of truth, constancy, can oppose itself to another, integrity. "True," and "truth" and "truly" in both senses characterize the young man in several sonnets, as in 54, 82, 93, 101, to name a few, but when the speaker's and hence the poet's voice utters these terms and also characterizes himself and his art, the results are sometimes ironic clashes of meaning directed both at the young man and the speaker. In one poem, Sonnet 57, the speaker elaborately catalogues his self-humbling slavery to the young man, concluding that "So true a fool is love that, in your will / Though you do anything, he thinks no ill" (13–14). This self-characterization of the speaker as both a veritable fool and a constant one, willingly accepting whatever the young man does, occurs elsewhere, notably in 35, "Myself corrupting, salving thy amiss" (7).

This strain of self-accusation, of admitting complicity in the young man's moral failures, notably his infidelity, invites comparison with a slightly different mood of hurt feelings in 83:

I grant thou wert not married to my Muse,
And therefore mayst without attaint o'erlook
The dedicated words which writers use
Of their fair subject, blessing every book.
Thou art as fair in knowledge as in hue,
Finding thy worth a limit past my praise;
And therefore art enforced to seek anew
Some fresher stamp of time-bettering days.
And do so, love; yet when they have devised
What strainèd touches rhetoric can lend,
Though, truly fair, wert truly sympathized
In true plain words by thy true-telling friend:
    And their gross painting might be better used
    Where cheeks need blood; in thee it is abused.

All of the issues reviewed so far return in this poem: the claim to
simplicity of style linked to honest emotion, the difficulty of praising a paragon without falsifying his nature, the poet's linking of
telling the truth (not lying) to accurate imitation or poetic representation, and the pretense that repetition is both a poetic and emotional virtue, not the embroidery of rhetoric. Yet once the speaker
mentions rhetoric's "strainèd touches," he immediately resorts to
close-packed verbal repetition and wordplay, so that once more
we have a poem biting its own tail, practicing the very modes it
despises and complaining where it pretends to praise. And we must
ask if the speaker is "true-telling." Does he accurately describe
his own poetic practice that is willy-nilly a kind of flattery and as
ornamental as one could wish? And does he not, by calling the
young man "truly fair," indict himself, more subtly perhaps, but
just as definitely as in Sonnets 35 and 57?

    In a rhetorical context the most confident assertions have a tem-
porary validity, and this is one of the features of the sonnet and
sequence forms that make them particularly useful for rendering
shifts and contradictions in mood. The irony of many of Shakespeare's speaker's assertions of constancy and truth is that they
may be contradicted in neighboring as well as in more removed
sonnets. As I have argued, the forms that distribute irony or wordplay or variations on a theme through several poems should prevent us from taking the speaker's language at face value, as do his
own contradictory statements. The poems themselves define the
elusive nature of the poetic voice, the poet's *ethos* in the poems
as both truth-teller and liar, telling the truth sometimes by lying
or claiming the lie, as in Sonnet 138, which I think defines the

speaker's relationship with the young man as well as with the dark lady, though with her, of course, more openly:

> O, love's best habit is in seeming trust,
> And age in love loves not to have years told.
> Therefore I lie with her, and she with me,
> And in our faults by lies we flattered be.

(11–14)

Notes

1. My texts are *Shakespeare: The Sonnets and A Lover's Complaint,* ed. John Kerrigan (Harmondsworth: Penguin, 1986) and *The Poetry of Sir Philip Sidney,* ed. William A Ringler, Jr. (Oxford: Oxford University Press, 1962.)

2. By fictional worlds I mean the virtual realities created by the speaking voices in each sequence. It is in that context—in rhetorical terms the *ethos* of each speaker—that the notion of the poet's place and the quality of his work is acted out. A useful caution against reading the sonnets as biography, rather than as fiction, is L. C. Knights, "Shakespeare's Sonnets," in *Elizabethan Poetry: Modern Essays in Criticism,* ed. Paul J. Alpers (New York: Oxford University Press, 1967), 277. Knights's alternative to regarding the poems as direct reflections of Shakespeare's personal circumstances and emotions is to study the sonnets as a stage in the development of his blank verse. This,needless to say, is not my own position.

3. Germaine Warkentin, "The Form of Dante's 'Libello' and Its Challenge to Petrarch," *Quaderni d'Italianistica* 2 (1981): 162. The metapoetic character of the sequence begins with Dante's *Vita Nuova* and the "acceptance of the idea that such a book could be put in order by the author himself, and that order might exemplify by its form his vision of his own creativity." This last proposition is not one I will argue for Shakespeare, at least insofar as the order of his entire sequence is concerned, but I will deal with the ways in which the speaker's concern for his place and purpose as a poet inhabit substantial numbers of the sonnets.

Rosalie Colie, in her published lectures entitled *The Resources of Kind: Genre Theory in the Renaissance* (Berkeley and Los Angeles: University of California Press, 1973), suggested that what she calls the "analytical element" in sonnets and sonnet-sequences was added to the lyrical, emotional, and psychological features developed by Dante and Petrarch (103–6). Shakespeare added "the plot element of the rival poet" and "justified literary criticism and theory as a sonnet-topic" (107). One might modify this generality to propose that these are not so much topics as dimensions of the persona in the sonnets.

4. I have addressed this issue at greater length and in somewhat different terms in "The Poetics of Astrophil," *Sir Philip Sidney's Achievements,* ed. M. J. B. Allen, Dominic Baker-Smith, and Arthur F. Kinney, with Margaret M. Sullivan (New York: AMS Press, 1990), 145–56.

5 Anne Ferry, *The "Inward" Language: Sonnets of Wyatt, Sidney, Shakespeare, Donne* (Chicago: University of Chicago Press, 1983), chap. 4. Here and in the previous chapter, Ferry demonstrates just how pervasive is Shakespeare's quotation of Sidney and offers a careful, developed argument to the effect that

130   ROBERT L. MONTGOMERY

both poets are concerned with "the speaker's struggle between what is in his heart and the language of poetry" (136), a formula she repeats often in the two chapters in question (e.g., 141, 149, 171). This theme is certainly evident in the metapoetic sonnets of both poets, but Ferry takes the utterances of both speakers more or less at face value. My reading suggests that the issue of "true" writing is itself a function of the rhetorical positions adopted by each speaker, and not necessarily the ingenuous, heartfelt expression of the poet's struggle to match words accurately to inner emotion. Furthermore, I would state the issue somewhat differently, especially in regards to Sidney's Sonnet 3 and Shakespeare's 84: the problem is not the expression of the poet-lover's inner emotion but whether Stella or the young man are to be praised transparently, imitated for what they are, or added to, embellished, flattered, and hence falsified.

6. Stephen Booth, ed., *Shakespeare's Sonnets* (New Haven: Yale University Press, 1977), 283. Booth adds, "The confusion and awkwardness of the syntax of lines 1–4 is so extreme—and so regularly patterned—that it seems studied" (284).

7. Joel Fineman, *Shakespeare's Perjured Eye* (Berkeley and Los Angeles: University of California Press, 1986), 181, first regards the poem only as hyperbole: "the self-surpassing height of praise consists of turning praise against itself to describe a paragon beyond compare." He notes further that "the young man's poet problematizes the exemplary tradition of praise, so that the merely epideictic poet—the poet who would say more than 'you alone are you'—will only write the hollow, repetitious writing of 'Lean *penury within* that *pen* doth dwell'" (248–49). This reading is incomplete if one remembers the turn given in the final couplet.

8. This last reading is apparently preferred by Fineman, ibid.

9. My text is *On Copia of Words and Ideas,* trans. Donald B. King and H. David Rix (Milwaukee: Marquette University Press, 1963), 11. For a more extended account of *copia,* as well as Erasmus's domination of the subject, see Terence Cave, *The Cornucopian Text: Problems of Writing in the French Renaissance* (Oxford: Clarendon Press, 1979), chap. 1. Cave points out that *inopia* cuts in two directions: it means either poverty of diction or prolixity, *"copia without varietas"* (5). For a brief account of the kind of rhetorical practice used in schools see Sister Miriam Joseph, *Rhetoric in Shakespeare's Time: Literary Theory of Renaissance Europe* (New York and Burlingame: Harcourt, Brace & World, 1962), 9.

10. Desiderius Erasmus, *De utraque verborum ac rerum copia* (London, 1650), 9.

11. *Cornucopian Text,* 19.

12. As just one example, see Petrarch, *Rime sparse,* 119.

13. Kerrigan, *Shakespeare,* 270–71, comments, "saying things *already* said, the poet 'once more counts over the coinage of love.'" Booth, *Shakespeare's Sonnets,* remarks that "although the line gestures toward several strange compounds, its sum is as simple and dull as its immediately obvious surface meaning would leave us to expect any lines by this speaker to be" (265).

14. *Shakespeare's Sonnets,* 244.

15. Kerrigan (*Shakespeare,* 279) offers three possible readings of this line, that already mentioned and something close to it: "'*Being fond* of the kind of panegyric which, praising the wrong things in you, debases itself (and so degrades you.'" The remaining reading is a bit strained: "*Being* that of being, in that you are *fond on.* 'Too fond of' carried as far as 'besotted by'. . . ."

16. Perhaps the most obvious example of *copia* is the way the first seventeen

sonnets variously repeat the injunction to the young man to marry and procreate in order to pass on to posterity his beauty at its zenith.

17. Quintilian *Institutio Oratoria* 8.3.52. I am indebted to Joseph Chaney for calling this passage to my attention.

18. Booth, *Shakespeare's Sonnets*, 339.

19. Kerrigan, *Shakespeare*, 311 and 309.

20. Booth, *Shakespeare's Sonnets*, 336–37, calls 105 a "playful experiment in perversity" in that the speaker seems deliberately to misunderstand idolatry, which usually referred to polytheism and to a puritan view of Roman Catholicism. Hence the speaker is arguing that by limiting his devotion and its expression to the young man and the three virtues he finds in him that he is not idolatrous, when in fact the worship of someone not the deity is just that.

Shakespearean Imaginations of the Other

Joseph H. Summers

I have come to think that any credible theory of the moral or educative usefulness of literature must derive from the imaginative perception through literature of the relations between the self and the other, the familiar and the alien. Such a perception can become central to a notion of how we acquire truly useful knowledge. Roger Ascham expressed it well enough, in *The Scholemaster* (1570) at a utilitarian psychological level, when he remarked, "There be that keep them out of fire, and yet was never burned"—or more generally, "Learning teacheth more in one year than experience in twenty." There is a further and more important knowledge that I glimpsed in 1940 when I was working on my senior honors essay on the modern poet, Louis MacNeice: I remember coming across a sentence in one of his semiautobiographical volumes (I believe it was *I Crossed the Minch*) concerning his failed first marriage: "Marriage at least made me conscious of the existence of other people in their own right and not merely as vicars of my godhead." I thought at the time that it would surely be less painful to acquire such a consciousness before marriage, and I wondered that all of MacNeice's reading in the classics had not at least suggested it. The imaginative realization of the existence of another or others is surely a more profound knowledge than the merely prudential knowledge of how to avoid getting burned.

But I think it may be even more miraculous to apprehend imaginatively the existence of other times and places. Such an experience almost inevitably entails some recognition of the fluidity of our own sense of being within time and space—the inevitability of growth and decay and change (and perhaps evanescence and death); it also eventually suggests, I believe, both the recognition of large repetitive rhythms of lives and seasons and also the irreducible individuality of any one age or society or life or moment. In Samuel Daniel's *Musophilus: Containing a generall defense of learning* (1599?), Musophilus, in his debate with Philocosmus (the

lover of the world), gives as moving a formulation as I know of the
way that, through reading, the past may become the present:

Whenas (perhaps) the words thou scornest now
    May live, the speaking picture of the minde,
    The extract of the soule, that laboured how
    To leave the image of herselfe behinde,
    Wherein Posteritie, that love to know
    The just proportion of our Spirits may finde.
For these Lines are the veines, the arteries,
    And undecaying life-strings of those harts
    That still shall pant, and still shall exercize
    The motion, spirit, and Nature both imparts,
    And shall, with those alive so sympathize
    As, nourisht with their powers injoy their parts.
Oh blessed Letters, that combine in one,
    All Ages past, and make one live with all:
    By you, we do conferre with who are gone,
    And the dead-living unto Councell call:
    By you, th'unborne shall have communion
    Of what we feele, and what doth us befall.
Soule of the world, Knowledge, without thee,
    What hath the Earth that truly glorious is?
    Why should our pride make such a stirre to be,
    To be forgot? What good is like to this,
    To do worthy the writing, and to write
    Worthy the reading, and the worlds delight?

(lines 177–200)[1]

With these general notions, and stimulated also by my discovery
of some of the marvelous writings in English that have come from
Africa, Asia, and the Caribbean during the past twenty-five years,
I proposed as my subject, when the Folger Institute asked me to
give a seminar in 1986, "Shakespearean Imaginations of the Other."
As I read over the applications for the seminar, I discovered how
ambiguous the phrase was: almost every member had a slightly
differing understanding of what "the other" is—or might be. I then
discovered that Martha Tuck Rozett had recently published a help-
ful note on contemporary uses of the phrase in her volume *The
Doctrine of Election and the Emergence of Elizabethan Tragedy:*

I have encountered the term "the other" in psychological, anthropological, philosophical, and theological contexts. In most usages, the

"other" is "not self," as in Emerson's distinction between "me" and "not-me." This does not necessarily carry any implication of value—the "not-me" need not be better or worse than the "me," simply different. Sometimes the difference plays on fundamental dichotomies—for Simone de Beauvoir, woman is the "other" from the perspective of man and vice versa. . . . Elsewhere the difference depends wholly on context. As Giles Gunn demonstrates in *The Interpretation of Otherness: Literature, Religion, and the American Imagination* (Oxford, 1979), American literature is rich in dramatizations of the relationship between self and other—Ahab and Moby Dick represent one form, Whitman's sense of the "other" as comrade is another. Robinson Jeffers' sense of the "other" as the opposite of the self who holds absolute dominion over the self is still another (p. 183). Gunn returns to a paradigm set forth originally by Perry Miller: man defines or redefines himself in response to an ideal "other," which he may confront in various human or non-human forms. From this process of encountering the "other" emerges a new understanding of the self. . . .[2]

I believe we should probably recognize a few other uses of "the other": economic, sociological, and political uses can be distinguished from the anthropological; and at least as subsets, national, regional, tribal, class, communal, and familial uses of "the other" can also be recognized. Literarily (and certainly in Shakespeare's plays), linguistic usages become the most immediately obvious characteristics of groups (or "selves") and their "others"; and genres, styles, and conventions are essential to the literary work and its definition of a "self" as distinguished from other literary kinds and other works.

In responding to Shakespeare's plays, we may have even more serious misunderstandings about the "self" than about the "other." Only recently I read a student's sentence about "the truth of man's essential isolation, anxiety, and alienation from the non-self or 'the other'", a formulation that I believe would strike most contemporary readers as unobjectionable. But I do not believe it would likely have occurred to Shakespeare or to most of his contemporaries, because they seemed to conceive as intrinsic to any self its relations to family, place, heritage, hierarchies, and roles. They seem to have found it easier to say "we" than we do. The notion of a "self" as possibly independent, even "absolute"—a naked ego to whom other human beings as well as animals and inanimate nature are essentially alien—Shakespeare seems to reserve for villains doomed to destruction (Gonerils and Regans) or a tragic individual in the last stages of self-destruction (a Macbeth).

Despite the fact that he was writing a semifictional dialogue,

Samuel Daniel in the passage from *Musophilus* that I quoted seemed to be concerned chiefly with authors who spoke in their own persons, remembering the past and anticipating future audiences. With Shakespearean drama we have a different situation. Here we have texts, which theoretically at least, are not the expressions of a single individual but supposedly the speech of differing individuals of varying and conflicting interests, thoughts, and emotions. We come to know them only indirectly by what and how they speak (to each other, to themselves, to the audience in the theater), what and how others speak to them and about them, and what they do. It is proverbial that most readers and viewers come to accept characters in the plays as "people" (real or "artificial"), and sometimes respond to them as if they were friends or acquaintances, if not actually other selves. Yet their languages, assumptions, and actions are frequently of another time and place. As we attend their performances, differences of history and geography, other times and places, frequently suggest "other" realities to which we respond imaginatively—almost as if they were present.

How the characters on stage meet, accept, oppose, or reject other characters usually serve as guides to how we respond to them. But in some situations we know more than most (or all) of the characters on stage, and the gap between our knowledge and theirs may prove disturbing. From Richard III's opening soliloquy until at least the midpoint of the play, we are repeatedly placed in a situation where we must identify dramatically with a malevolent and morally repugnant figure. Richard addresses us directly and he explains his actions, attitudes, and purposes—and his contempt for his opponents. He knows how to play his various roles with masterly cunning and hypocrisy, and he is supremely intelligent. He is the initiator of nearly all the action in the first half of the play (audiences naturally find more interest in active characters than in passive ones), and in the representation of a society of knavish fools, we tend to identify with the more intelligent. Richard dazzles us when, as in his wooing of Lady Anne over the corpse of her murdered royal father-in-law, his brilliant histrionics carry all before them; we are likely to be both startled and disturbed when he then turns to us and remarks on the incredibility of his success and the stupidity and moral abtuseness of Anne:

> Was ever woman in this humor woo'd?
> Was ever woman in this humor won?
> I'll have her, but I will not keep her long.
> What? I, that kill'd her husband and his father,

To take her in her heart's extremest hate,
With curses on her mouth, tears in her eyes,
The bleeding witness of my hatred by,
Having God, her conscience, and these bars against me,
And I no friends to back my suit at all
But the plain devil and dissembling looks?
And yet to win her! All the world to nothing!
Hah!
Hath she forgot already that brave prince,
Edward, her lord, whom I, some three months since,
Stabb'd in my angry mood at Tewksbury?
A sweeter and a lovelier gentleman,
Fram'd in the prodigality of nature—
Young, valiant, wise, and (no doubt) right royal—
The spacious world cannot again afford.
And will she yet abase her eyes on me,
That cropp'd the golden prime of this sweet prince
And made her widow to a woeful bed?
On me, whose all not equals Edward's moi'ty?
On me, that halts and am misshapen thus?

                              (*Richard III* 1.2.227–50)

The clarity of Richard's self-condemnation is breathtaking. As he draws our attention to his physical as well as moral deformity, I think we are likely to be both fascinated and repelled—the figure of a bird fascinated by a snake may suggest our predicament.

Richard III is an early Shakespearean example of a figure that haunted the dreams of the period. A major assumption of the sixteenth-century humanists was that a study of the writings and history of the past (a reading of the "great books") *should* lead to enlightenment, greater human sensitivity, and moral discrimination. The idea (and even more, the evidence) that extraordinary intelligence and learning could be put to the service of an amoral pursuit of power and the gratification of the ego, totally divorced from law or love or the consideration of others, was for them the ultimate nightmare. When Roger Ascham called an "Italianate Englishman" "the devil incarnate," he was speaking both passionately and, from his point of view, literally. For only the devil was defined as a self-affirming intelligence and will incapable of any true love for another, who delighted in destruction rather than creation and who possessed an insatiable desire for power. Since he was also a supreme hypocrite who could deceive almost everyone, he was a figure against whom the innocent were horribly vulnerable. Human incarnations of the devil fortunately possess human limitations: as treacherous and murderous Richard becomes the scourge for the past treacheries and murders of the Lancastrians and Yorkists, as he either destroys the rival claimants to power or unites the survivors in opposition to himself, as he loses his ability to dominate the action, we begin to lose our sense of dramatic identification with him and to anticipate his ultimate defeat and death. Shakespeare, seemingly deliberately, gave no real development of character to Richmond, the future Henry VII. The most important thing about Richmond is that he is not Richard, and he is presented with only tenuous relations to those around Richard. Richmond represents an "other" to Richard and his world—an end to the bloody cries of vengeance of the dead and to the civil war, the union of the roses, the sun without the ominous crooked-back shadow, a new beginning and a blessed future. (Among the early audiences of the play, some at least must have associated the dramatic promise of Richmond with the later accession of Elizabeth and the hopes for an end to the violence and uncertainty that characterized the reigns of Henry VIII and Mary.)

In *The True Confessions of an Albino Terrorist,* the distinguished South African poet Breyten Breytenbach remarked, "At the heart of the South African prison system is the denial of the humanity of 'the tother'—and in that it is only a reflection of the larger South African cosmos": he implies that such a denial characterizes all totalitarian and racist regimes.[3] Shakespeare's satanic villains do appeal to such denials for political and incendiary purposes—witness Iago's shout to Brabantio in the opening scene of *Othello:*

> 'Zounds, sir, y' are robb'd! For shame, put on your gown;
> Your heart is burst, you have lost half your soul;
> Even now, now, very now, an old black ram
> Is tupping your white yew. Arise, arise!
>
> (1.1.86–89)

But as Richard III's speech suggests, when they speak in soliloquy or without disguise to others, their own deepest contempt is reserved not for members of other races or cultures, but for the good or the ordinary—those "others" who do not share or even suspect their villainy. In *King Lear* Edmund exclaims about

> A credulous father and a brother noble,
> Whose nature is so far from doing harms
> That he suspects none; on whose foolish honesty
> My practices ride easy.
>
> (1.2.179–82)

And although Iago seems occasionally to believe what he frequently suggests—that all men are knaves and all women whores—yet at times he recognizes Othello as a contemptible exception:

> The Moor is of a free and open nature,
> That thinks men honest that but seems to be so,
> And will as tenderly be led by th' nose
> As asses are.
>
> (*Othello* 1.3.399–402)

I think it is this contempt as well as their intelligence and skill at destruction that usually prevents the audience from accepting Richard III and the villains in the tragedies with any sort of easy tolerance—as if to understand all really were to pardon all. Rather, because we come to see them as beyond the tolerable bounds of human society, we sympathize with those who refer to Richard III as "cockatrice" (4.1.54) and "That bottled spider, that foul bunchback'd toad" (4.4.81) and to Goneril and Regan as monsters—"Tigers, not daughters" (*King Lear* 4.2.40). For smaller, less developed, or even deceived villains in the differing worlds of the comedies and the romances, there are other possibilities. For Duke Ferdinand and Oliver in *As You Like It,* sudden, total conversions are available; and repentence and ritual purgations restore Leontes and Alonso to the human community in *The Winter's Tale* and *The Tempest.* But for such figures in the tragedies (for Macbeth and Lady Macbeth most notably), we are led to the anguished perception that human beings can indeed become inhuman beings—even lose their sense of being—before physical death.

But in most of the plays we are concerned with characters within a narrower human range; and with them, particularly in the comedies, the most ordinary "others" may be simply sexual. With anticipations and misgivings young men and women meet, and if a conventional happy ending is achieved, it represents a discovery of an "other self," a commitment, and an anticipation of a wedding that implies a new beginning for both and the establishment of a new family. But there are generic limits to the roles of the two sexes in plays in which we are invited to laugh at the lovers during their courtship and yet to rejoice in their marriages. We are not likely to find it an acceptable happy ending if a nice and intelligent girl marries a fool or weakling or a man who has shown himself callous and unimaginative. Any number of readers and viewers have found the endings of *Much Ado About Nothing, All's Well That Ends Well,* and *Measure for Measure* less than completely satisfying. A man at whom we laugh incessantly may very well seem a fool, but a woman may sacrifice little admiration if we laugh at her in a romantic situation—particularly when the laughter is partly occasioned by masculine disguises or other violations of convention. (Elizabethan staging, in which boys imitated girls who were frequently imitating boys, must have provided additional laughter about sexual conventions as well as sexual ambiguities and identities; but the characters represented on stage seem to delight in their disguised roles as much as any actor might.)

It may be that the male roles must be smaller than the female in most Shakespearean romantic comedy because of basic incompatabilities between the presumably admired characteristics of masculine heroes, the nature of laughter, and the nature of sexual love. The hero should supposedly be a happy combination of practical and idealistic youth, rationally successful in his pursuit of his purposes or goals, and to some extent master of his destiny; but a man who has fallen in love is by definition irrational, and his success (at least on stage) usually depends upon a number of elements hardly within his conscious control. Shakespeare's male lovers are at their most absurd when they insist that they are behaving perfectly rationally. In *A Midsummer Night's Dream,* after Lysander has received Puck's magic eyedrops and awakes to see Helena, he insists to her,

> Not Hermia, but Helena I love.
> Who will not change a raven for a dove?
> The will of man is by his reason sway'd;
> And reason says you are the worthier maid.
> Things growing are not ripe until their season;
> So I, being young, till now ripe not to reason.
> And touching now the point of human skill,
> Reason becomes the marshal to my will,
> And leads me to your eyes, where I o'erlook
> Love's stories written in Love's richest book.
> (*MND* 2.2.113–22)

The women, on the other hand, recognize easily that their love is irrational: "How now? Even so quickly may one catch the plague?" Olivia in *Twelfth Night* asks just after she has met Viola in the masculine disguise of Cesario (1.5.294–95). But that recognition does not for a moment prevent them from recognizing also the power and seriousness of their emotions. Except possibly for Katherine in *The Taming of the Shrew,* they are more intelligent than the men (in wit combats Beatrice always beats Benedick—as Rosalind/

Ganymede always does the hardly competitive Orlando), and part of their intelligence lies in recognizing the limits of reason—theirs and others. They recognize that they are in complete control of neither their emotions nor their destinies.

It may be partly a reflection of masculine fantasy, but Shakespeare's heroines are also usually remarkably direct in their declarations of affection and their lack of coyness. When Juliet discovers that Romeo has heard her avowal of love, she insists that she *would* blush if there were light enough for Romeo to see her face clearly (2.2.86–87), but she does not. Hermia and Helena spend midsummer night chasing the men they love. Rosalind falls for Orlando at first sight, hints broadly at her feelings, and gives him her chain—actions to which most lovers would respond more openly than the tongue-tied Orlando. Miranda insists to Ferdinand that her imagination cannot "form a shape, / Besides youself, to like of" (*Tempest* 3.1.56–67), and when she is unsure of the implication of his elaborate courtly compliment, she effectively proposes marriage to him: "My husband then?" (3.1.88). Their refusal to employ the usual social protective subterfuges is endearing: our laughter is directed at least as much at the conventions as at the ladies.

It is remarkable how frequently the traditional learned or "philosophical" assumptions about the hierarchical relations between the sexes, the generations, and even the social classes are questioned or tested—if not turned upside down—within the plays. In *Love's Labor's Lost,* feminine superiority seems clearly to be a group rather than an individual phenomenon. The Princess of France and her ladies win every engagement in their wit combats with the King of Navarre and those gentlemen who have vowed a three-year's fast from food, sleep, and female companionship as they devote themselves to supposedly higher studies. Berowne, the wittiest of the men, objects to the unnaturalness of their endeavor, but nevertheless joins in their vows and leads the others in establishing a standard of proper language and behavior in the play—until the entrance of the ladies. The courtly gentlemen are quick to laugh at the absurdities of the fantastical Armado, the pedantic Holofernes, the clownish Costard and the rest; but in the wonderful sonnet scene, they become the objects of our laughter and their own, as, serially, they expose their obsessions, their poetic tastes and abilities, and their hypocrisy. The climax of our pleasure is when the pretensions of Berowne to be the one honest man in the "academy" are thoroughly exploded—and by the ignorant and bumbling Jaquenetta and Costard, at that. When Costard remarks before his exit, "Walk aside the true folk, and let the traitors stay" (4.3.209), he speaks more truly than he seems to know.

Love's Labor's Lost is full of such reversals—when the alien unexpectedly enters. Berowne encourages the King of Navarre to allow the low characters' absurd performance of their pageant of the Three Worthies: "We are shame-proof, my lord; and 'tis some policy / To have one show worse than the King's and his company" (5.2.512–13). The new performance does deflect the laughter from themselves, and both they and we enjoy it. But as the courtiers, particularly Berowne, bait the unimaginative performers, we become alienated from them; we are surprised when the discountenanced Holofernes (whose pomposity had seemed to insulate him from our sympathies), has a moment of protest that distances us further from the laughers: "This is not generous, not gentle, not humble" (629). And when Marcade enters with news of the death of the King of France, the Princess's father (the one sort of intrusion that the nature of the play had seemed absolutely to bar), we discover that Shakespeare can surprise us by what seems a last-minute shift of genre. The ladies' insistence on a period of trial and penance of a year and a day before they answer their lovers' suits ("That's too long for a play," Berowne protests—at least it is too long for a conventional comedy) may be another surprise, but it is one necessitated by what has just happened. If there can be a happy ending after that intrusion of loss and death, it can be imagined only if there is some evidence that those charming young men have grown up enough to be sure of what they want—and that they will recognize their ladies as other persons with minds and judgments and desires, and not merely as images or symbols or idealized forms. The final songs of spring and winter, the cuckoo and the owl, remind us of just those things that comedy often helps us to forget: the paradoxical separation of times and experiences, the discomforts of spring and the comforts of winter.

It is notorious in Shakespeare studies that in these plays so largely concerned with kings and princes, nobles, or at least affluent gentle folk, the lower orders are usually represented as comic or ignorant "others." (After all, the central characters represent the groups that primarily possessed literacy as well as power.) But the uses of lower-class characters in the plays are hardly single; they serve much wider purposes than simply as objects of our laughter. Sometimes they express general human responses, undistorted by private, frequently falsifying intents. Collectively, when manipulated by an Antony or an Aufidius, they can become fearful and destructive mobs; but sometimes they resist manipulations to

which their betters succumb. The first time in *Richard III* when
Richard fails to achieve his ends is when Buckingham cannot get
the crowd to shout, "God save Richard, England's Royal King"
(3.7.1–43); and Richard's stage-managed scene with prayer book
and two bishops takes in the Lord Mayor long before the citizens
join him in an "Amen" to Buckingham's later "Long live Richard,
England's worthy king!" (3.7.240–41).

Individually, the lower orders may at moments become the sole
representatives of humane response. It is the First Servant in *King
Lear* who protests against Cornwall's cruelty to Gloucester, challenges him, and mortally wounds him. (It is Regan who is shocked
by this violation of chivalric decorum; she exclaims, "A peasant
stand up thus?" [3.7.8] as she stabs the servant in the back.) In
the Quarto text of *Lear,* it is the Third Servant who reminds us of
the persistence of an ordinary human world of comforting responses and remedies outside the cruelty and torture that we have
just witnessed, when he encourages his companion to go to the
blinded Gloucester's aid:

> Go thou. I'll fetch some flax and whites of eggs
> To apply to his bleeding face. Now, heaven help him.
>
> (107–8)

It is the gardener and his servants who understand Richard II's
failures, pity his fall, and plant rue "even for ruth," "In the remem-
brance of a weeping queen" (*Richard II* 3.4.106–7).

The simple clowns are usually obviously from the lower classes,
while the witty ones may seem outside the class structure altogether. Both groups are frequently truth-tellers, whether knowingly
or unknowingly. With them, malapropisms may explode into meaning: it makes a good deal of sense to say, for example, as Elbow
does in *Measure for Measure,* that someone is "void of all profana-
tion in the world that good Christians ought to have" (2.1.55–56)
in a society where an Angelo wields nearly absolute power. And
Hamlet can learn from the gravediggers that if a man's primary
purpose in life is to defeat the worms as long as possible, he should
be a tanner. Touchstone casts a good deal of light as he cynically
parodies both romantic love and gentlemanly pretensions to honor,
and we get a fresh perspective from Stephano and Trinculo's parody of their betters' murderous plots for power. If Francis's job as
tapster in *1 Henry IV* has reduced him to parroting "Anon, Anon"
to the calls of his customers, Hal also insists that Hotspur's mecha-
nized devotion to military honor has reduced him to a role as in-

flexibly limited as Francis's (*I Henry IV* 2.4.4–111). The major characters in *Measure for Measure* and *The Winter's Tale* would have a much more difficult time in avoiding catastrophe if they were not aided by a drunken, unrepentant Barnardine, who refuses to take seriously the mortal rituals and judgments of church and state, by a brothel-haunting and scandal-mongering Lucio (who may not be lower class but is certainly no gentleman), and by a cheerfully amoral Autolycus, who does good despite his attempts to remain true to his profession as a thief. Feste shares with Viola the central perspectives of *Twelfth Night,* and the Fool in *Lear* shares the role of painful truth-teller with Lear's "poor fool," Cordelia.

Similarly, attitudes toward generational differences are at least as double on stage as off. The Latin *senex* was originally a title of honor, implying an association of wisdom with age institutionalized in the Senate. But as *Julius Caesar, Coriolanus,* and other plays remind us, the honorific implications soon wore thin. When Brabantio calls Iago a villain and Iago replies "You are a senator" (*Othello*1.1.18), he is not paying him a compliment. Age is as frequently associated with timidity, cowardice, avarice, anger, and oppressive use of arbitrary power as with wisdom and patriotism. In the comedies and sometimes also in the tragedies the older generation are frequently brutal in their opposition to the young: in *Midsummer Night's Dream* Egeus would prefer to have his daughter, Hermia, executed than to have her refuse the husband he has chosen for her; Lady Capulet says "I would the fool were married to her grave" when she tells her husband of Juliet's refusal to marry Paris immediately (*Romeo and Juliet* 3.5.140) and Capulet swears to Juliet:

> And you be mine, I'll give you to my friend;
> And you be not, hang, beg, starve, die in the streets,
> For, by my soul, I'll ne'er acknowledge thee,
> Nor what is mine shall never do thee good.
>
> (3.5.191–94)

Capulet speaks as if Juliet were simply his disposable property. Despite some Renaissance notions of parental authority, I doubt that any audience in the theater ever sympathized much with these parents. But there are plenty of contrasting aged characters. In *As You Like It,* Duke Senior is as benign as Duke Frederick is malign, and he welcomes his daughter's unexpected marriage; and old Adam is as faithful to his new master, Orlando, as any "new Adam" a theologian could imagine: Old Adam's virtues seem to be from an age before the fall. Henry IV, a sometimes grim, disapproving, and suffering father is reconciled to his son when Hal proves his bravery and loyalty. The dying John of Gaunt opposes Richard II's abuses and fearlessly prophesies the ruin of Richard and England. York is torn between justice and legitimacy, and tries desperately to be loyal. But despite all the benign and sympathetic old, I believe the audiences of the plays usually identify with the young—those for whom the future has still to be proved. Perhaps a major reason why a number of readers and viewers have found *King Lear* almost unbearable is that it is the one play in which the crimes and inhumanity of the young are so much more horrible than the violence, injustice, and foolishness of the old. For those who have never yet become reconciled with the "injustices" that they feel they have suffered from their own parents, the dramatic prospect that children might become infinitely more treacherous, brutal, and inhuman than their "unjust" parents may be devastating.

More alien than the aged, the lower classes, or even the opposite sex for most viewers in ordinary social life are probably members of other races or foreigners—those who do not look or dress or speak the way that we do. Shakespeare uses a great many of the popular xenophobic clichés and frequently seems to invite our laughter almost equally for the aliens and for the clichés: the foppish French, the drunken Danes, the proud Spaniards, the lecherous Italians, the lying Welsh, the quarrelsome Irish usually seem little more serious than the crazy English at whom he invited his English audiences to laugh in both *Hamlet* and *The Tempest*. The clichés can be used for one or two characters and then forgotten, since whatever their supposed nationalities, the most important Shakespearean stage figures have a habit of acting like contemporary Englishmen as they speak an eloquent English language. But in *The Merchant of Venice* and *Othello,* something different happens. As G. K. Hunter has demonstrated, with the Jew and the Moor (two figures who, along with the Turk, represented on stage cultures outside Christendom), Shakespeare used (and to a large degree transformed) prejudices much deeper than those commonly felt toward other Europeans. Anthony Hecht has recently demonstrated that in *The Merchant of Venice* Shakespeare used or assumed a great deal of the traditional medieval anti-Semitic association with blasphemy and perhaps ritual murder as well as the Old Law, lack of charity, revenge, miserliness, and usury. In one of the most familiar passages, when Solanio quotes Shylock's response to his discovery of Jessica's elopement,

My daughter! O my ducats! O my daughter!
Fled with a Christian! O my Christian ducats!
Justice! the law! my ducats, and my daughter!

(2.8.15–17)

we are invited to laugh at Shylock's implicit equation of the two losses (of daughter and ducats) as well as at the notion that coins could become "Christian"—or could have been Jewish, for that matter. And we cannot sympathize with Shylock when he exclaims, "I would my daughter were dead at my foot, and the jewels in her ear!" (3.1.87–88). The passage most often cited as a sympathetic assertion of Shylock's humanity, "Hath not a Jew eyes? . . . . If you prick us, do we not bleed?" (3.1.59–64) is ironically distanced by his following claim that a Jew has the right to behave as badly as a Christian: "The villainy you teach me, I will execute, and it shall go hard but I will better the instruction" (71–73). I think more disturbing to our responses to the play are the moments when Shylock breaks out of the predictable mold: "It was my turkis, I had it of Leah when I was a bachelor. I would not have given it for a wilderness of monkeys" (3.1.121–23). When Shylock is given a past, a courtship, and a gift to a named woman who became his wife and is now dead, we cannot laugh, and I think we must sympathize. (Something similar happens to our attitudes toward Caliban in *The Tempest,* I believe, when he describes his dreams of happiness and music.) The horrors of anti-Semitism in the twentieth century may make it impossible for many of us to respond to *The Merchant of Venice* as Elizabethans did when they grouped it among the comedies and supposedly considered the ending a satisfactorily happy one. But a number of the problems must also have been present for some of them—suggested simply enough by Portia's first question when she enters the court disguised as Balthasar: "Which is the merchant here? and which the Jew?" (4.1.174). We can respond easily enough to the notions that mercy should triumph over legalism, and most of us can be attracted (if not enchanted) by the mood of light and harmony, playful love and generous forgiveness in the final scene. It is also easy enough to see the major flaw in Shylock's question, "What judgment shall I dread, doing no wrong?" (4.1.89). But what can we feel for the others in the play when he goes on to insist that it is as unreasonable to expect him to give up his pound of flesh as it would be if he asked them to free their slaves, allow them an equal standard of living, and "marry them to your heirs?" (89–94).

There have been many incompatible modern interpretations of

Othello, but I find convincing Helen Gardner's insistence that above all, the title character of that play is "The Noble Moor." G. K. Hunter declares that he is unique: earlier stage "Moors" are either stupid or evil—if not both. In *Othello* Shakespeare pushed to a painful extreme his frequent oppositions between appearance and reality: it is the black Moor whose soul is noble and dangerously innocent; and it is the white Iago who gives us perhaps our most horrifying glimpse into a blackened soul. That basic and paradoxical opposition involves us in the action of the drama in complicated ways, since the issues extend far beyond the stage. As Hunter remarked,

> Shakespeare's choice of a black man for his Red Cross Knight, his Rinaldo, has a further advantage. Our involvement in prejudice gives us a double focus on his reality. We admire him—I fear that one has to be trained as a literary critic to find him unadmirable—but we are aware of the difficulty of sustaining that vision of the golden world of poetry; and this is so because *we* feel the disproportion and the difficulty of his social life and of his marriage (as a social act).[4]

In *The Merchant of Venice* and *Othello* Shakespeare made central to his dramas two of the major cultural and racial prejudices that have haunted and disgraced the Western world. It is no wonder that for many years in our enlightened century, those two plays have frequently been considered too embarrassing or disturbing or incendiary to allow them to be taught in our schools.

In comparison to modern drama, we may think that there is a good deal of the superhuman (and perhaps subhuman) that is truly "other" within Shakespearean drama, but if we compare it with the preceding miracle plays or moralities or with Greek and Roman tragedy, there seems remarkably little. The powers of even the most extraordinarily gifted human characters within the plays are severely limited. Richard II cannot understand how one can be a king and also be subject to ordinary human frailties and limitations, but all of Shakespeare's kings are so subject. When a ruler comes closest to something like supernatural power or insight (resembling that of a divine figure, a playwright, or director), we find surprising limitations. Duke Vincentio in *Measure for Measure* prevents catastrophe, but he discovers that his human characters refuse to follow his intended script, and he finds himself subject to scandal and laughter as he plots and quickly improvises. Prospero has achieved his extraordinary mastery for a limited period only; the happy ending for which he anxiously works involves his giving up his superhuman power over nature and his enemies as well as his father's authority over his daughter, and rejoining the ordinary, limited, human community—it could hardly be a happy ending for the young lovers if he did not.

There are plenty of omens within the plays, and fairies, spirits, ghosts, apparitions, and witches may appear, but at least until the late romances, their roles and influences are ambiguous or severely limited. They appear only selectively to individuals, or within visions or dreams, to inspire or encourage or terrify human beings, and their status is frequently questioned—most notoriously in *Hamlet.* Hymen may lead a concluding wedding masque and Time can serve as an explanatory chorus for the audience. But Puck and Ariel's remarkable powers are exercised only within their limited roles as servants. In Prospero's wedding masque, it is not the gods themselves who perform, but spirits who imitate gods. Before the late romances, I think the ancient gods come nearest to appearing with power in *Antony and Cleopatra;* but we only hear the music as "the god Hercules, whom Antony lov'd, / Now leaves him" (4.3.16–17), we glimpse an image of him in Antony's final agony ("The shirt of Nessus is upon me"—4.12.43), and we glimpse Mars and Venus only in the final transformations of the human lovers. The danger of the entrance of unambiguously divine power onto the stage is that it may put an end to the kind of drama Shakespeare was usually concerned with: fallible human actions within time.

It is within the late romances that we are continually faced with an "other" more wonderful than anything most of us have known: the recovery of the lost—children, dukedoms, the dead, love— even, it would seem, time. And it is no wonder that within these plays we find a vision of Diana, a Jupiter who descends in a dream (sitting upon an eagle and throwing thunderbolts), and an oracle of Apollo; these divinities lead to revelations and resolutions that almost seem beyond the capacities of a secular theater. Yet an increasing number of secular theatergoers in recent years respond to them with delight. I now believe the most magical moment in these plays is when, at the end of *The Winter's Tale,* the statue of Hermione becomes living flesh—a scene I thought impossible to bring off when I first read the play, but which I can now testify usually works on stage even on occasions when very little else does. Where else does a postclassical, "modern" dramatist present a "miracle" on stage, dramatize the problems of perception and disbelief, and then lead his audience to accept it and to rejoice?

I find almost equally moving those occasions when we come to recognize that characters we had thought existed within our ordi-

nary human possibilities and limitations have truly become
"other"—have gone far beyond us in experience or insight or intelligence or suffering. That discovery seems central to the great
tragedies: as we witness the sufferings and deaths of heroic figures,
we recognize that they have surpassed not only what we have
known, but even what we had imagined before we had experienced
their dramas. Lear's rage and suffering and discovery of a world
beyond power and justice, ceremony and obligations; Othello's passionate love and murderous jealousy and appalled recognition of
both the truth and what he has done; Hamlet's torment, agility,
brilliance, doubt, and final carelessness; Macbeth's discovery of
tedium and despair within the expanding circle of blood—these
are things I think we could not have anticipated and cannot forget
after attending decent performances of the plays or reading them
with care. And sometimes we recognize that the imaginations of
tragic figures may be almost as far beyond ours as their experiences. Cleopatra describes to Dolabella her dream of Antony:

> His legs bestrid the ocean, his rear'd arm
> Crested the world, his voice was propertied
> As all the tuned spheres, and that to friends:
> But when he meant to quail and shake the orb,
> He was as rattling thunder. For his bounty,
> There was no winter in't: an autumn it was
> That grew the more by reaping. His delights
> Were dolphin-like, they show'd his back above
> The element they liv'd in. In his livery
> Walk'd crowns and crownets: realms and islands were
> As plates dropp'd from his pocket.
>
> (5.2.82–92)

When Cleopatra asks him whether he believes there could be such
a man, I think we anticipate Dolabella's answer: "Gentle madam,
no" (94). It is not really the figure of Antony that we have seen
thus far in the play. But the passion of Cleopatra's response ("You
lie up to the hearing of the gods") and her insistence that Antony
was "nature's piece 'gainst fancy" disturb our certainty. We come
to believe, even if we cannot fully share, the reality of Cleopatra's
transformed image of the dead Antony; I think we attend it with
awe, as a vision other than ours, but one we might share if we had
truly experienced heroic passion and heroic loss.

Almost as touching and equally unexpected are those smaller
moments when we recognize a difference in perspective with some
characters on stage, a difference so profound as to make us respond

emotionally to the gap of otherness. Everybody remembers Miranda's exclamation as she first views the group of chastened courtiers, usurpers, and would-be murderers at the end of *The Tempest.*

> O wonder!
> How many goodly creatures are there here!
> How beauteous mankind is! O brave new world
> That has such people in't!
>
> (5.1.181–84)

We can hardly imagine a first viewing of mankind, and we wonder how we might respond to it, even as we rejoice in Miranda's innocence and delight. This sort of moment happens more frequently than we may realize, and sometimes we hope that our distance from the speaker's perspective is more obviously to our advantage. In the Quarto of *King Lear,* when Edmund warns the Captain that he should act in accordance with the times and obey his as yet unread orders, the Captain replies:

> I cannot draw a cart, nor eat dried oats,
> If it be man's work, I'll do't.
>
> (5.3.37–38)

Our initial response may be one of amused cynicism if not horror at the implication that killing a defenseless woman and a very old man who are prisoners of war might be considered proper "man's work," while drawing a cart is not. But our immediate dissociation from the Captain and his sentiments is surely soon complicated by memories of the various inhumanities and horrors that are frequently practiced under the guise of necessity, with the implication that "man's work" is often defined by whatever seems necessary for a man (or woman) to enjoy the social role and standard of living to which he is accustomed—or to which he aspires. It is a fortunate reader or viewer who can remain comfortably sure that the Captain's sentiment is totally "other."

I find one of the most touching moments of all in the fourth act of *Othello* at the end of the willow-song scene, when Desdemona, thinking of Othello's furious charges against her, suddenly remarks to Emilia,

> O, these men, these men!
> Dost thou in conscience think—tell me, Emilia—
> That there be women do abuse their husbands
> In such gross kind!
>
> (4.3.60–63)

It is a startling question. Surely, every member of the audience must agree with Emilia's understated "There be some such, no question." And a large number must find sympathetic (if not exactly admirable) Emilia's response to Desdemona's following question, "Wouldst thou do such a deed for all the world?": "'ud's pity, who would not make her husband a cuckold to make him a monarch? I should venture purgatory for't." (75–77). But Emilia's response only reinforces Desdemona's doubt and disbelief: "I do not think there is any such woman" (83). Such innocence and ignorance of the world are almost beyond our imaginations: I do not think we would be likely to believe a narrator who told us of them. But Desdemona's words make us believe them, at least for this moment of the drama, and I think we are touched by awe as well as astonishment and pity. That Shakespeare's plays can make us imagine so many kinds of others, including Desdemona's astonishing ignorance of others less innocent than she, is one of the miraculous things about the plays.

Notes

1. Rev. ed. R. Himelich, Purdue University Studies (West Lafayette, Ind., 1965), 67–68; *u* and *v* modernized.

2. (Princeton, N.J.: Princeton University Press, 1984), 28, n. 24.

3. Breyten Breytenbach, *The True Confessions of an Albino Terrorist* (Emmarentia, South Africa: Taurus, 1984), 247.

4. G. K. Hunter, "Othello and Colour Prejudice," *Dramatic Identities and Cultural Traditions: Studies in Shakespeare and His Contemporaries* (Liverpool: University of Liverpool Press, 1978), 59.

Love's Labor's Lost: Finding a Text, Finding a Play

HOMER SWANDER

Among those disciplined acts of the imagination available to us in the 1990s, which would bring us closest to the mind and imagination of Shakespeare—the playwright of the 1590s?

For the special purpose of this collection of essays, allow me to translate my question into something more personal. Is there any way to become so intimately Shakespeare's collaborator that one could legitimately feel one's own creativity to be a shared act with him? In what sense and to what degree could one's mind and imagination be not only inspired and freed but directed and disciplined by those acts of imagination titled—for example, and to stay within the 1590s—*A Midsummer Night's Dream, The Taming of the Shrew,* and *Love's Labor's Lost?* After nearly fifty years of enjoying myself with what is called "work" in the academy and the theater, these questions, more than any other, matter to me. They happen also to be questions to which I believe I have found unromantic, unsentimental, unillusory answers—answers that have led me further and further into a rewarding—and perhaps unique?—exploration of Shakespeare's scripts.[1]

The activity that I shall be describing allows of no single descriptive term. Its essential but not concluding consequence is a work of art: one of Shakespeare's scripts fully, vigorously, deeply staged. But I am not speaking simply of a theatrical performance. The activity is, in its complete nature, at once theatrical, pedagogical, scholarly, analytical, literary, aesthetic, and creative. As it is each of these at every moment, the description could begin with any one of its elements. Quite arbitrarily, then, let it begin with textual scholarship.

As I am seeking collaboration, not appropriation (that popular sport of the 1980s), what I most need to know, to the degree possible, are the exact words, forms, and signs that Shakespeare put down on paper. Oddly enough, after four centuries of editorial work to provide such matters, there exists no modern edition of any one of the three scripts that we can fully trust. To read any modern Shakespearean text is to read a text that is at significant points devised not by Shakespeare but by editors who have deliberately altered not only important words but speech assignments, entrances, exits, crucial punctuation, even structure. A production of *Dream, Shrew,* or *Love's Labor's Lost* based on any of the available modern editions would not be a satisfactory collaboration with Shakespeare.[2] Yet it is such productions that one encounters, almost always, even in the finest professional or university theaters in this country, Canada, and England.

Early in *Love's Labor's Lost,* for example—at a point that proves crucial for an understanding of nearly everything else—there is no widespread editorial or theatrical agreement about the content of the script. Amazingly, there is in the 1990s no agreed-upon script of this play upon which reasonably to base either an interpretation or a production. In the first moments of the first meeting between the women of France and the men of Navarre (the third scene of the play) the words and actions of five of the major characters— Katherine, Rosaline, Berowne, Boyet, and Dumaine—remain a matter of textual controversy: who says and does what, and with whom? To proceed responsibly to criticism or performance, one must face that question, and if one is seeking to collaborate with the playwright by submitting as far as possible to his authority, nothing, obviously, is more important than the accuracy of the script.

Such a collaborator, finding modern texts caught in a dead end of conflicting speculation, is forced to expand the arena of textual scholarship. Without deserting the study or the library, he or she must move also into the rehearsal hall and onto the stage. To do so adequately, however, one needs a theater, dedicated actors, and freedom—freedom, especially, from the triple bondage that most theaters cannot escape: time, money, and union rules. The collaborator also needs, I believe, a long apprenticeship in bringing scholarly demands to the service of theatrical processes. The academy and the theater are both jealously demanding when called equally into the same creative act: a modern collaborator with Shakespeare must live a variety of lives in both houses.

In order properly to return to the textual challenge of *Love's Labor's Lost* I should admit that I live in an ideal world. I have the theater, the actors, and the freedom that make the needed textual scholarship possible. Through fourteen-hour days and seven-day weeks that no Equity company would ever be allowed, and probably would never want, we in the American Shakespeare Company (of which, more later) find ways of getting behind the editorial confusion and literary masks that, even, in the best professional companies, hide Shakespeare from the actors and the audiences. Ours is, precisely, an archaeological enterprise. Sifting through the debris of centuries, we discover in the original texts amazing plays that long ago dropped out of sight. We are then privileged to perform them: quite literally, "new" plays—by Shakespeare.[3]

Different scripts yield different plays. And in that part of *Love's Labor's Lost* to which I have referred, the flight from Shakespeare's original started very early. The Quarto (1598) offers one play, the Folio (1623) quite another; and no modern editor or theatrical production that I know of has fully accepted either. All editors agree that in the third scene of the play (2.1) just as the young men and women are meeting for the first time, there is some kind of confusion between Katherine and Rosaline, between Berowne and Boyet, and, for a brief moment, involving Dumaine. The editors also agree upon their clear duty: they must create a text that is *not* confused.

They have in fact created several. In various ways and to various degrees, they conflate, emend, and/or cut. Theater companies follow after or, occasionally, create their own versions. As a result, anyone diligently seeking *Love's Labor's Lost* has at least seven distinctly different scripts from which to choose.[4] But do these differently scripted brief moments (fewer than forty lines) really give us, in a major way, different plays? Am I, that is, speaking with scholarly care? As in rehearsal and performance we explored the territory and we found—not surprisingly, I suppose—that what happens in that first meeting of the men and women has a defining impact on what happens in the rest of the play: on who these characters are, how they respond to one another thereafter, and the tone, texture, and color of the gender relationships throughout.

It was surprising to us, however, that the version we chose, at last, was the first one of all, the Quarto, the one that has been universally blamed for all of the confusion. It certainly wasn't, for us, the most obvious choice; and it came only after ten weeks of rehearsal, five preview performances, and two more weeks of work before we opened—a fact that proves, for me, the extraordinary power of editors. I think it fair to say that we had been at least as brainwashed by what now appears to us to be an editorially created confusion as has any other group of readers who assume (or hope) that the editors have done their homework fruitfully. As we do not want our archaeological bent to turn us into antiquarians, we wish, surely as much as any other theater company, to benefit from valuable editorial work. Thus we started, as nearly all companies do, with the version of the play that appears in most modern editions: *Editorial Play #1*. It is for most readers (as it was for us) *The Play,* and it was especially etched into my consciousness because it was the play that I had directed twice before.[5]

The story it offers goes like this: four young men, having taken an oath to study for three years and to see no women, are confronted by four young ladies, three of whom bring with them a strong interest in three of the men, thus creating three couples before the men have anything to say about it; but as soon as the men enter, each chooses the "right" lady, as the fourth couple is creating itself before everyone's eyes; and the two who compose the most articulate couple—Rosaline and Berowne—twice spar wittily with one another, Rosaline winning both matches but (as we learn later) only in such a way as to drive Berowne into a more passionate interest. The first match goes as follows:

Berowne.   Did not I dance with you in Brabant once?
Rosaline.   Did not I dance with you in Brabant once?
Berowne.   I know you did.
Rosaline.   How needless was it then to ask the question?
Berowne.   You must not be so quick.
Rosaline.   'Tis 'long of you that spur me with such questions.
Berowne.   Your wit's too hot, it speeds too fast, 'twill tire.
Rosaline.   Not till it leave the rider in the mire.
Berowne.   What time a day?
Rosaline.   The hour that fools should ask.
Berowne.   Now fair befall your mask.
Rosaline.   Fair fall the face it covers.
Berowne.   And send you many lovers.
Rosaline.   Amen, so you be none.
Berowne.   Nay then will I be gone.

After some fifty lines of governmental matters between the King of Navarre and the Princess of France, Berowne tries again:

Berowne.   Lady I will commend you to my own heart.
Rosaline.   Pray you, do my commendations, I would be glad to see it.
Berowne.   I would you heard it groan.
Rosaline.   Is the fool sick.
Berowne.   Sick at the heart.

Rosaline. Alack, let it blood.
Berowne. Would that do it good?
Rosaline. My physic says "ay."
Berowne. Will you prick't with your eye.
Rosaline. No point, with my knife.
Berowne. Now God save thy life.
Rosaline. And yours from long living.
Berowne. I cannot stay thanksgiving.

Immediately thereafter, the three young men, one after the other, ask Boyet to identify the "right" young lady: Dumaine points at Katherine, Longaville at Maria, Berowne at Rosaline. It is clear that Rosaline's sharp wit has in no way discouraged Berowne.

Nothing could be more neat, more symmetrical, more artificial, more romantic, more charming, more satisfying. We know at once where we are. As Gerald Freedman, who has also twice directed the Editorial Play, says, we are in the world of "sunny . . . light, charming comedy."[6] But is it the world of Shakespeare's play? The longer we rehearsed it, the less interesting, the less fruitful it became; and that is not the experience we normally find when rehearsing Shakespeare. Without any preconceived plan to try something else, our confidence in the scene began to crumble. For it really did begin to seem mildly boring, especially the second Berowne-Rosaline sparring match, which seemed so close to repeating the first that we could understand why many productions (that of the BBC, for example) cut the second one: very little, if anything, is lost, certainly nothing essential.

But one of the basic rules of our company is that we do not cut. We make the script work as a play, or we embarrass ourselves—and it sometimes comes to that. In the face of our shaken confidence, we needed to turn back to the originals, away from the perhaps too-plausible world of the editors, in order to do our own kind of searching and testing, a kind that can take place only in the theater. After much disagreement, analytical work in rehearsal, and a bit of wavering—even against some pretty severe doubts—we put our money on the play offered by the Folio, though the editors still convinced us to emend so that Berowne and Dumaine would ask Boyet for the names of the "right" ladies instead of (as the Folio has it) Berowne asking for Katherine and Dumaine for Rosaline.

The Folio version is fascinating because its very existence means that someone—actors in the company? the first editorial revisionist? Shakespeare himself?—was so unhappy with the Quarto as to

shape a new play. The story it offers gives us the same four couples
we meet in the modern version, but when Berowne makes his move
on Rosaline, and she immediately rebuffs him, she then (in the
second duet) seems to pretend, apparently for his benefit, to be
interested in another man (Boyet), causing the rebuffed and
scorned Berowne suddenly to stalk off with, as he says, no
"thanksgiving," and to show a brief interest in another lady (Katherine) even as Dumaine shows an interest, never developed, in
Rosaline by asking Boyet for her name. That is, in the second duet
quoted above, all of Berowne's lines, except the last, are given to
Boyet, with Berowne now clearly an irritated observer—as Rosaline must intend him to be—of her relationship with another man.
It is in this irritation, then, that he inquires about Katherine
(though by the next time he appears he has, without explanation,
recovered his interest in Rosaline).

This story makes, we still think, a more interesting play than
the editorial version. It contains all the romance, the charm, the
satisfying symmetry of the Editorial Play, and it is a lot more fun.
As a story idea—what Hollywood calls a treatment—my actors
loved it. And the possibility that it is a revision made for the Elizabethan stage, perhaps even by Shakespeare himself, gave us every
motivation to make it work. We had great fun with it, and so did
the audiences for our five preview performances. We still don't
understand why it has been so completely ignored by modern editors, who usually don't even bother to dismiss it. Whoever invented it was a clever fellow.

But in fact it does not work. In performance, two problems are,
we believe, insurmountable:

1. What in the Editorial Play (and, as we will see, in the Quarto)
is a sparring match between Berowne and Rosaline really *is* a sparring match. To make the passage work for a Rosaline using Boyet
to annoy Berowne one would have to rewrite it. The Berowne-
Rosaline dialogue is at last unconvincing as a Rosaline-Boyet maneuver (or as anything else between them that we could discover).

2. However hard we tried—and try we did—we couldn't believe
that a Berowne who has just watched the Rosaline-Boyet duet and
walked off in a huff would go almost at once to that very same
man to ask the name of any lady; and a momentary interest in
Katherine seemed quite pointless, having no context in which to
function. That is, the Folio text, with Berowne asking Boyet about
Katherine, is unconvincing; but so is the editorially unanimous
substitution of Rosaline.

At last, we found that we had to clear our heads of every revisionist speculation, of every plausible editorial version, and—hardest of all—of that conventional satisfaction with artifice, formality, and symmetry that are universally said to be the staples of *Love's Labor's Lost*.

Suddenly, released from four hundred years of well-meaning obscurantism, we fell in love with the Quarto: what an amazing script! And how quickly—through the simple elements of that so-called confusion in the third scene—it frees an acting company into something real, creating the joyful burden of finding a deeper, truer play. We didn't have enough time—we could have used another four months—but in rehearsal and performance through the next three weeks, we did what we could. At last, we felt, we were collaborating with Shakespeare instead of with all those critics, scholars, editors, actors and directors whom we had been allowing to shut us away from the scripted signals that reveal the world of his imagination.

Profound embarrassment of course accompanied the discovery, for the story the Quarto tells is perfectly simple and clear. Why didn't we see that from the beginning? This "new" story, furthermore, drew us into a world we recognized: our world, the world of students at any American university. What a lovely irony: Shakespeare's script from the 1590s seemed, as soon as we started doing it, closer to the 1990s than any of the versions offered by "modern" editors. My young actors could finally stop merely pretending to believe what was going on. To be sure, at first the same four men, the same four women, but Berowne—who has, even while signing the oath, been dreaming of "some mistress fine"—is here at once on the prowl, making (in the first duet) a fast, macho play for Katherine, then (in the second) for Rosaline, back briefly to Katherine (checking on her name), and at last settling (apparently, but not until next we see him) on Rosaline. "The young Dumaine," as Katherine significantly characterizes him in her first words about him, is also making his move: Rosaline looks good to him, and the editors haven't told him about symmetry.

So what is confusing? Who is confused? Not the characters, not the actors, not the audience. We could at last begin to feel the pleasures of archaeological discovery. We would, in fact, rather find *Love's Labor's Lost* than the foundations of the Rose Theatre.

But what did we really find? In this new-old play we found Berowne trying his line—and it is so sophomorically a "line"—on Katherine: "Did not I dance with you in Brabant once?" Ah, Katherine: she whose beloved sister—"melancholy, sad, and heavy" (5.2.14)—died of love; she who late in act 5 will say even to Du-

maine, "Then if I have much love, I'll give you some" (822); and
she who knows that her dear friend Rosaline (standing right over
there, listening and watching) has a very special interest in this
man. Berowne couldn't have found a less promising way to break
his oath, and for his pains gets the verbal equivalent of a knee to
the groin. Retreating in haste—"Nay then will I be gone"—he almost at once brazenly puts an even more outrageous move on
Rosaline: "Lady, I will commend you to my own heart." Ah, right:
he for whom this is the second lady in the last three minutes. Her
replies—if taken simply as they come—are stunning: she has a
knife for his heart and wishes him soon dead. When Boyet later
says that the "tongues of mocking wenches" are like arrows and
bullets (5.2.256–61), we will know what he means.

No wonder that after this defeat, Berowne decides at once to
switch back to his first choice: even Katherine seems a more likely
pickup than this brunette fury. And in the playing, as we soon
realized, the actor (speaking to Boyet) needs only to hesitate at the
right second: "What's her name"—pause, eyes roaming over the
field, finger pointing at last to her—"in the cap." Katherine!—"by
good *hap*"?—yes, indeed, as Boyet says. Apparently the Elizabethan audience recognized this brash young man; certainly our modern audience did. Laugh at him or loathe him, he is as familiar—
especially to women—as a street corner, a college party, or a day
at the beach. And he's infinitely more interesting for the actors
and the audience than the bland editorial Berowne—funnier and
yet a more serious threat to comic form, more problematic for the
female characters, and with a more complex impact on the rest of
the play. As we thought about it, he seemed a far more likely
candidate for a play in which the "Labor" of "Love" is "Lost."

Our reward came in many forms. It is a critical commonplace
that Armado is some kind of parody of the oath-breaking, romantic
young men of the court, especially, perhaps, of Berowne. Discovering how to convert the scripted signals of the parody into
amusing and revealing stage action is, however, not as easy as one
might wish. It was, therefore, always a moment of pure joy when,
with the insight provided by the Quarto, we saw signals that had
been hidden from us by the other scripts. In the fourth scene (3.1.),
the major elements of the parody are, in all versions, clear enough:
Armado, melancholy in love, asks Costard to deliver a letter to
Jaquenetta and tips him a "remuneration"; Berowne, melancholy
in love, asks Costard to deliver a letter to Rosaline, and tips him
a "guerdon." There is no missing the parallel. But why, for example, does Armado forget Jaquenetta's name—"But o but o"—and

Moth drive home so emphatically (in some eighteen lines: 3.1.26–43) the forgetting: "Negligent student, learn her by heart"? The moment, just in itself, is funny enough; but could there be another payoff?

In all versions of this scene, Berowne enters with the letter, but the Quarto is by far the most interesting; for there the audience cannot know at once which lady (Katherine or Rosaline) he is now pursuing. Groaning for love and begging Costard to deliver the letter to a "gentle Lady," he says:

> When tongues speak sweetly, then they name her name,
> And *Rosaline* they call her. . . .
>
> (160–61)

Suddenly in rehearsal, we knew that the Berowne of the Quarto would (of course) forget her name, that—even in the midst of his moony talk about naming her name—he would have to glance quickly at the letter to name "Rosaline." An action of two or three seconds only; but it is true to character, is based (we believe) firmly on the script, enriches the function of Armado, and employs the parody wonderfully to ridicule Berowne's ability to "love." Our audiences loved it. And we, once more, were grateful to the Quarto.[7]

Another consequence of playing the Quarto script is that the women, too, become more interesting. Startled and challenged by the disorderly surprises of life instead of simpering into the prearranged simplicities of neatly symmetrical patterns, they blossom into real women, women with more passions than parasols. Katherine is suddenly on the front line, deeply offended, even wounded (she may have known just such a man as the lover of her sister), and deeply embarrassed, suffering for Rosaline. But what Katherine (and the audience) won't know until much later is that Rosaline has lied about Berowne, lied outrageously, and this in a play that is prominently about the value of honesty. Only minutes earlier, in the same scene, she has said to her friends that Berowne's wit— unlike that of the men the two of them fancy—remains always "Within the limit of becoming mirth," that his tongue is "fair," his words so "apt and gracious" that older folk are delighted and the young "quite ravished" by his "sweet . . . discourse." What a lovely man! He has, in Rosaline's description, no faults. What a contrast to Longaville—of whom the painfully honest Maria has just confessed that his "sharp Wit" and "blunt Will" spare "none . . . that come within his power"—and to Dumaine, of whom Kath-

erine, in a bonding with Maria, says that he has "Most power to
do most harm" and "wit to make an ill shape good." But Rosaline
is hiding the truth, trying perhaps to hide it even from herself.
Berowne is, as she has known from the beginning but does not
admit until her next-to-last speech in the play, at least as dangerous
as the other men:

> a man replete with mocks,
> Full of comparisons and wounding flouts:
> Which you on all estates will execute,
> That lie within the mercy of your wit.

(5.2.835–38)

The actress playing the Quarto will know that, as Rosaline watches
Berowne trying to manipulate first Katherine and then herself, she
is already beginning to pay for her lie. The passion of her response
to him has its source in guilt as well as anger. No such complication
troubles the life of the editorial Rosaline.

Maria has watched it all, heard it all: heard Rosaline's unqualified
praise for Berowne, felt the force of the comparison against Longaville and Dumaine, and watched as Berowne puts his arrogant,
oath-breaking moves on her two friends. With all that, we suddenly
discovered that it isn't easy to find Maria's tone of voice when,
upon Berowne's exit, she says, "That last is Berowne, the merry
madcap Lord / Not a word with him but a jest." In his exchange
with Boyet just before leaving, he has in no sense justified such a
comment: nothing "merry," nothing of the madcap, no jesting. She
must, then, be commenting on Berowne's behavior with Katherine
and Rosaline—with an ironic look back at Rosaline's glowing characterization of him. As Maria doesn't know that Rosaline has been
lying, there need be no resentment toward her in the irony. What
Maria does know is the great contrast between Berowne's "apt and
gracious" ways in Rosaline's report and his ungracious ways in the
last few minutes. Our actresses came to believe that the women
are united in their feelings about this man who seems to think that,
even as he breaks his oath, he is God's gift to any lady; and we all
agreed that Maria, with her scornful and amazed irony, is speaking
for them all. "So why do I continue to put up with the guy?"—an
anguished question from the actress playing Rosaline, and a very
good question it is, revealing a level of difficulty, of complexity, a
depth of characterization that challenged us only once we had
switched to the Quarto.

In each succeeding rehearsal and performance, we discovered

that, under the impact of the Quarto script, this kind of deepening continues right through the play. It would be easy to present more examples of the transformation and more points at which the Quarto is textually superior, but for the purpose of this essay it will be more useful to turn to a quite different kind of reward— though it, too, came from the effort of trying to collaborate with, instead of merely to study or interpret, Shakespeare. Sitting in my study as a reader, I would never have entered, even fancifully, into the strange world of masks. But in the theater, these things happen, often a bit mysteriously. The simple fact is that if you direct *Love's Labor's Lost,* you need masks. You have decisions to make: what kind of masks? what size, shape, texture, color? And the wonder of it is that through the masks (or whatever else, on some other occasion, it may be) you come, if you are lucky, to feel closer to the secret and the power of the play.

When the young men enter disguised as Russians, the women— having exchanged with one another their gifts from the men—don or hold face masks. The men are totally deceived. Not one of them is able to identify his beloved by height, weight, figure, color of hair, shape or color of hands, sound of voice, gait or manner. Instead, each follows the gift that he has given—diamonds, pearls, gloves—and, as Berowne says later, "woo'd but the sign of she" (5.2.469). Well, if we were ever in an artificial world of make-believe, this is surely it. In most productions that I have seen, what matters most—and it can be delightful—is the color and swirl of costume, the high vocal style, the patterned style of movement as the women either hold in their hand elegant masks or wear delicately lovely quarter-face masks. As we went into rehearsal, something of this kind is certainly what I had in mind; it is what I had employed in my two previous productions.

In such productions, with the women not in any real sense disguised, the audience is always vividly aware of each female identity as each man amazingly fails to see or hear that he is wooing the wrong woman. The error of the men is gross, obvious, incredible; and the theatrical device is close to being a mere joke, a dip into elegant farce. The point—that these men do not know the women they are wooing—is clearly and amusingly made; and the play goes on well enough.

But there are other possibilities. We discovered ours one day when, in the hands of an actress, the "wrong kind" of mask showed up from a rental costume shop: full-face masks, the vivid likenesses of animals and mythical creatures. Well, we'll try anything, however skeptical we may be; and after a while we began to sense that something important was happening. We rented two of the masks and later made two of our own. Our four ladies became a brown-faced antelope with horns, a white unicorn, a black cat, and a pink rabbit with very long ears. No human face was even partly visible. The difference for the play was amazing. The mysterious, trans-forming force of such distinctive masks, under which the human face disappears, is such that members of the audience, not just Berowne and his fellows, tend to be distanced from the actual person behind the mask. The personal identity of the woman is weakened, and a surreal sense is created of four strange creatures swirling about the stage, saying and doing very strange things. Theatrically, a quite different and more subtle point gets made. While the audience can still laugh at men who cannot recognize the women they praise so fulsomely and claim to love so deeply, we also experience sufficient nightmarish confusion to be reminded of how difficult it is really to know anyone, even the person one loves. The scene is thus more complex, more oddly, perhaps para-doxically, real and believable, even disturbing in its nightmarish reality.

For the men, the only way through this sudden nightmare is the gifts they have given to the women. The whole matter of the gifts takes on a new urgency, a deeper significance. The men *must* cling to the gifts as the only means of identification in a world of women who are suddenly refusing to be knowable. The women's strategy deliberately reveals the men to be capitalists of female flesh, each content—and only able—to identify his love by the money (in Be-rowne's terms, the "copper": 4.3.382) they have spent on them. As the women play out their roles for the purpose of such a strat-egy, they can seem to become the "Light wenches" (381) of the men's imaginations and desires, easily purchased women whose only identity is placed upon them by men, women apparently de-fined wholly by the purchases of men, women who are no more than the possessions of men.

For such a scene, we discovered that the gifts should be in as poor taste as the accompanying poems that the women find so ridiculous and hypocritical. The signal for this is, after all, clearly in the script. Even a princess is impressed by the conspicuous wealth now entering the game:

> we shall be rich ere we depart,
> If Fairings come thus plentifully in.
> A Lady wall'd about with Diamonds.

Is the Princess "wall'd about"—captured, imprisoned—by a wide, garish diamond belt? Has Rosaline received a brooch nearly the size of a saucer? Are Katherine's gloves garishly sequinned, bejeweled, or furred? Can Maria's chain of pearls—though shorter (as the Princess points out) than Longaville's ludicrously long letter— be far too long for its purpose? If the gifts are going to function fully (and I think they never did in our production), they must be emphatically visible to the audience: as Rosaline says, "wear the Favours most in sight." The more the women can, in their false personae, apparently define themselves by the gifts—the more that they become merely the "signs of she"—the more successful is their strategy, with two consequences: the scene is funnier, and at the same time contributes more seriously and powerfully to the exploration of male-female relationships.

Women defined by material tokens can trade identities in a flash, are infinitely and instantaneously self-malleable, so easily known as not to be known at all. And thus, again, the masks: such women to such men can only be strange beasts or mythical creatures, ultimately unloving and unlovable, their real selves locked away somewhere forever out of sight. The experience for the audience is complex and unstable. In one moment, the women, because of masks, are mysterious, unknowable; in the next, because of the obtrusive gifts, wholly, though falsely, knowable and defined. The scene embodies and projects one of the nightmares of a culture in which, as in ours, the male gaze and easy male assumptions tyrannize the grotesquely gendered landscape. The women adopt their strategy of disguise only when they learn that the men are coming disguised (as Russians) to "parle and court and dance" (5.2.122) and thus behind false identities to offer love when in their own persons they are sworn to abstain from female society, and when in their own persons they blame the women for forcing them, through the power of beauty, to break their oaths. Always, Eve is to blame for Adam's fall.

But in what sense can I claim that presenting such masks and such "Fairings" is "collaborating" with Shakespeare? In what way can they share a place with textual scholarship in the process I am describing? Am I claiming the same kind of validity for the masks or the size of the favors as for the text of the Quarto? Do I believe that the script demands full-face masks or the masks of animals and mythical creatures? The short answer to the last two questions is of course no. But there is more to be said.

The Act of Imagination that occurred in the 1590s took place in a theater; and it is not even accurate to say that a set of words, a literary work, initiated it. The theater—its stage, its actors, its audience—was, from the first inkling of an idea, active in the mind and imagination of the man who wrote the words. The words—that is, as they were brought together and became a script—already contained the theater. They were never a language for a book and a reader. They were but one part of a theatrical language, only fully to be experienced and understood when in the profoundest union with space, sound, color, bodies, movement. The Act was collaborative; that was its nature. The Act is still collaborative; that is still its nature. The Act was and is theatrical. When Shakespeare wrote the script of *Love's Labor's Lost* he was a playwright in the most precise sense of the word "wright": the maker of a play, a staged event, a theatrical (not a literary) work of art.

I am, as you can see, fighting three perverse notions: (1) that a theater company can develop an intimate relationship with Shakespeare while altering his scripts or performing scripts that have been altered by editors; (2) that scripted words, written down, constitute a work of art; and (3) that a script can be properly or fruitfully explored, assessed, or interpreted as if it were literature. Editing, criticism, scholarship, or theater that has been touched by these notions closes the doors to Shakespeare's theater, and thus to his imagination.

I'll take my chances with a discovery about masks that appears to deepen a play, especially when the masks work—as these certainly did—in mysterious harmony with the fascinating complications served up by Shakespeare's original script. I don't know what kind of masks he imagined as he wrote the script or actually used as he and others presented the play. But it is unarguable that his completed Act of Imagination required his actors to wear real masks. And we made the same journey from thinking to doing, from the words of his script to the sights and sounds of a real stage before a real audience.

So as I watched our show night after night I grew increasingly convinced that we were working with the right script, and that working with it in the same art form that disciplined the playwright, we had found our way to a play that was close to him. Each night those masked women who had suddenly become so strangely alien, even nightmarish—and whom I kept failing, in a sense, to recognize—taught me something about the horror of women disfigured by men who are bent on possession, and it taught me something too about grief we must feel for men who, in the name of love, have lost their way. That it did this while still allowing me to laugh at the surface silliness of it all convinced me that I was experiencing a true Shakespearean complexity. And that is what we always hope for—by collaborating with his words, to experience the complexity, profundity, and power of great art. How long, I thought, will it take us all to learn that *Love's Labor's Lost* is a very great play?

To discuss masks, however, does not take us directly into either of the areas in which, over the centuries, so many objections to the play have been raised: plot or language. The plot is said to be too thin, the language too dense, convoluted, obscure, excessively clever. But, at once, two observations: as for plot, the very title announces that this is a play in which something will *not* happen; as for language, no one complains about its complexity, ambiguity, inflation, and obscurity more than do the characters themselves. Now the purpose of such observations is to provide—from the script itself—some sense of direction for a theater company in the initially dark thicket of rehearsal. Our attempts to collaborate with Shakespeare are based on the belief that everything in a Shakespearean script is, in fact, scripted: the script, when taken as the thing it is—a script—yields nothing of value to literary, political, sociological, or psychological interpretation. In and of itself a script is partial, incomplete, does not reveal itself accurately even to the most brilliant and searching interrogation by experts in these other areas of human endeavor. It functions only to enable the process of collaboration that results in a play. For *Love's Labor's Lost,* then, there are no essentially literary observations to be made. Everything is theatrical.

But how, in the theater, are we to take, for example, what seems like a thousand puns? *Love's Labor's Lost* surely contains more puns than any other script by Shakespeare: it is, I believe, the only script to have generated a book entirely devoted to but one category of its punning.[8] A pun admits the instability of meaning in language, but at the same time rejoices in the athletic possibility of communicating more than one meaning at a time. Whenever puns are as plentiful as they are in *Love's Labor's Lost,* we are likely to feel ourselves simultaneously on the brink of chaos—for nothing means simply what it at first seems to mean—and at a wild, thrilling celebration of the power of words to speak two or three (sometimes four or even five) meanings at once. For a theater company, such a ride can be perplexing. As a script, it presents its pleasures for those actors who can enjoy the giddy sense of being lost in a whirling twist and mist of words, and who can, at the same time, be thrilled by the lights that shine in bright precise colors from words that keep dancing, as it were, until dawn.

One of the great challenges of *Love's Labor's Lost* is how to take this scripted dance of words as a set of signals for staged action. The major requirement in meeting that challenge is to find the structure within which the puns and other noisy rhetorical figures function. It is clear, I think, that they are in a state of structural tension with the insistent call in the play for "honest, plain words." At the heart of that call—evoked in the first three minutes through Berowne's line "By yea and nay, sir, then I swore in jest"—is the great passage from Matthew (5:33–37) about swearing oaths and speaking simply:

> Again, ye have heard that it hath been said by them of old time, Thou shalt not forswear thyself, but shall perform unto the Lord thine oaths: But I say unto you, Swear not at all; neither by heaven, for it is God's throne: Nor by the earth; for it is his footstool: neither by Jerusalem; for it is the city of the great King. Neither shalt thou swear by thy head, because thou canst not make one hair white or black. But let your communication be, Yea, yea; Nay, nay: for whatsoever is more than these cometh of evil.

Berowne is having his fun even with the Bible: instead of saying merely Yea or Nay to Longaville, as Christ directs, he says both Yea *and* Nay, mocking the structure of the biblical sentence; in addition, he swears by the words—which is, precisely, to violate Christ's directive: "Swear not at all." And there is surely some irony in the fact that it is the talkative and rhetorically ornate Berowne who evokes a passage that urges us all to speak simply. But this is not all. At last, the play goes even further than to call for plain speaking. It ends with an explicit call for silence; its last words are:

> The Words of Mercury
> Are harsh after the songs of Apollo:
> You that way; we this way.

> (5.2.922)

The irony here is that this call comes from Armado the Braggart, the man for whom words are food (though he may feed, as Moth says, only on stolen scraps).

In a sense, the silence will last only, as the King says, a "twelve-month and a day" (869), ending—if all goes well—"when the King doth to my Lady come" (821). But in another and truer sense, it will last forever, as Berowne well knows. It is that knowledge that causes his final burst of anger (aimed at the King, perhaps at the audience)—"That's too long for a play" (870)—and why, in our production, he tries to speak again. For he knows that once the play ends, there is no more time, no "latest minute of the hour" (779) even, and no more words. For the "Jack [who] hath not Jill" (867)—and Berowne insists on pointing out that none of these Jacks has his Jill—there is, after this play, only silence, a uniquely defined silence, because, unlike most plays, the silence begins *in* the play, is (in Armado's speech) the last action signaled by the script: "You that way; we this way"—silently. Even the songs of Apollo turn to silence before the play ends, leaving, in our production, Berowne and Marcadé on stage—with no words to speak, the playwright having deserted them. Marcadé, clothed in black and with a white full-face mask, has accepted the end of speech: "my tale is told" (713). But Berowne, in our production, struggles to the bitter end—longs for words, fights for words, hates the silence that form imposes. It is both the silence and the angry struggle that we wanted the audience to feel. And when Berowne exits, there remains only the silent, unmoving, inhuman figure of Marcadé—now a statue of Death—towering above the tiny figure of Cupid: that "Giant dwarf" (3.1.175) who has occupied center stage throughout the play. We meant to make it clear who, in this play, has won and who has lost: the final silence was very long—long enough to discourage applause and encourage thought.

But to write this way, with the advantage of hindsight, about the structure of language and silence in the play is drastically to misrepresent the process of discovery, which was of course slow and disorderly. One desperately needs the structure before one sees it, while still struggling with bits and pieces, but it is only through the tangle of bits and pieces that one begins, slowly, to sense a shape. "I learn by going where I have to go," Theodore Roethke said about living and dying. Rehearsal, too, is like that. At last, we found that it was only with the help of the silence that we could trust, comprehend, and perform the energy (sometimes fierce, sometimes bursting with delight) of each pun, each "taffeta phrase" (to use Berowne's term), each wild syntactical turn. And as we worked, in arduously specific detail with each flamboyantly rhetorical moment, through to the final silence that seemed increasingly to force itself upon us, we were of course also learning about that thin (as the critics see it), that very thin, plot: it will demand a word or two in a moment.

First, however, a confession: the silence as I have described it, and as we performed it, comes from the Folio, not the Quarto. How do self-styled "collaborators" justify that? Does collaboration allow us to hop from one script to another, merely to follow our own playwrighting notions? Whenever the Folio and the Quarto differ, as they do again here, do I believe I can tell which is Shakespeare or (if, perhaps, they both are) which is his most considered choice? *I do not, I certainly do not.* What, then, is collaboration at such a moment? And what, if anything, disciplines our choices? Although a reasonable bibliographical argument can, in fact, be made to support the Folio's assignment of the last speech—with six additional words not in the Quarto—to Armado, the discipline we seek is, as always, rehearsal and performance.[9] Such a discipline is, we know, not a science. We are making artistic decisions, employing the materials and methods of art. We immerse ourselves in the script, its particular ways and idiosyncratic demands, submit ourselves to those demands, commit ourselves to following the scripted signals even (and perhaps especially) when they go against our own desires or beliefs, and learn to empower one another as watchdogs against any drift away from the privileged demands of the script. In the rough give-and-take of rehearsal, we listen to every voice, especially any voice that is at the moment trying to speak for the playwright. Any actor waving overhead a text of the Quarto or the Folio is, for us, and until proved otherwise, the privileged voice of Shakespeare. We stop and listen. Discussion and argument follow—often for hours—with always one fundamental point of agreement: the play we are seeking is the play authorized by Shakespeare's script. This means, of course, that we believe there is such a play, that he was not trying to provide a skeleton on which the rest of us could fashion any body we happen to fancy at the moment. For us, the author is not dead.

Although we reject the nonsense that deprives a work of art of its authorial identity and privilege, we are aware that a script is not a work of art, is not even an exact blueprint for such a work. Yes, yes, yes, the cliché is The Truth: there can be no "definitive" production (or interpretation) of a play by Shakespeare. But that does not mean that the collaborative method of production or the collaborative goal is rendered pointless, or even reduced in value. We collaborate with the Wright-as-Artist partly because we believe Shakespeare's exploration of life is likely to have been deeper and more illuminating than ours; and partly because, even if this is not so, we wish to know the Other as well as the Self, and we commit ourselves to honoring and defending the rights of the Other. We are also comfortable with and delighted by, stimulated and empowered by, the opportunity to create in the context of legitimate authority. By submitting, as far as possible, to the same collaborative discipline that produced *Love's Labor's Lost* on Shakespeare's own stage, we seek not a museum replica of that production but a vital play for our own stage and our own time, a play with all of the energy, form, and currency of great art. Ezra Pound was right: art is news that stays news. Our production of *Love's Labor's Lost* was ours, was new, and was news—otherwise it couldn't have been Shakespeare or art.

Our decision to accept the Folio's version of the last speech and to give it, as the Folio does, to Armado, could not, then, depend upon some personal (or even collective) preference, or upon the bibliographical speculations of the editors. Our task was to find, through rehearsal and performance, if the Folio speech rises harmoniously out of all that precedes it *in the Quarto,* and joins with all that precedes it in the Quarto, to produce a convincing unity and a satisfying theatrical complexity. We found that, in our judgment, it does. Would we, therefore, swear on a stack of Bibles that the speech is Shakespeare's? No, not ever. But, well, we don't keep that many Bibles around, anyway. So we are happy enough. Quite wonderfully happy, in fact.

Let me offer as partial justification of our euphoria one small piece of the script-as-puzzle, a piece that contributes importantly (but not, by itself, conclusively) to our belief that the Folio's last words are compellingly scripted—function, that is, as an integral part of the Quarto script. As Armado (5.2.655)—in the face of savage heckling from Boyet and three of the young men of Navarre (all but the King)—insists that he will continue his "device" (His presentation as Hector), he appeals to the Princess: "sweet royalty bestow on me the sense of hearing." In both original texts at this point, "Berowne steps forth." That is all. He doesn't speak, and is given nothing else to do—except in nearly all modern editions (eight of the eleven), where, in an added stage direction, he "whispers to Costard," prompting that "Worthy" to accuse Armado of getting Jaquenetta pregnant. In the rehearsal room, however, the original script as it stands is perfectly clear: Armado says he will continue and hopes the Princess will listen; Berowne steps forth to continue the hazing; the Princess stops him in favor of Armado— "Speak brave Hector, we are much delighted"; Armado thanks her—"I do adore thy sweet Grace's Slipper"; and Boyet and Dumaine, unstoppable, continue the cruel hazing. There is no mystery about any of that. It is scripted as clearly as one could wish. And then, upon the instant that Marcadé has delivered his message— "my tale is told"—Berowne again *steps forth.* This time no stage direction is needed, and none appears, for he speaks. He, not the King (whom one might expect), takes charge: "Worthies away. . . ." And it is Armado who refuses to go quietly. It is the moment of his great and mysterious declaration of freedom: "For mine own part I breathe free breath."

At the end of the play, after the song, it was certainly no surprise to our audiences when Berowne stepped forth for a third time (even more vigorously), was about to speak, and was silenced by Armado: "The Words of Mercury, / Are harsh after the songs of Apollo." In every sense that we could discover, the action served the play, creatively collaborated with the Quarto script to do so. Most important, perhaps, it provided a clear and theatrical motivation for Armado to speak; his speech became part of the play, in no sense an epilogue. For the audience it was of course again a pleasure to see Berowne silenced, never an easy task, and this time by Armado himself. But the audience could also see that Berowne was continuing his rebellion against the play he is in: to hell with that song, so obviously (to him) a patched-up ending for a play that is refusing to be "an old Play . . . a Comedy." He is going to keep the play going until he gets his "Jill"; or, at least, to register another objection. The one thing that everyone (on stage and off) knows about Berowne is that he does not easily or often shut up. It is wonderful, then, that not even the end of a play will silence him; that even when words run out, he will try to speak. That Armado is the one to stop him seems just right, too, for it completes the action started in his declaration of freedom—"I breathe free breath"—and in his threat of revenge with which the declaration ends: "I have seen the day of wrong through the little hole of discretion, and I will right my self like a Soldier."

Need I return now, as I said I would, for "a word or two" about the plot that is, in the conventional sense, so very, very thin? I hope it is clear already that the play we found pushes something like "plot"—an action that involves Berowne and Armado—to the very end. But I promised. In Shakespeare (as I first learned from my great teacher, Hereward T. Price) there is always story, plot, and design.[10] Most complaints about story or plot come from those who don't care for design unless it can plainly be seen to contribute directly to the other two. But Shakespeare was a guerrilla artist, constantly shooting down establishment notions of dramatic form. *Love's Labor's Lost* is, as Berowne tells us, not like "an old Play." That is, it is not like most plays (then or now), and it differs more radically than even Berowne knows. Is there any other play in which the fourth, fifth and sixth scenes—over five hundred lines early in the play—could be dropped with no harm to what seems to be the plot? Yes, we could have jumped from the third scene

(2.1) to the seventh (4.3), and in our audience no stranger to the play would have sensed the smallest gap in the "plot." Collaboration certainly requires coming to terms with that stunning fact. In the face of it, the collaborative discipline—the refusal, for example, to cut any of those "superfluous" lines—may seem a mindless bardolatry.

But we insist: the script is our authority, though it is not authoritarian. One of the activities it authorizes, sponsors, stimulates, and even insists upon is creativity: acts of the imagination. The severest challenge to our collective imagination was those three scenes, their way of functioning in the dramatic design. In fact, the final, surprising key remained a secret, out of our grasp, until after—yes, painfully after—our final performance; and this is not the place to discuss it. My point here is that, in this kind of work— in these "acts of the imagination"—the learning never stops. The "last" night is not the end, for there is never a final, packaged product. There is only the continuing process, a work of art that, in spite of, or even in opposition to, its highly ordered state, keeps moving: playing the script increasingly reveals the script. On opening night the audience arrives to help in our research, enlarging the community of seekers, providing us with new knowledge and new perspectives, educating us into an awareness of our mistakes. Performance is, for us, only rehearsal after a shifting of gears, with a new degree of intensity, alertness, and discipline. And after the last performance, the process continues—into the sentence I am now writing and beyond, the thinking and writing still informed and disciplined, one believes, by the experience of the rehearsal hall and the theater.

Now who are we? What is the American Shakespeare Company? The story I am telling is not simply about discoveries or performances or a discipline; it is also about what makes such things possible. My actors are undergraduate students at the University of California, Santa Barbara, most of then enrolled in a course that is certainly unusual for an English department. They and former students compose the company. Though the course lasts only ten weeks, from early January to the middle of March, the students must commit themselves from early December to late April. During the ten-week rehearsal period (the Winter term), they are required to be available seven days a week—on weekdays from 4 P.M. to midnight (or later); and on weekends, from 10 A.M. to midnight (or later). The *Love's Labor's Lost* company had one day off in ten weeks. Until the last week of April—several days after our last performance—they were students, actors, *and* textual scholars. Everyone does everything: designing, building, sewing, whatever. No professional football team headed for the Super Bowl ever worked harder.

Talent and experience (though we have some of both) play almost no part in company membership or in casting. Casting is done entirely on the basis of student preferences; each student lists, in order of preference, the four roles he or she would like to play. To enable as many students as possible to be in the company, we rehearse and perform with two complete casts. In the casting I am obliged, as far as possible, to follow the student requests instead of my own prejudices, preconceptions, or judgments. Type casting is out; surprises are in.

We are amateurs, and I do not think we fool ourselves about that. Robert Brustein has somewhere said that to think amateur theater production preferable to that done by people with training is to show contempt or indifference toward the stage. We believe that this is especially true of Shakespeare's plays. We are an amateur company with profound respect for professional standards. And yet we take it as a sign of something important that our two most lively audiences for *Love's Labor's Lost* were also the two most surprised by their own response: an audience of high school students who had not read the play and an audience of scholars from a research conference on class structure in the Renaissance (scholars from such universities as Harvard, Stanford, Princeton, Pennsylvania, Michigan, Chicago, and California).

Delighted as we have been with the positive response to our recent shows—*A Midsummer Night's Dream, The Taming of the Shrew,* and *Love's Labor's Lost*—the impressive laughter and the stimulating intellectual and emotional engagement of all kinds of people no longer mystify us. The success of *Love's Labor's Lost* was, for us, the final clarification. Probably more than any other play by Shakespeare, it is thought to be "relentlessly Elizabethan" and relentlessly filled with incomprehensible jokes.[11] Even the scholars in our audience were prepared for boredom. And yet we know that the play we presented was, in its turn, relentlessly faithful to the script, and that we owe our success (about which I shall be no more immodest than is essential to the point) directly to that incomprehensible Elizabethan script from the 1590s. Isn't that, as the Murphy in me would say, a darlin' thought? But is it such deadly words as "bardolatry" and "academic purism" you would, instead, be thinking? Consider, then, the simple truth: our actors get to explore and perform a Berowne and a Rosaline, an Oberon and a Titania, a Petruchio and a Katherina, in the complexity of fantastic scripts unavailable in modern editions; and our audiences are plunged into the wonderfully funny, moving, delicate, intricate, challenging moral worlds of those original scripts. No professional actor I know of has had the privilege and the pleasure of playing, for example, any but the relatively bland Berowne created by the editors. This does make a difference, giving us an enormous head start.

Our actors are fortunate, too, that we do not mask them or Shakespeare's script behind a directorial or design concept, and we do not put them in competition with elaborate light shows or spectacular mechanical effects. The concept and the spectacle we are looking for are Shakespeare's. We believe, as he did, in the centrality of the actor. It was an actor's theater for which his scripts were scripted, in which his plays were wrought; and in such scripts we mine an extreme physical energy that lifts any receptive actor (amateur or professional) to the rarest levels of mental, vocal, and physical activity.

For our young actors—most of whom are English majors—it is an extraordinary opportunity to live, for over four months, in the world of *Love's Labor's Lost,* a world in which language and the uses of language, intelligence and the uses of intelligence, are prime moral matters. It is a world inhabited by people who are responding—sometimes gracefully, sometimes inanely, sometimes cruelly—to the power, beauty, and infinite challenge of the English language. For the actors, it is wonderful fun to be, through the characters, so clever with language, so filled with a love of words, and to find in themselves the ability to communicate that love and that fun to a modern audience.

The students, too, collaborate with Shakespeare. They learn that to read Shakespeare as literature (which is what most of them have been taught to do) is to intervene in and drastically diminish the only life for which, as far as anyone knows, the words were gathered together. As actors, these undergraduates get to work with every word, pause, or syntactical subtlety, every rhyme and metrical strategy, every pattern of images or sonnet form—everything that came to Shakespeare's mind and imagination, survived the process of selection, and ended up on the page, placed there specifically in and for the theater. No student is ever the same after such a discipline.

Nor am I, of course. At first, twenty years ago, I began directing Shakespeare in my English "literature" classes because I had begun to sense that it was, quite simply, the best way to teach the plays. It soon became clear to me that nothing else could so vividly and lastingly bring Shakespeare into the lives of my students. And although that pedagogical motivation is still strong, there is now much more. I now direct Shakespeare because it is the most direct and comprehensive way to learn about a script and because it possesses a legitimacy unavailable to any literary form of exploration. I know what it is like to interpret, and to try to understand, the plays as literary works, and to do so from a theological or political point of view. I have lived—and thought the wells were deep—in that desert. It took me years to learn the pure joy of a rehearsal room that is also a classroom that is also a laboratory that is also a research workshop that is also a center for the practical use of any or all scholarly knowledge and that is, first and last, a preparing place for live performances. What a thrill it is to join with thirty others and to let no foreign motivation come between us and the script, to allow no foreign goal to control (or even guide) our actions in the rehearsal process—no ideological conviction, no theological preference, no political agenda, no literary theory, no goal or desire or strategy extraneous to the theatrically driven words. Of course, no hard knowledge of any kind can ever be foreign to the rehearsal room; what we reject as foreign is only the manipulation of knowledge, or of the script itself, in order to serve a belief or theory or concept that one brings to rehearsal from some other area of life: religion, politics, literature, whatever. We are not naive about the difficulty of succeeding in such a rejection and we hear the voices of those who say it is an impossible task. But through the tough checking and disciplining power that we give to every member of the company, we strain to achieve a single goal: we want the script to speak, through us, for itself. If that is an "impossible" goal, we don't mind. I suppose it is the only kind of goal that would interest us.

To meet the script under the instruction of three disciplines—theater, teaching, and scholarship—is to create a new discipline for which there is, I believe, no name. To submit to this demanding discipline is to enter a world of new and previously unguessed possibilities. For me it is the ultimate validation of the academic life: where else could I have found the freedom, the opportunity, and the privilege to create works of art based radically and richly on scripts by Shakespeare that have been relieved of the literary masks they normally wear even in the theater, and that have thus been allowed the full power of their theatrical origin? I know of no other way and no other place in which I could have become so intimate a collaborator with the greatest genius ever of the art form I most treasure.

Notes

1. To claim uniqueness for anything may only be a way of exposing one's ignorance: there may be dozens (hundreds?) of others in the academy or the theater engaged in work identical to the kind I have more or less stumbled into. I would be grateful to learn of them and from them. If they have written about their work, I want to read it; if they have not, I urge them to share their discoveries with all of us.

2. Elsewhere I have offered what I hope are constructive criticisms of current editorial practice: "Menas and the Editors: A Folio Script Unscripted," *Shakespeare Quarterly* 36, no. 2 (Summer 1985): 164–87; "Editors vs. A Text: The Scripted Geography of *A Midsummer Night's Dream*," *Studies in Philology* 87, no. 1 (Winter 1990): 83–108; "No Exit for a Dead Body: What to do with a Scripted Corpse?" *Journal of Dramatic Theory and Criticism* 5, no. 2 (Spring 1991): 139–52.

3. I am also able to pursue this kind of textual scholarship as director of ACTER (A Center for Theatre, Education and Research). The ACTER professional company of British actors has engaged in research workshops with our research associates on such plays as *Hamlet, King Lear, The Winter's Tale,* and *Much Ado About Nothing,* and has recently begun to tour productions *(A Midsummer Night's Dream* and *Much Ado About Nothing)* based on our research.

4. The eleven modern texts on which I am relying include both popular and scholarly versions, ranging over time from 1951 to 1992: Pelican, Penguin, Signet, New Cambridge, Arden, Riverside, HarperCollins, The Guild, both Oxford editions (the one-volume and The Complete Works), and The New York Shakespeare Festival edition. For line references I use the Arden. For quotations I use the Quarto text (normally modernizing spelling but not punctuation) from *Shakespeare's Plays in Quarto,* ed. Michael J. B. Allen and Kenneth Muir (University of California Press, 1981), 292ff.

5. This version of the play is offered with no questions raised by HarperCollins, Signet, Pelican, and the New York Festival; with warning brackets by both Oxford editions; with brackets and notes explicitly rejecting it by Arden and New Cambridge. However, as brackets and textual notes mean little to most readers, this version (created by conflation and emendation) receives effective support even from the two editions that thoroughly reject it in favor of another version. A third version appears in Penguin, a fourth in both Riverside and Guild. A fifth is to be found in the BBC television production. The other two (to make up seven) are of course the Quarto and the Folio, of which I will have more to say.

6. "Directing *Love's Labor's Lost,*" the Festival Shakespeare edition, eds. Bernard Beckerman and Joseph Pap (New York: 1968), 41–42. Productions and interpretations vary, of course, and some are darker than Freedman's, but in my experience, most have seen sunshine at the end of the tunnel.

7. It is perhaps necessary to say that we know the Quarto does not dictate such moments. We believe that it does, however, offer strong scripted signals, of a very rich kind, that all later versions blur or hide entirely.

8. Herbert A. Ellis, *Shakespeare's Lusty Punning in "Love's Labor's Lost"* (The Hague: Mouton, 1973).

9. In the Quarto, the song is followed (in a larger type, with no speech heading) by "The wordes of Mercurie, are harsh after the songes of Apollo." The Folio adds, "You that way; we this way," assigns it all to Armado, prints it in normal type as three lines of verse, and provides a stage direction, *"Exeunt Omnes."* Editorial speculation about these differences varies widely.

10. He has illuminated the point in *Construction in Shakespeare,* Contributions in Modern Philology 17 (Ann Arbor: University of Michigan, 1951).

11. The quoted phrase is from Anne Barton's introduction to the play in *The Riverside Shakespeare* (Boston: Houghton Mifflin, 1974), 174.

Falling in Love: The Tragedy of *Romeo and Juliet*

John F. Andrews

What happens in *Romeo and Juliet?*[1] What did a dramatist of the 1590s want the "judicious" members of his contemporary audiences to see and hear, and how did he expect them to feel, as they attended the play[2] a later age would laud as the most lyrical of all love tragedies? Before I hazard a response to what is admittedly an unanswerable question, I should make it clear that what I'm really posing is a query about the "action"[3] of Shakespeare's drama, and more specifically about the effect such an action might have been intended to have on a receptive Elizabethan playgoer.[4]

O. B. Hardison emphasizes in the commentary that accompanies Leon Golden's 1968 translation of Aristotle's *Poetics,*[5] there is much to be said for interpreting the earliest technical term for tragic effect, *catharsis,* as a word that means "clarification," and for conceiving of the experience it describes as one that takes place, not in the characters of a dramatic work, but in the audience that participates vicariously in those characters' thoughts, emotions, and interchanges. Hardison reminds us that Aristotle defines tragedy as that category of imitation *(mimesis)* which produces pleasure through a cogent representation of fearful and pitiable incidents. He and Golden stress the passage in which the great philosopher observes that realistic renderings of even the most displeasing subjects delight the viewer by assisting perception and eliciting insight. And they infer that when the father of dramatic theory speaks of the purgation that results from a tragedy, he is focusing primarily on the learning any coherently constructed work of art fosters: the sorting out, the clearing away of confusion or temporary misapprehension, that occurs as a responsive spectator notices, and appreciates, an aesthetically satisfying pattern of logical connections. When Aristotle refers to the catharsis that derives from a well-devised imitation of fearful and pitiable incidents, then, Hardison and Golden deduce that he is probably thinking of the enlightenment—the sense of mental relief and psychic release—that a member of the audience enjoys when he or she is able to make sense of a sequence of happenings that initially strike an onlooker as disparate and disorderly.

When we bring this concept of catharsis to bear upon the various species of tragedy, we discover that in some instances the intellectual, emotional, and ethical clarification attained by an attentive theatergoer parallels the hard-earned wisdom of a character who has arrived at self-knowledge through a siege of suffering. In tragic actions which feature this kind of recognition (*anagnorisis*) the central figure is divested of any impurities of mind or heart that impede "clearer Reason" (*Tempest* 5.1.68), and he or she acquires a degree of awareness that approximates the comprehension a perceptive member of the audience obtains by tracing and assessing the character's fortunes.[6]

In some instances the clarity a tragic figure realizes is a judgment that amounts to self-condemnation, as happens in *Richard III* and *Macbeth.* In these dramatic sequences the protagonists acknowledge their own guilt and wretchedness in ways an audience can endorse. In other instances the down-cast hero goes beyond an accurate mental evaluation of himself to a remorse that penetrates the conscience, as with the title characters of *Othello* and *King Lear.* Here the protagonists feel sorrow for what they perceive themselves to have done, and in the second case if not the first the audience may be led to conclude that the hero has gone a step further—from remorse to repentance, to a resolve to do whatever is required to make amends for the pain he has inflicted on others and cleanse his own soul.

In rare instances a tragic protagonist proceeds all the way to a complete reconciliation with himself, with those he has injured, and with the Heavens. In these sequences the protagonist arrives at a sense of "at-one-ment" that signifies redemption. In dramatic actions in which this kind of conversion occurs the central figure wins deliverance through an epiphany that transports him or her past the point where even the most sage of witnesses can hope to follow. In Sophocles' *Oedipus at Colonus,* for example, or in Milton's *Samson Agonistes,* the central character is granted a culminating vision in which death is swallowed up in a kind of victory. The hero completes his mission nobly, and as he expires he crosses the threshold to a mysterious but presumably more exalted realm on the unseen side of this world's veil of tears. Here the clarification that takes place in the protagonist surpasses the apprehension of the viewer, and the catharsis that issues in the well-tuned playgoer is akin to ecstatic rapture: a "calm of mind"[7] that accompanies the "wonder"[8] evoked by powers that move us to awe.

In most tragic actions the audience's catharsis is something that can be more aptly described as a sense of "woe" or "pity"[9] for a character whose grasp on reality is shown to be in some way defective. As we watch a misguided protagonist come to grief under the lamentable circumstances that tragedies usually depict, we feel a wrenching disparity between our own observations and those of the focal figure. If we receive the kind of catharsis the usual tragedy is designed to provide, in other words, we emerge with an understanding that is both broader and more lucid than the impaired perception of the lost hero or heroine.

So what do we find when we turn to *Romeo and Juliet?* Do we sense that the protagonists share our view of what undoes them? Do we feel that in the end they transcend our vantage to claim a better world elsewhere? Or do we finally conclude that they fail in some manner, and lack the insight to assess their failure with the acuity an alert audience acquires by contemplating their "misadventur'd piteous Overthrows" (Prologue.7)?

Adherents can be found for all of these interpretations and more. Many accept the title characters at their own estimate, perceiving them as helpless pawns of conditions they have no means of countering. Some react to them with admiration, even reverence, canonizing them as pure "Sacrifices" of their families' "Enmity" (5.3.304). And a few blame them for intemperance and hold them responsible not only for their own tragedies but for the untimely deaths of several other characters.

Perhaps the best way to enter the world of the play is to take note of its cosmic imagery, its all-pervasive references to Fortune, Fate, and the Stars. If we hope to recapture something of the experience *Romeo and Juliet* provided its original audience, we need to come away from the tragedy with a conception of what it would have meant in Shakespeare's time to be a victim of "fatal Loins," to feel like "Fortune's Fool," and to seize upon the extremest of measures to "shake the Yoke of inauspicious Stars" (Prologue.5, 3.1.144, 5.3.111).

The most important locus for medieval and Renaissance thinking about Fortune and Fate was Boethius's *Consolation of Philosophy,* a Latin dialogue that had probably been written in A.D. 524. Chaucer had used the *Consolation* extensively in the fourteenth century, and it remained so popular in the late sixteenth century that it was translated into Elizabethan English by no less a personage than the Queen herself. When Shakespeare alluded to the *Consolation,*

then, he would no doubt have assumed that any literate member
of his audience would be nearly as familiar with this masterwork
as with the Bible and the Book of Common Prayer.

Any playgoer who had read Boethius would have known that
the *Consolation*[10] involves a conversation between Lady Philosophy and a statesman who has fallen into disfavor and now awaits
death. The imprisoned political leader is the author himself, and
he calls upon a personification of Wisdom to explain why Fortune
has treated him so cruelly. During the exchanges that ensue, Lady
Philosophy points out that "Fortune" is properly to be regarded
as a fictional abstraction, a symbolic embodiment of the role of
mutability in human affairs. To those who view her aright, Dame
Fortune is nothing more than a convenient name for the fickle and
seemingly irrational "Goddess" who bestows and withdraws such
worldly gifts as riches, honors, political office, fame, and pleasure.
Lady Philosophy acknowledges that many people mistakenly believe that happiness is to be found in the possession of goods that
are subject to Fortune's caprices. But she insists that those who
examine their lives carefully will eventually realize that the only
felicity which lasts and is free from anxiety is that which is fixed
on a supreme good higher than, and unaffected by, the vicissitudes
of Fortune. Lady Philosophy doesn't deny that Misfortune is painful, but she insists that if we take it in the right spirit it provides
a salutary reminder that everything in this life is fleeting. In the
process it encourages us to focus our sights on Heaven, where,
according to an even more authoritative, spiritual guide, "neither
moth nor rust doth corrupt, and where thieves do not break
through nor steal" (Matthew 6:20).[11]

Many writers used the terms "Fortune" and "Fate" interchange-
ably, but Boethius drew a subtle distinction between them. For him
Fortune was a name for mutability itself, for what we now refer to
as blind chance. Fate, on the other hand, was his term for a higher
authority that presided over Fortune's seeming arbitrariness. For
Boethius, and for subsequent Christian philosophers, Fate (or Destiny, as it was often called) was actually a pagan disguise for Providence, and the author of the *Consolation* saw it as a cosmic
principle that was ultimately benign, though forever shrouded in
obscurity.

Boethius was valued in Renaissance England for the way he had
adapted Christianity to a quasi-Stoic frame of reference. In similar
fashion, Saint Augustine was revered for the way he'd made Christianity fit a quasi-Platonic framework two centuries earlier. Augustine's treatise *On Christian Doctrine*[12] and his monumental

discourse on the *City of Gold* were both familiar to educated Elizabethans, and Shakespeare's contemporaries would have seen the
author of these two works as a theologian whose writings were
fully compatible with Boethius's philosophy. Boethius's dichotomy
between those pursuits directed the Supreme Good (which is immutable) and those directed to all lesser goods (which are mutable)
would have been accepted, then, as merely another means of expressing Augustine's distinction between those pursuits that lead
to the supreme felicity of the City of God (Jerusalem) and those
that leave one mired in the confusion and frustration of the City
of Man (Babylon).

According to Augustine, all movement of the soul is prompted
by the will, and that which moves the will is love. Love, then, is
the basic motivating force in human behavior, and it falls into two
categories: (a) Sacred Love, or *caritas* (charity), which urges the
will in the direction of eternal life, and (b) Profane Love, or *cupiditas* (cupidity), which pulls the will in the direction of temporal life.
From Augustine's viewpoint, the sole purpose of religion and ethics
is to teach believers what things are to be loved and enjoyed in and
of themselves and what things are to be employed in the service of
true (sacred) love. In his system the proper relation to things (loving and enjoying only the things of God, and using the things of
this world solely in obedience to God) is *caritas;* the improper
relation of things (loving and enjoying the things of this world,
and abusing the things of God for the sake of temporal things)
is *cupiditas.*

The cohesion between Augustine's theology and Boethius's philosophy becomes evident as soon we note that only those things
which are temporal are subject to Fortune. To be under the sway
of Fortune, then—to seek happiness by setting one's heart on those
goods that are subject to Fortune's bestowal and removal—is to
be guilty of *cupiditas* (misplaced or inordinate love). On the other
hand, to rise above Fortune's sphere by aspiring to the immutable
Supreme Good—to seek happiness through union with that which
lies beyond the realm of Fortune—is to live in accordance with
caritas (well-placed and duly ordered love).

But what about the stars? How did they relate to Boethian and
Augustinian thought? According to most medieval and Renaissance
thinkers, "the Stars" (the Sun, the Moon, the Planets, and the
constellations of the Zodiac) exercised a degree of influence on
Earth, and this influence conditioned the general and particular
destinies of human beings. But it was commonly believed that the
Stars could directly affect only the material and corporeal levels

of existence. Since will and reason were regarded as spiritual rather than physical (material or corporeal) in nature, it followed that these faculties of the human soul could not be influenced directly by the Stars. Will and reason could be affected by the lower parts of the soul (the senses and the passions), however, if they did not maintain proper control over these earth-bound dominions; and the lower nature (since it was corporeal in composition) could, in turn, be influenced by the stars. If the will or the reason allowed themselves to be usurped by the senses or the passions, then, they became subject to indirect astrological influence and thus to Fortune.[13]

Let me sum up. As I have observed, Fortune, Fate, and the Stars were perceived in Shakespeare's time as interwoven concepts, and all three were integral to a system of ethics that drew heavily on the writings of Boethius and Augustine. Through these concepts, errant behavior could be depicted by any of several interchangeable means of expression: as unfortunate behavior caused by the influence of the Stars; as irrational behavior caused by the whims of Fortune; as improper and intemperate behavior caused by reason or will's subjection to the senses or the passions; or as disobedient, sinful behavior caused by misplaced or inordinate love. For an alert Elizabethan, the name one applied to wrongheaded behavior was of little moment; the only thing that mattered was that sooner or later a person recognize it as a course that would result in disaster if it continued unchecked.

We should now be in a position to return to the questions posed at the outset. What "happens" in *Romeo and Juliet?* Do the lovers succumb to forces beyond their control? Do they somehow triumph over the circumstances arrayed against them and emerge as martyrs, as unblemished agents of redemption? Or do they "fall in love" in some ethical and theological sense that would have been meaningful to an audience familiar with Augustine and Boethius?

Suppose we begin our scrutiny of the action by reviewing some of the perspectives the play offers on the protagonists' romantic attachment. The Chorus who speaks the Prologue to Act 2 describes Romeo's sudden infatuation with Juliet as "Young Affection" gaping to be the "Heir" of "Old Desire" (lines 1–2); he goes on to suggest that the only reason Juliet has replaced Rosaline in Romeo's heart is that this time Romeo's feelings are requited (line 5). From the Chorus's point of view, then, what draws Romeo to Juliet is no different in kind from what attracted him to Rosaline. The young hero is simply shifting his attention to a more receptive subject as he responds to the erotic spurring implicit in his name.[14]

Friar Lawrence's initial response to Romeo's news about "the fair- Daughter of rich Capulet" (2.2.58) echoes the Chorus's sentiments:

> Is Rosaline, that thou didst love so dear,
> So soon forsaken? Young Men's Love then lies
> Not truly in their Hearts but in their Eyes.
>
> (2.2.66–68)

In a way that recalls Mercutio, who refers to his friend as "Humours, Madman, Passion, Lover" (2.1.7), and Benvolio, who comments that "Blind is his Love, and best befits the Dark" (2.1.32), Friar Lawrence appears to feel that, notwithstanding its intensity, Romeo's zeal for Juliet is as likely to be a manifestation of "Rude Will" as of "Grace" (2.2.28). Hence the old man's admonition to "love moderately" (2.5.14).

Despite his solemn advice, however, the Friar does nothing to impede the "wanton Blood" (2.4.71) that he and Juliet's Nurse both see in their eager charges. Before he even speaks with Romeo's betrothed, Friar Lawrence agrees to channel the youths' ardor into a clandestine marriage. With the Church's sanction, then, they consummate their vows within twenty-four hours of their initial encounter. So much for moving "Wisely and slow" (2.2.94).[15]

There can be no question that what draws Romeo and Juliet to each other at the outset is physical attraction. But would it be just to assert that their union is based on nothing more elevated than erotic desires? I think not. The poetry with which they declare their feelings makes it well nigh impossible for us to conceive of any situation in which the protagonists could ever again be severed, let alone drift apart. After all, to preserve herself for the husband to whom she has plighted troth, Juliet defies and deceives her parents, evades a match that would advance both her own fortunes and her family's, dismisses the Nurse when the old retainer's pragmatism becomes the voice of "Auncient Damnation" (3.5.235), and drinks a potion she fears may be lethal. Meanwhile, for his part Romeo proves more than willing to "give and hazard all" (*Merchant of Venice* 2.7.16) to uphold his pledge to Juliet. As we see the lovers increasingly isolated by events and, more important, by the folly of their elders and the insensitivity of even their closest confidants, we cannot help responding with sympathy for their predicament and admiration for the courage their consecration to each other inspires. By the end of the play it is patent that no one in their society really understands them; they're left completely alone in a world that seems at best indifferent, at worst hostile. In soul-trying times their loyalty to each other is severely tested, and it never falters.

But if the tie that binds Romeo and Juliet is the most precious treasure the setting of Shakespeare's tragedy affords, does it follow that we are meant to regard the lovers' "extreme Sweet" (2.Chorus.14) as a delicacy that supersedes all other treasures? Are we to join our hearts and minds with the protagonists' fathers and erect statues of "pure Gold" (5.3.301) to honor the title characters' fidelity to each other and to love?

Perhaps so, but I find it difficult to locate a lot to celebrate in the events with which the play concludes. Old Capulet and Old Mountague clasp hands at long last, and if only by default a feud that has wrought untold devastation appears to be history. But at what cost? According to the city's sovereign, the only thing that remains when all is said and done is "A glooming Peace"—that and the Prince's haunting pronouncement that "All are punish'd" (5.3.307, 297).

So what are we to make of the mood with which the final scene draws to a close? Is it possible that Shakespeare expected his audience to include the lovers themselves in the Prince's stern accounting of Verona's "Woe" (5.3.311)? Can it be that a relationship so rare it has become proverbial, a bond that appears indissoluble, was meant to be viewed as in some way wrong? The answer, I submit, is yes. I think it more than likely that the playwright intended to have his earliest theatergoers see Romeo and Juliet as protagonists whose tragic flaw derives from the same source as their strength and beauty: the very fact that their devotion to each other is so all-consuming that it eliminates everything else from consideration.[16]

At their first greeting Romeo bows before Juliet as if she were a "holy Shrine" and he a "Pilgrim"; Juliet accepts this description of their venue and grants Romeo's "Pray'r" "lest Faith turn to Despair" (1.4.209, 212, 217, 219). In the Balcony Scene, the next time the protagonists meet, Romeo describes Juliet successively as "the Sun," "bright Angel," and "dear Saint," and he tells her "Call me but Love, and I'll be new baptiz'd" (2.1.45, 68, 97, 92). Juliet responds in kind and declares Romeo's "gracious Self" to be "the God of my Idolatry" (2.1.155, 156). What this imagery implies is that Romeo and Juliet are forswearing an old creed in favor of a new; their professions, accordingly, are to be understood as the religious vows of converts to a faith that differs from that of their fathers.

In act 3, having just learned of his banishment, Romeo says "'Tis Torture and not Mercy! Heav'n is here / Where Juliet lives" (3.3.29–30). To be exiled from Juliet's presence is, for Romeo, to be condemned to outer darkness. A few hours later, as the lovers are saying farewell on the morning that ends their one night together, their aubade suggests that their lives are now fundamentally "out of Tune" (3.5.27) with the lark, the daylight, and other manifestations of a harmonious natural order. It is thus apropos that after Romeo's departure Juliet asks, "Is there no Pity sitting in the Clouds / That sees into the Bottom of my Grief?" (3.5.198–99). Shortly thereafter she cries "Alack, alack, that Heaven should practice Stratagems / Upon so soft a Subject as my self" (3.5.211–12).

These and numerous other passages demonstrate that the relationship between Romeo and Juliet is a species, however refined, of *cupiditas*—a form of pseudo-worship in which one's deity is a creature rather than the Creator. Each lover views the other as the Supreme Good. Each accords the other a degree of adoration that Augustine (and innumerable later theologians) had defined as properly directed only to God. Their love becomes a universe unto itself, and when they are deprived of it each of the protagonists concludes that there is nothing left to live for.

But of course if Romeo and Juliet fall victim to idolatry, it is because they also succumb to passion. By indulging the senses and emotions, they allow first the concupiscible (pleasure-driven) and later the irascible (wrath-driven) divisions of the lower, sensible soul to gain hegemony over the rational soul (the reason).

At the beginning Romeo is subject to the melancholy of a frustrated suitor. He keeps to himself, and when he is sighted by even his closest friend he slips into a "Grove of Sycamour" (1.1.124). Romeo is himself a "sick-amour," a youth afflicted with love-sickness, and his father observes that

> Black and portendous must this Humour prove
> Unless good Counsel may the Cause remove.
>
> (1.1.144–45)

Romeo's reason emits warnings, both in the dream to which he several times refers in 1.4 and in the misgivings he expresses at the end of that scene (1.4.106–11), but the protagonist allows Mercutio's set-piece about Queen Mab to convince him, against his better judgment, to put his fear of "Consequence" out of mind. As the title character consents to attend the Capulet ball, his pivotal

comment makes it obvious that what his intellect tells him is being
suppressed by an act of will: "he that hath the Stirrage of my
Course / Direct my Suit" (1.4.112–13).[17]

From this point on the hero plunges headlong into action. At his
first glimpse of Juliet his senses are so entranced that he is oblivious to the threat posed by Tybalt. Later, in the Balcony Scene, it
is Juliet, not Romeo, who expresses apprehensions; he declares
"thy Kinsmen are no Stop to me" (2.1.111) and defines himself as
a bold mariner (2.1.124–26). Disregarding her instinctive caution,
Juliet allows herself to be seduced by such bravado and agrees,
against *her* better judgment, to become the partner of her suitor's
rash ventures.

Up to this juncture the concupiscible passions have dominated
the behavior of both lovers. Following Romeo and Juliet's hasty
marriage, however, the irascible passions begin asserting themselves. Almost as soon as he departs from his wedding Romeo
comes upon an incipient quarrel between Mercutio and Tybalt.
The fresh bridegroom is not yet ready to reveal his new kinship
with the Capulets, and as a result his conciliatory reply to a challenge Tybalt thrusts at him is misinterpreted by Mercutio as an
expression of "calm, dishonorable, vile Submission" (3.1.76). Romeo's hotheaded friend steps in to defend the honor he assumes
a lethargic and cowardly Mountague is incapable of maintaining
for himself. In an urgent attempt to prevent needless conflict, Romeo lunges between the two duelers. Unfortunately the protagonist's efforts at peacemaking prove fatal to Mercutio, and Romeo's
ally dies cursing the house of Mountague as vehemently as he had
earlier scorned the Capulets.

To this moment in the scene Romeo has "thought all for the
best" (3.1.111) For the first time in the play, he has acted with
judgment, restraint, and genuine valor. But now he finds himself in
an unaccustomed position. By turning the other cheek and trying
to comport himself as an honorable gentleman, he has unwittingly
made himself appear dishonorable and contributed to a calamity.
After a too-brief pause for reflection, he reacts to the "Plague" in
his ears by accepting Mercutio's erroneous judgment on measured
behavior that the audience will have recognized as anything *but*
"Effeminate" (3.1.113, 121). Casting aside his momentary self-
control and rationality, and yielding to an idolatrous concern for
the kind of male "Reputation" that demands vengeance,[18] Romeo
spurns "respective Lenity" to make room for "Fire-ey'd Fury"
(3.1.118, 130–31). He disregards the Prince's prohibition against

further bloodshed and takes the enactment of "Justice" into his own hands (3.1.187–88).[19]

The slaying of Tybalt functions as the turning point in the action. Before this development there has been at least a possibility of success for Romeo and Juliet. Capulet and Mountague have both shown a willingness to end the feud, and there has thus been some basis for the Friar's optimism that the marriage of a Capulet to a Mountague might bridge the way to a more harmonious future. With the deaths of Mercutio and Tybalt, however, the hostility between the two factions is rekindled, and the Prince can see only one way to prevent further carnage: by removing Romeo from "fair Verona" before more "Civil Blood" makes more "Civil Hands unclean" (Prologue.2–4).

By the time Romeo arrives at the Friar's cell in 3.3 he is practically beside himself. Upon learning that he has been banished, he falls to the ground, his abject posture symbolizing the topsy-turvy state of a soul no longer led by reason. In this condition he draws a dagger, and only the Friar's intervention forestalls an instant suicide:

> Hold thy desperate Hand.
> Art thou a Man? Thy Form cries out thou art.
> Thy Tears are Womanish; thy wild Acts
> Denote the unreasonable Fury of a Beast.
>
> . . . .
> Hast thou slain Tybalt? Wilt thou slay thy Self?
> And slay thy Lady that in thy Life lies
> By doing damned Hate upon thy Self?
>
> (3.3.107–17)

The answer to the Friar's last two questions will turn out to be affirmative. And the questions and answers that precede them explain why.

In 4.1 Juliet comes to the Friar's cell, like Romeo with a knife, and like Romeo determined to take her own life. Seeing in her "the strength of Will to slay [her] self" (line 72), the Friar suggests a less desperate remedy for her difficulties. He then gives her a potion that will suspend her bodily functions for enough time to allow her to be mourned and buried. Meanwhile he sends a message to Juliet's husband. Due to unforeseen difficulties Romeo fails to receive it, and a day later he has no way of knowing that there is literal truth in his servingman's euphemistic report that the heroine is "well" and "sleeps in Capel's Monument" (5.1.17–18).

Now the protagonist descends into an even deeper depression.

Purchasing poison from an apothecary whose appearance resembles that of Despair in Spenser's *Faerie Queene*,[20] he makes his way to Juliet's tomb. Upon his arrival, as he dismisses his man Balthasar, Romeo depicts himself in language that summons up memories of the Friar's rebuke in 3.3.107–17:

> The Time and my Intents are savage wild,
> More fierce and more inexorable far
> Than empty Tigers or the roaring Sea.
>
> (5.3.37–39)

The pertinence of these words is almost immediately borne out when the desperate title character is provoked by an uncomprehending Paris and kills him. Moments later Romeo's portrayal of his "Intents" is illustrated yet again when he downs the liquid he has brought with him to the cemetery:

> Come, bitter Conduct, come unsavory Guide,
> Thou desperate Pilot, now at once run on
> The dashing Rocks thy seasick, weary Bark.
>
> (5.3.118–20)

Within seconds Juliet awakens to find her dead husband, and his example inspires her to plunge his dagger into her own breast. Thus does Romeo "slay" his "Lady" by "doing damned Hate" upon himself (3.3.116–17). And thus does Shakespeare emblematize the fatal consummation of a union forged in unregimented idealism.

We should now be in a position to return to the roles of Fortune, Fate, and the Stars in *Romeo and Juliet*. As we have observed, the protagonists are prompted by their concupiscible passions into an idolatrous relationship that makes them vulnerable to forces beyond their ken. As chance would have it, these forces combine to unleash the irascible passions that destroy Mercutio, Tybalt, Paris, and eventually Romeo and Juliet themselves. To put it another way, by forfeiting rational governance over their own behavior, the lovers subject themselves to the waywardness of happenstance. They become Fortune's fools (3.1.143). In a sense that they don't recognize, they become "fated."

In the process, by reducing themselves to menial servants of emotional and astral influences that would have had no power to manipulate them if they had kept their souls under the guidance of reason, they become "Star-cross'd" (Prologue.6). Ironically and sadly, at no point in the action are the "Stars" more securely in command than at the moment when a tragically misled Romeo commits a mortal sin in a futile effort to "shake" their "Yoke" from his "World-wearied Flesh" (5.3.113–14).

It should not escape our notice, of course, that most of the play's other characters are also culpable victims of Fortune, Fate, and the Stars. The Capulets have sought to rise in worldly status, using their daughter as an unwilling instrument to that end, and that is one of the reasons we cannot bring ourselves to blame Juliet for disobeying her unfeeling parents. It seems altogether apt that the Capulets' "ordained Festival" turns to "black Funeral"; they learn by bitter trial that on the Wheel of Fortune "all things change them to the contrary" (4.3.170–71, 176). Meanwhile Mercutio, Tybalt, and Paris all submit in their own ways to Fortune's turns and suffer the consequences.

Even the sententious Friar can be seen as Fortune's plaything. For a man of the cloth he seems inordinately preoccupied with his worldly standing (hence his well-intended but ill-advised efforts to use unauthorized means to end the city's feuding, and hence his frantic scurrying about to cover his traces and avoid being caught at the graveyard in Act 5), and all of his error-prone judgments and makeshift expedients presuppose an improvident reliance on Fortune's notoriously unreliable cooperation.

In many respects the play's society as a whole is shown to be at the mercy of Fortune, Fate, and the Stars. The setting for Shakespeare's tragedy is, after all, a microcosm of postlapsarian humanity. And in this context the fates of Romeo and Juliet turn out to be a "Scourge" (5.3.294), a divine judgment, in senses that exceed the meaning intended by the Prince.

But how should all of this affect an audience experiencing the drama? Ultimately, like most of Shakespeare's tragedies, *Romeo and Juliet* appears designed to leave us with an enhanced appreciation of what it means, in Christian terms, to be human. If we've profited as we ought to from the action, we will know the protagonists better than they know themselves. And we will understand—alas, in a way that they do not—what brought their story to its grievous denouement.

And how will we appraise the "Death-mark'd Love" (Prologue.9) of these beautiful and pitiable youths? If we have attended to what we have seen and heard, our sentiments will echo the humility and compassion implicit in a sixteenth-century cleric's prayer of thanksgiving. As he witnessed a small company of wrongdoers being carted off to their dooms, he said "But for the grace of God, there goes John Bradford."[21]

Notes

1. I realize, of course, that "What happens in *Romeo and Juliet*" varies each time the tragedy is performed; this was no less true of productions in the playwright's own lifetime than of those that have occurred in "After-hours" (2.5.2). For a provocative discussion of the impossibility—if not indeed the undesirability—of "definitive" realizations of a dramatic script, see Jonathan Miller's *Subsequent Performances* (New York: Viking, 1986). For a thoughtful application of Miller's principles to recent interpretations of Shakespeare's most famous love-drama, see Barbara Hodgdon's "Absent Bodies, Present Voices: Performance Work and the Close of *Romeo and Juliet*'s Golden Story," in *Theatre Journal* 41 (1989): 341–59. Hodgson's article can also be found in my collection *"Romeo and Juliet": Critical Essays* (New York: Garland, 1993), as can an earlier version of the present essay.

2. I am acutely conscious of oversimplification when I refer to "the play" as if there were a single rendering of *Romeo and Juliet* (or of any of Shakespeare's works) that can answer to such a term. What a given person sees or hears on a particular occasion depends not only on the sensibility he or she brings to the encounter but also on what text of the drama is presented and how that text is treated by those who present it.

In 1597 and 1599, respectively, two versions of *Romeo and Juliet* appeared in quarto printings. The later version is less crude and appears to be more directly related to an authorial manuscript than the earlier; it advertises itself as "Newly corrected, augmented, and amended," and (appropriately, in my view) it constitutes the control text for modern editions of the title. Because the Second Quarto is itself flawed in places, however, it too is usually "corrected, augmented, and amended" by modern editors, frequently with material spliced in from the comparatively corrupt First Quarto and less frequently with material drawn from the derivative later quartos—Q3 (1609), Q4 (undated but evidently issued around 1622), and Q5 (1637)—and from the 1623 First Folio (whose *Romeo and Juliet* appears to have been set from the Third Quarto). An inevitable consequence of the plethora of options afforded the post-Elizabethan editor, director, and commentator is that no two *Romeo and Juliet*s are exactly the same.

In this essay all quotations from the plays and poems are referenced to the text in *The Everyman Shakespeare* (London: J. M. Dent, 1993), an annotated edition I have recently completed for the Orion Group. Other Shakespearean quotations derive either from the Everyman set or from its predecessor, *The Guild Shakespeare* (New York: Guild America Books, 1989–92), an edition produced for the Doubleday Book & Music Clubs. The Everyman text retains a number of features from the early printing that are altered in most of today's editions, and one consequence is that some of the line references in *Romeo and Juliet* will seem unfamiliar. Everyman treats as a single scene, 1.4, what modern editions usually render as two, 1.4 and 1.5; in similar fashion Everyman's 2.1 combines the usual 2.1 and 2.2, and Everyman's 4.3 combines the usual 4.3, 4.4, and 4.5.

3. For Shakespeare's own use of the words "judicious" and "action," see *Hamlet* 3.2.1–52.

4. I would underscore the word "might" in this sentence. We have very little

information about how Elizabethan playgoers responded to Shakespeare's tragedies, and much of what we do have is subject to debate.

5. See *Aristotle's Poetics: A Translation and Commentary for Students of
Literature* (Englewood Cliffs, N.J.: Prentice Hall, 1968), particularly 115–20. My
thinking on catharsis in Shakespeare has also been richly informed by Hardison's
"Three Types of Renaissance Catharsis" in *Renaissance Drama*, n.s., 2 (1969):
3–22, and by the writings of the late Virgil K. Whitaker, especially in *The Mirror
Up to Nature* (San Marino, Calif.: Huntington Library, 1965), and Roy Bat-
tenhouse, above all in *Shakespearean Tragedy: Its Art and Its Christian Premises*
(Bloomington: Indiana University Press, 1969).

6. The situation I describe here is the norm for Shakespearean comedy and
romance, where catharsis ("dis-illusionment") must occur in the central characters to bring about the resolution that constitutes a happy ending. I've written in
more detail about the relationships between tragedy and comedy in "Ethical and
Theological Questions in Shakespeare," in *William Shakespeare: His World, His
Work, His Influence*, ed. John F. Andrews (New York: Scribners, 1985), vol. 2.
For further comment on the relationship between "disillusionment" and catharsis
in Shakespearean tragedy, see the Editor's Introduction to *Antony and Cleopatra*
in *The Everyman Shakespeare* (London: J. M. Dent, 1993).

7. *Samson Agonistes*, line 1758.

8. *Hamlet* 5.2.375. Among Shakespeare's tragedies, the only one that strikes
me as approaching this kind of denouement is *King Lear*, where (depending on
how the final moments of the play are staged) a long-suffering protagonist can be
construed either as dying in despair or as departing from "this tough World" with
a glimmer of faith and hope that promises to "redeem all Sorrows" (5.3.311, 264).
Some see *Hamlet* and *Antony and Cleopatra* as tragedies that also carry us to
the verge of "divine comedy." I can find some basis for this reading of the Prince
of Denmark's final moments, but up to the point where Hamlet and Laertes
exchange forgiveness I see little reason to take at face value the allusions to
Providence that are usually interpreted as indicating a "sweet Prince" with his
heart in the right place. In *Antony and Cleopatra* I discern no textual warrant
for the view that an audience is to be persuaded by the protagonists' grandiloquent
assessments of themselves or by the "New Heaven, New Earth" they claim to
win by disavowing the "dungy" clay kingdoms they cede at last to Caesar (1.1.17,
35). I discuss Milton's appropriation of tragic form in "'Dearly Bought Revenge':
"*Samson Agonistes, Hamlet*, and Elizabethan Revenge Tragedy," *Milton Studies*
11 (1979): 81–108. For a fascinating new analysis of the different types of Christian
tragedy, I recommend Sherman H. Hawkins's "Religious Patterning in Shakespeare's Major Tragedies," *Transactions of the Connecticut Academy of Arts and
Sciences* 50 (June 1991): 151–88.

9. See *Hamlet* 5.2.375, and *King Lear* 5.3.231–32.

10. The edition of *The Consolation of Philosophy* that I have used is the translation and commentary by Richard Green (Indianapolis: Bobbs Merrill, 1962).

11. Friar Lawrence invokes "Philosophy" in 3.3.55–56 of *Romeo and Juliet*
when he explains to a desperate Romeo that he should welcome "Adversity's
sweet Milk." Both here and later in the play (see 4.3.151–69), the Friar calls
attention to Lady Philosophy's teaching that "bad" fortune is actually better for
us than what we incorrectly think of as good fortune. In *As You Like It*, 2.1.1–17,
Duke Senior sounds a Boethian note when he observes that "Sweet are the Uses
of Adversity." And in *King Lear*, 4.1.19–21, Gloster speaks similarly when he

says that "Full oft 'tis seen / Our Means secure us, and our mere Defects / Prove our Commodities."

12. I am indebted to the translation and commentary by D. W. Robertson, Jr. (New York: Liberal Arts Press, 1958). Robertson also discusses *On Christian Doctrine* extensively in *A Preface to Chaucer* (Princeton: Princeton University Press, 1962).

13. For a detailed exposition of the relationship between astrology and medieval and Renaissance psychology, see Walter Clyde Curry's "Destiny in *Troilus and Criseyde*" in *Chaucer and the Medieval Sciences* (New York: Oxford University Press, 1926). Also see John W. Draper, "Shakespeare's Star-Crossed Lovers," *Review of English Studies* 15 (1939): 16–34; Douglas L. Peterson, "Romeo and Juliet and the Art of Moral Navigation," in *Pacific Coast Studies in Shakespeare,* ed. Waldo F. McNeir and Thelma N. Greenfield (Eugene: University of Oregon Books, 1966), 33–46, and James L. Calderwood, "*Romeo and Juliet:* A Formal Dwelling," in *Shakespearean Metadrama* (Minneapolis: University of Minnesota Press, 1971).

14. Romeo's surname in all the original texts is spelled "Mountague." Given Shakespeare's wordplay on "ague" (fever) in "Sir Andrew Ague-cheek" (as the name of the foolish suitor is rendered in the First Folio text of *Twelfth Night*), it seems reasonable to assume that the playwright was fully aware of the symbolic potential in "Mount-ague," a word that related not only to the erotic drives of both lovers but also to the aspirations of the Capulets and to the celestial imagery of much of the play's language. See *Love's Labor's Lost* 4.1.1–4, for related play on "Mounting," and compare the aptness of such additional Shakespearean names as *Launcelet* ("small lance") in *The Merchant of Venice* and *Fortinbrasse* (a rendering of the French *Fortinbras*—"strong in arms"—that picks up on "Brazen" and "Mettle" when the name is introduced in 1.1.65–102) in the Second Quarto of *Hamlet*. In 5.3.159 of *All's Well That Ends Well*, we learn that Diana, the maiden Bertram believes himself to have mounted, derives from "the ancient Capilet," an Italian family whose surname can be translated "small horse." In *Twelfth Night,* III.4.310–11, Sir Andrew Ague-cheek surrenders his horse, "Grey Capilet," to avoid a duel with the fierce "Cesario." What's in a name, then? Quite a lot, particularly if we disregard modern editors' "corrections" of Shakespeare's spelling and retain the designations the playwright himself provided. See *The Guild Shakespeare,* 16:468, for a note on "Doctor Buts" and other symbolic nomenclature in *Henry VIII.*

15. See James C. Bryant, "The Problematic Friar in *Romeo and Juliet,*" *English Studies* 55 (1974): 340–50, for background that might have been pertinent to an Elizabethan audience's perception of the Friar and his role in the events that lead to tragedy.

16. A. C. Bradley is seldom recalled nowadays, but one of the wisest and most memorable observations ever uttered about Shakespearean tragedy is his remark that "In the circumstances where we see the hero placed, his tragic trait, which is also his greatness, is fatal to him." In my view, Romeo and Juliet illustrate both this and another of Bradley's generalizations about Shakespeare's tragic protagonists: "In almost all we observe a marked one-sidedness, a predisposition in some particular direction; a total incapacity, in certain circumstances, of resisting the force which draws in this direction; a fatal tendency to identify the whole being with one interest, object, passion, or habit of mind." See *Shakespearean Tragedy* (London: Macmillon & Co., 1904), 26–27.

17. Here I retain the Second Quarto spelling "Stirrage," which plays on "stir"

(compare 1.1.9, where Gregory observes that "To move is to stir") and reminds us that Romeo's "Steerage" will prove that "Love" can be considerably more "rough" (1.4.27) than the jesting Mercutio suspects. Romeo's nautical imagery anticipates what he will say to Juliet in 2.1.124–26 ("I am no Pylat, yet wert thou as far / As that vast Shore wash'd with the farthest Sea, / I should adventure for such Marchandise") and what he will say just before he expires in 5.3.118–22. The *Pylat* spelling in 2.1.124 may be an authorial allusion to Pontius Pilate; if so, it casts an ironic light on the sacrificial imagery in Capulet's benediction at 5.3.305–6.

18. We sometimes forget that an excessive love of "Reputation" was regarded as a form of idolatry in the Renaissance. For a consideration of this theme in another Shakespearean love tragedy, see David L. Jeffrey and J. Patrick Grant's "Reputation in *Othello*" in *Shakespeare Studies* 6 (1970): 197–208. Meanwhile, for perceptive observations about the part gender plays in male codes of behavior, see Coppèlia Kahn's "Coming of Age in Verona," *Modern Language Studies* 8 (1977–78): 5–22; Marianne Novy's *Love's Argument* (Chapel Hill: University of North Carolina Press, 1984); Edward Snow's "Language and Sexual Difference in *Romeo and Juliet*," in *Shakespeare's Rough Magic*, ed. Peter Erickson and Coppèlia Kahn (Newark: University of Delaware Press, 1985); and Eve Kosofsky Sedgwick's *Between Men: English Literature and Male Homosocial Desire* (New York: Columbia University Press, 1985).

19. In doing so, of course, he disregards the teaching Elizabethans would have been familiar with from the homily *Of Obedience* (1547) and the later homily *Against Disobedience and Willful Rebellion* (1574), both of which drew on the Apostle Paul's Epistle to the Romans (12:17–13:7) to remind subjects that they should "Recompense to no man evil for evil," instead leaving to God and his ordained "powers that be" the judging and punishing of crimes. The popularity of revenge tragedy in the Elizabethan and Jacobean theater was an implicit acknowledgment that men who prized their honor (their self-respect and their social standing) frequently found it difficult, if not impossible, to submit themselves to passive, long-suffering forbearance, even though they recognized that the code duello was explicitly condemned by the Lord they claimed to worship (see the Sermon on the Mount, especially Matthew 5:38–44). For a fuller discussion of the ethical, social, and political tensions that resulted from the disparity between supposedly "masculine" and "feminine" approaches to the resolution of conflict, see Fredson Bowers's *Elizabethan Revenge Tragedy, 1587–1642* (Princeton: Princeton University Press, 1940), and Eleanor Prosser's *Hamlet and Revenge*, rev. ed. (Stanford: Stanford University Press, 1971).

20. See 1.9.27–54 of *Faerie Queene*. I owe this observation to Professor Joan Hartwig of the University of Kentucky, who shared it with me in 1971 when we were fellow faculty members at Florida State University.

21. The earliest version of this essay, "The Catharsis of *Romeo and Juliet*," appeared in *Contributi dell'Istituto di Filologia Moderna* (Milan: Università Cattolica, 1974), 142–75. I grateful to the editor of that volume, Professor Sergio Rossi of the University of Turin, for permission to publish a revision of the original article. I also wish to acknowledge the degree to which my thinking about *Romeo and Juliet* has benefited from the writings of others not previously cited in these notes, among them Ralph Berry, "The Sonnet World of Verona," in *The Shakespearean Metaphor* (London: Macmillan, 1978); James Black, "The Visual Artistry of *Romeo and Juliet*," *Studies in English Literature* 15 (1975): 245–56; Franklin M. Dickey, *Not Wisely But Too Well: Shakespeare's Love Tragedies* (San

Marino, Calif.: Huntington Library, 1957); Harley Granville-Barker, *Prefaces to Shakespeare,* vol. 4 (Princeton: Princeton University Press, 1946); Jack J. Jorgens, "Franco Zeffirelli's *Romeo and Juliet,*" in his *Shakespeare on Film* (Bloomington: Indiana University Press, 1977); Harry Levin, "Form and Formality in *Romeo and Juliet,*" *Shakespeare Quarterly* 11 (1960): 3–11; M. M. Mahood, *Shakespeare's Wordplay* (London: Methuen, 1957); Thomas E. Moisan, "Rhetoric and the Rehearsal of Death: The 'Lamentations' Scene in *Romeo and Juliet,*" *Shakespeare Quarterly* 34 (1983): 389–404; Norman Rabkin, "Eros and Death" in *Shakespeare and the Common Understanding* (New York: Free Press, 1967); Susan Snyder, "*Romeo and Juliet:* Comedy and Tragedy," *Essays in Criticism* 20 (1970): 391–402; and Stanley Wells, "Juliet's Nurse: The Uses of Inconsequentiality," in *Shakespeare's Styles,* ed. Philip Edwards, Inga-Stina Ewbank, and G. K. Hunter (Cambridge: Cambridge University Press, 1980).

"Begot of nothing"? Dreams and Imagination in *Romeo and Juliet*

JOAN OZARK HOLMER

CRITICS have seen the witty Mercutio's Queen Mab speech as his most imaginative flight in *Romeo and Juliet*. But the extent to which Shakespeare himself is imaginative in his fusion of dream lore and a diminutive demon has not been fully understood. The idea of small fairies does not originate with Shakespeare. They appear in old folklore traditions, recorded in the late Middle Ages by authors such as Giraldis Cambrensis and Gervase of Tilbury, and particularly in Welsh lore; John Lyly often is credited with being the first to introduce into Elizabethan drama the small fairies, who would be aptly played by the smaller of his boy actors.[1] Lyly's language, however, reveals that his small fairies in *Endimion* are not meant to be imagined as extremely diminutive, but rather as childlike in their stature because he calls them "fair babies."[2] Shakespeare breaks new dramatic ground in *A Midsummer Night's Dream* and *Romeo and Juliet* when he combines the subject of mortals' dreams with small fairies (Titania and Oberon, who can assume mortal size) and with very diminutive fairies (in *Dream* the courtly attendants who can wear coats of bats' wings and in *Romeo* the agate-stone-sized Queen Mab).

This originality of Shakespeare's coupling of fairy and dream has been overlooked. In *An Encyclopedia of Fairies* Katherine A. Briggs presents comprehensive information about fairies, but there is no entry for dreams as a subject directly related to fairies.[3] Indeed, Shakespeare's description of Queen Mab as "the fairies' midwife" (1.4.54)[4]—the fairy whose role it is to bring to life the dreams of sleeping mortals—should surprise us. The idea of a fairy playing midwife to humans reverses the popular idea, recorded by Briggs, of mortal women who act as midwives to fairy mothers in the delivery, not of dreams, but of fairy offspring.[5] Is Shakespeare's demon-dream association "begot of nothing but vain fantasy" (1.4.98)?

195

I suggest that Shakespeare's stylistic habit of borrowing and transforming material found in other literary sources applies as well in this situation. The source I propose for considering Shakespeare's imaginative transformations is also markedly original in presenting the first literary association of extremely diminutive spirits and their causative roles in the dreams we mortals have: Thomas Nashe's *The Terrors of the Night, or a Discourse of Apparitions* (1594).[6] In his work Nashe greatly develops much of the earlier work on demonology done for his *Pierce Pennilesse* (1592),[7] but his two most substantive additions are diminution and dream lore as he spoofingly expatiates on his wide-ranging single "theame . . . the terrors of the Night" (1:360). Just as Robin Goodfellow in *A Midsummer Night's Dream* provides his audience with the option to think they "have but slumbered" and "this weak and idle theme, / No more yielding but a dream" (5.1.403–6), so also Nashe with a puckish gesture of self-depreciation dismisses his work as "but a dream": "& to say the troth, all this whole Tractate is but a dreame, for my wits are not halfe awaked in it" (1:360–61).

To begin, dreams and the Romeo-Mercutio exchange about dreams are Shakespeare's innovative additions to the acknowledged source for his play, Arthur Brooke's poem, *The Tragicall Historye of Romeus and Juliet* (1562).[8] Despite extensive critical discussion of the possible influences on Mercutio and his Queen Mab speech on dreams and despite a growing awareness of Nashe's influence on Shakespeare,[9] it is surprising that Nashe's *The Terrors of the Night,* with its satirically spirited use of diminutive demonology and dreams, has been overlooked as a possible source for Shakespeare's paradoxical use of dream and his characterization of Mercutio as a dream-mocker and Romeo as a dream-believer. Mercutio's very debunking of dreams, those "children of an idle brain, / Begot of nothing but vain fantasy" (1.4.98–99), closely apes Nashe's own dismissal of dreams as "fragments of idle imaginations" (1:355) or "ridiculous idle childish invention" (1:356) of "the phantasie" (1:354). When Romeo interrupts Mercutio's supportive spoof on dreams, "Peace, peace, Mercutio, peace! / Thou talk'st of *nothing*" (1.4.95–96; my italics), he echoes Nashe's denouement: "But this is *nothing* (you will obiect) to our journeys ende of apparitions" (1:377). And Romeo's conclusion regarding his belief about his dream, that "with this night's revels" (1.4.109) begins some dire consequence, changes the mood but recalls that phrase from Nashe's conclusion: "my muse inspyres me to put out my candle and goe to bed: and yet I wyll not neyther, till, after all these *nights reuells,* I haue solemnly bid you good night . . . and sleep quietly without affrightment and annoyance" (1:384; my italics).

Perhaps one reason that might help explain the oversight of Nashe's possible influence is the impoverished reputation of *The Terrors of the Night.* Ronald B. McKerrow concluded about Nashe's piece, "It is a slight production . . . a hasty piece of work . . . and on the whole of very little importance either as regards Nashe's biography or the history of letters in his time" (5:23). McKerrow's dismissal rests chiefly on his view that Nashe's work is very unoriginal: "a mere stringing together of matter taken from elsewhere"; most of it "might well have been gathered by miscellaneous reading" (4:107). But as Donald J. McGinn rightly observes, McKerrow "admits being unable to identify any of these sources."[10] Especially for Nashe's dream lore McKerrow can cite no particular source.[11] Even Briggs dismisses Nashe's work: "He has, however, nothing to add to our knowledge except a remark on the small size of spirits, which makes them even smaller than Drayton's fairies."[12]

G. R. Hibbard revises this negative appraisal. Although he does not suggest any connection between Shakespeare's *Romeo* and Nashe's *Terrors,* he praises Nashe's work—its spirit and style—in terms suggestive for recalling Mercutio's spirit and style in his Queen Mab speech:

> This combination of over-wrought description on the one hand, and mocking skepticism on the other, is the outstanding characteristic of the whole pamphlet and the real unifying factor in it, for *The Terrors of the Night* is essentially a *jeu d'esprit* . . . one of the most sophisticated prose-works of the age . . . too sophisticated for Nashe's contemporaries; only one edition of it appeared during his lifetime. . . . It seems to me, further, that *The Terrors of the Night,* although it had no influence on anything written after it, does have its place in the history of letters in Nashe's time. . . . It is one of the first, if not the first, prose works in English that exists for no other end than to give pleasure a discriminating reader can find in a . . . display of stylistic ingenuity that carries with it the impress of a personality. . . . In essence, *The Terrors of the Night* is a piece of literary clowning, and good clowning in writing, no less than in the theatre or the circus, is neither a common nor a contemptible thing.[13]

Shakespeare is precisely the sophisticated audience, the "discriminating reader," on whom Nashe's "literary clowning" was not lost. Shakespeare reshapes it to develop Mercutio's character as a mirthful scoffer, not unlike Tom Nashe himself, and to craft the tenor, tone, and function of his Queen Mab "improvisation."[14]

Shakespeare uses much of Nashe's dream lore, but he also recasts what he borrows, chiefly through the cultivation of paradox, personalization, and tragic irony, all elements conspicuously absent from Nashe's work. His adaptive borrowing from Nashe covers a wide range: tone (chiefly Mercutio's satirical stance on credulity); text and context (the opposition between serious belief and comic nonbelief regarding spirits and dreams as species of nightly "terrors"); and language (the lexicon used to describe these terrors and how they are interrelated). Even the tonal framework for Nashe's work, which shifts from a serious and religious tone (1:345–48) to witty spoofing (1:349–84) and back again to a graver concluding tone of admonition (1:384–86), might have provided Shakespeare with a hint for comic-tragic juxtaposition, a hint that Shakespeare improves upon throughout his scene by interplaying these opposing moods between melancholic Romeo and mirthful Mercutio.

Within this context the purpose for the Romeo-Mercutio exchange on dreams reveals itself. Romeo clearly believes in the truth of dreams, and because his love melancholy has been the butt of Mercutio's humor from the beginning of this scene, Mercutio probably anticipates some ominous announcement when Romeo implies why they show "no wit" in going to this mask, "I dreamt a dream tonight" (1.4.50). Mercutio attempts to deflect Romeo's gravity, "And so did I" (1.4.50), to which the polite Romeo falls pat, "Well, what was yours?" (1.4.51). Mercutio's rejoinder concisely expresses his attitude "that dreamers often lie" (1.4.51), which Romeo refutes in a clever pun, "In bed asleep, while they do dream things true" (1.4.52). Mercutio's Queen Mab speech is a loquaciously witty rejoinder, even a *jeu d'esprit,* wherein he tries to laugh Romeo out of his lover's melancholy and restore him to his "sociable" (2.4.73) self by debunking Romeo's belief in dreams as cleverly as he can. Mercutio's sportive wit that seeks to uplift Romeo's downcast spirit informs all his previous rejoinders in this scene—"You are a lover, borrow Cupid's wings, / And soar with them above a common bound" (1.4.17–18)—because Mercutio, eager to go to the Capulet feast, seeks to draw Romeo from "the mire, / Or (save your reverence) love, wherein [Romeo] stickest / Up to the ears" (1.4.41–43).

Mercutio's wittily skeptical attitude toward dreams and Queen Mab, who delivers these fancies, parallels Nashe's treatment of dreams and diminutive spirits in both language and thought as

Nashe seeks to counsel his reader about nightly terrors, even to the point of providing a good-night prescription for how to avoid bad dreams. In his pamphlet Nashe's shift from a serious to a comic tone begins with his introduction of tiny spirits who inhabit the four elements, as well as humans whose humors correspond to those four elements and indeed inhabit everything in our world, and who are so diminutive as to be almost microscopic: "In *West-minster* Hall a man can scarce breath for them; for in euery corner they houer as thick as moates in the sunne" (1:349). Mercutio's extremely diminutive depiction of Mab as "in shape no bigger than an agate-stone / On the forefinger of an alderman" (1.4.55–56) is a very similar, if more elaborate, version of Nashe's description of men who "haue ordinarily carried a familiar or a spirite in a ring in stead of a sparke of a diamond" (1:350). Shakespeare's use of "an alderman" as the "spritely" ring bearer seems to be his speci-fication of Nashe's general "man" likely to be found in Westmin-ster Hall.[15]

But far more telling than these verbal parallels is Shakespeare's debt to Nashe for the idea and imagery that lie behind Shake-speare's imaginative depiction of his Mab as the fairies' midwife. Hibbard implies that Nashe merely juxtaposes spirits and dreams because Nashe "rambles on" so that "ultimately spirits lead to melancholy and melancholy back to dreams."[16] But Nashe actually forges the causative relation between the tiniest of spirits and dreams; he uses language of birthing to define the causal relation-ship in which diminutive, elemental spirits use melancholy to "en-gender" dreams in mortals: "the spirits of earth and water have predominance in the night; for they feeding on foggie-brained mel-ancholly, engender thereof many vncouth terrible monsters . . . engendereth many mishapen objects in our imaginations . . . many fearfull visions . . . [and] herein specially consisteth our senses defect and abuse . . . [that] by some misdiet or misgouernment being distempered . . . [they] deliuer vp nothing but lyes and fa-bles" (1:353–54). Friar Lawrence echoes this concern about dis-temperature when he sees young Romeo up too early, suggesting such behavior "argues a distempered head," a Romeo "uproused with some distemp'rature" (2.3.32–40) or imbalance of humors. Mercutio's view, however, that dreamers "lie" (1.4.51) is more sa-tirically dismissive and parallels Nashe's quip: "What heede then is there to be had of dreames, that are no more but the confused giddie action of our braines, made drunke with the innundation of humours?" (1:370). For Mercutio's sporting with fairy and dream, Shakespeare enhances Nashe's causal relationship by personalizing the diminutive earthly spirits into one chief figure who is both "queeñ" and "quean," who is specifically named as "Mab," and whose function is to be the fairies' "midwife" in the delivering of mortals' dreams.

Nashe interrelates tiny spirits (chiefly earthly ones, whose identifying element of earth corresponds in Renaissance psychology to the humor of melancholy), mortals' melancholy, and dreams in order to mock dreams as "ridiculous idle childish invention" (1:356), "trifling childish" (1:371), "toyish fantasies" (1:373), "froth of the fancie" (1:355), "an after feast made of the fragments of idle imaginations" (1:355), and "but the Eccho of our conceipts in the day" (1:356). Nashe rambles but manages to sum up concisely: "When all is said, melancholy is the *mother of dreames,* and of all terrours of the night whatsoeuer" (1:357; my italics). Shakespeare cultivates Nashe's generalized use of "childish" by personifying dreams as "children of an idle brain, / Begot of nothing but vain fantasy" (1.4.98–99). But Shakespeare probably derives his "midwife" image from Nashe's "mother of dreams" and his linguistic emphasis on "engendering" for how spirits use melancholy to create dreams.

Various sources have been suggested for Mercutio's descriptions of different dreamers and their appropriate dreams (1.4.70–88n). Shakespeare's depiction of Mab as a midwife who delivers dreams that are dreamers' wish-fulfillments finds an analogue in Nashe's far less succinct but similarly satiric and decorous presentation of the elemental natures of spirits and their corresponding inhabitation of like-minded mortals who live, and who, it is implied, dream accordingly. For example, "terrestriall spirits" ally with soldiers and "confirme them in their furie & congeale their mindes with a bloodie resolution" (1:352). Spirits of the air are "all show and no substance, deluders of our imagination," and "they vnder-hand instruct women" in how "to sticke their gums round with Comfets when they haue not a tooth left in their heads to help them chide withall" (1:353). Nashe's violent soldiers and comfit-comforted women are not far from Mercutio's throat-cutting soldier and his ladies whose eating of sweetmeats (or "kissing-comfits") cannot cover up their blistered lips and "tainted" breaths (1.4.75–76). This descriptive matter immediately precedes Nashe's explanation of how spirits engender dreams (1:353). But Shakespeare also refashions Nashe's hints into his own imaginative dreamscape by appropriate amplification, and he attributes all power specifically to Queen Mab's role, deftly versified, in the delivery of appropriate dreams, such as the lovers' dreams of love, the ladies' dreams of kisses, and the soldier's dreams of violence.

Although Romeo dismisses Mercutio's words, "Thou talk'st of nothing" (1.4.96), and Mercutio concurs, "True, I talk of dreams, / Which are the children of an idle brain, / Begot of nothing but vain fantasy" (1.4.96–98), their exchange is not for naught within the context of the play. Fundamental to their exchange is the opposition between two views of dream that frame their dialogue: Mercutio's belief that dreams are lies or fantasies and Romeo's belief that dreamers "dream things true" (1.4.52). Nashe's general attitude toward his subject as trivial and his view of dreams as delusions, ensconced in a variety of popular superstitions (1:361–62), parallels Mercutio's dismissal of Romeo's apparent belief in the truth of dreams as prophetic. Some of Nashe's remarks are quite pertinent for Shakespeare's treatment of dream in his play; he imitates Nashe and improves Nashe's associations chiefly through tragic effect heightened by irony and paradox. In Nashe's attack on excessive credulity, he debunks some popular superstitions concerning dreams—for example, the belief that a happy dream foreshadows misfortune and a sad dream good luck (1:362). Nashe develops his double-pronged view of dreams as caused immediately by melancholy and ultimately by night-dominant spirits when he adds his cautionary emphasis on the danger of emotional extremes that induce "most of our melancholy dreames and visions" (1:377). Romeo's susceptibility to dreams correlates with his temperamental imbalance due to excessive extremes of grief and joy, inviting our sympathy for his plight. The danger of excess is a philosophical idea that Friar Lawrence expounds, chiefly in proverbial terms (2.6.9–15).

Romeo has two dreams that resemble Nashe's dream psychology. His first dream probably is caused at least partially by his too-much-changed emotional state that his father so fears: "Black and portentous must this humour prove, / Unless good counsel may the cause remove" (1.1.132–33). Romeo's persistent suffering of love melancholy is Shakespeare's significant change of Brooke's handling of Romeus's decision to attend the Capulet feast. Brooke's Romeus responds positively and immediately to his friend's advice that he forswear his unrequited love and seek another love; his healing process is well underway before he goes to the Capulet feast (ll. 141–50). Although Shakespeare's Romeo may appear fickle to us and even to Friar Lawrence, who persists in seeing him as but a "young waverer" (2.3.89), Romeo does intend at least, unlike the far more fickle Romeus, to remain true to Rosaline until experience itself, the vision of Juliet, thwarts his faithful intention. Shakespeare's change here effectively keynotes one of his recurrent themes, that experience often changes intention, and in many ways *Romeo and Juliet* gains tragic poignancy through the persistent pattern of good intentions that run amuck. In Romeo's unhealthy state of love melancholy his dream of ill portent could be interpreted as being engendered by his continued grief over Rosaline's rejection of him. Nashe commonsensically observes that when "a solitarie man [lies] in his bed" (1:376), he tends to think over his recent experiences. If his experiences have been sad, then he feels overwhelmed by misfortune. Given the popular superstition that dreams prove contrary, "that euery thing must bee interpreted backward . . . good being the character of bad, and bad of good" (1:361), an idea that Romeo seems not to know, his sad dream of "untimely death" that begins "with this night's revels" (1.4.109–11) should foreshadow good luck. And in one respect it does. That very "blessed, blessed night" (2.2.139) Romeo doffs his inky cloak of melancholy to wrap himself in the joy of Juliet's love, despite his fear that this might be "but a dream / Too flattering-sweet to be substantial" (2.2.141).

On the other hand, Shakespeare invests his use of dream with more paradox than Nashe because the same dream can be interpreted as false and as true. This same seemingly blessed night does begin, for various reasons, the cycle of time that will ultimately cost much more than just the "vile forfeit" (1.4.111) of his life. Although Nashe argues against "the certainety of Dreames" (1:371) and focuses on the folly of "anticke suppositions" (1:378), he does not completely deny the prophetic power of all dreams, especially of those heaven-sent "vnfallible dreames" foretelling the deaths of the saints and martyrs of the Primitive Church (1:372), or even some of the historical "visions" that were "sent from heaven to foreshew" the rise and fall of "Monarchies" (1:361), the usual stuff of tragic drama so foreign to Shakespeare's new matter here, the rise and fall of young lovers. And Nashe closes with "the strange tale" of an English gentleman's "miraculous waking visions," which are left to the reader's judgment to decide whether they be "of true melancholy or true apparition" (1:378). But Nashe believes that fearful dreams provoke much more terror than the reality they foreshadow: "the feare of anie expected euill, is worse than the euill it selfe" (1:376). Romeo's dream proves an exception to this general truth when the audience finally sees the stage as a graveyard, littered with dead bodies—Romeo, Juliet, Paris, and Tybalt—and knows of the deaths of Mercutio and Lady Montague, with Lady Capulet's death imminent. Although Romeo, like Hamlet (2.2.256), is susceptible to bad dreams because he is melancholic enough to refer to his life as "a despised life" (1.4.110), his "terror of the night" proves no idle apparition by the play's end.

Nashe makes a point of focusing exclusively on the time of night for his "terrors," and Shakespeare adapts this setting of night, the time when dreams usually occur, to suit the genre of the play he is writing. In the romantic comedy, *A Midsummer Night's Dream*, night becomes the time when friendly fairies help to resolve the waking nightmares of mortals. But Shakespeare's use of night in *Romeo and Juliet* is more complicated and parallels his paradoxical presentation of dream. Nashe strikes the expectant tragic chord regarding night: "When anie Poet would describe a horrible Tragicall accident; to adde the more probabilitie & credence vnto it, he dismally beginneth to tell, how it was dark night when it was done, and cheerfull daylight had quite abandoned the firmament. Hence, it is, that sinne generally throughout the scripture is called the workes of darknesse; for neuer is the diuell so busie as then, and then he thinkes he may aswel vndiscouered walke abroad, as homicides and outlawes" (1:386). But in the benighted world of Verona's hateful feud, night contrarily becomes the lovers' friend so that Juliet's knight can come to her safely, and "civil Night," their "sober-suited matron," can teach them how "to lose a winning match / Played for a pair of stainless maidenhoods" (3.2.10–13). "Love-performing Night" (3.2.5) is love's traditional element. On the other hand, the joyful nights of their first meeting and marital consummation change to the contrary when Romeo returns in the night, once again as a torchbearer (5.3.25, 283), this time, however, going not to life's celebratory feast with his fears submitted to the guidance of a higher power (1.4.11–12, 35–38), but rather journeying passionately in a spirit of defiance to death's feast to be feasted upon:

> . . . then I defy you, stars! . . .
> Thou detestable maw, thou womb of death,
> Gorged with the dearest morsel of the earth,
> Thus I enforce thy rotten jaws to open,
> And in despite I'll cram thee with more food.
>
> (5.1.24, 45–48)

When Romeo first saw Juliet, he found her beauty brilliant: "O she doth teach the torches to burn bright!" (1.5.43). Likewise in death her beauty makes the vault "a feasting presence full of light" (5.3.85–86). Romeo's own mood, "a light'ning before death" (5.3.90), may recall for the audience, through memorial wordplay,

Juliet's premonitory warning about the "lightning" nature of their love (2.2.117–24).

Shakespeare adds Romeo's dark dream, which, like the opening choric Prologue, signals the genre of tragedy within the predominately comic context of the first two acts. Brooke warns that Romeus would have remained happier if he had never forsworn his first love (ll. 151–54), but he presents no dream of ominous premonition. With the Mercutio-Romeo exchange over dreams, Shakespeare heightens dramatic tension for the audience's hopes and fears, and he also elevates the sense of mystery involved in human tragedy and the problem of epistemology. Whence comes Romeo's dream? If heaven-sent, then no mere delusion, or as Nashe might say, it is "true melancholy or true apparition" (1:378). Romeo links his mysteriously fatal dream to "some consequence yet hanging in the stars," and this imagery reflects the "star-crossed" motif of the Prologue and anticipates "a greater power" (5.3.153), a punitive "heaven" that kills with love (5.3.153, 293), to which Friar Lawrence and Prince Escalus submit. Romeo resolves to journey onward by committing his direction to a higher power (1.4.112): "But He that hath the steerage of my course / Direct my sail!" (1.4.111–12). Likewise Nashe, in his discourse on nightly terrors, comforts the reader by indicating that "looking to heauen for succor" (1:346) is the only way to fight the blinding power of darkness.[17] Nashe illustrates this idea with the true story that partially motivated him to write his treatise, the story of a sick English country gentleman who had various visions that took the form of temptations (1:379). The gentleman, whose physical eye could not determine whether the seductive apparition was an angel or fiend, relied on his "strong faith" in God "to defie & with-stand all his iugling temptations" (1:380).

Although Romeo has no waking visions, Juliet does have one, the germ of which is in Brooke's poem, while the superstition regarding such a vision is recorded by Nashe. The articulation of this palpable vision is Shakespeare's own, however, and he uses it for negative premonition that begs to be construed correctly by the audience as it vacillates painfully between fear and hope for the lovers. Juliet's soliloquy as she deliberates whether she should or can take the sleeping potion, with all its attendant dangers, climaxes with a vision that so fires her imagination that she resolves to drink immediately. Like Romeo, Juliet is now suffering from deep melancholy, and her feverish state also makes her susceptible to such apparitions. Juliet's waking vision might prompt some members of an Elizabethan audience to fear for her life.

Nashe mentions one popular superstition that "none haue such palpable dreames or visions, but die presently after" (1:383). In Brooke's poem the provocative part of Juliet's vision is the vivid reseeing by "the force of her ymagining . . . / The carkas of Tybalt, / . . . in his blood embrewde" (11. 2378–82), which in turn spawns her fear of "a thousand bodies dead" (1. 2393) around her; before she can lose her nerve, she frantically drinks the potion.

But Shakespeare goes beyond Brooke by having his Juliet drink to save her beloved from Tybalt's hate. She thinks she "see[s]" (4.3.54) the rancorous ghost of Tybalt carrying the feud beyond the grave in order to revenge himself on "Romeo that did spit his body / Upon a rapier's point" (4.3.56–57). This specific recollection of their duel ironically anticipates the next deadly duel. Juliet's palpable vision proves paradoxically true and false, and as Nashe might gloss it, Juliet's vision is born of her own fears and her overwrought psychological state. It is not dead Tybalt but live Paris who seeks Romeo when he misconstrues Romeo's intention—"Can vengeance be pursued further than death?" (5.3.55)— and who pays with his life for his misguided but well-meant interference. However, as a gentleman Romeo honorably seeks both Paris's and Tybalt's forgiveness (5.3.101).[18] Tybalt does not seek Romeo's life; Romeo seeks his own. One principle of dreams in Nashe, which Shakespeare only partially acknowledges, concerns the role of personal responsibility in the shaping of one's fortunes and one's dreams: "of the ouerswelling superabundance of ioy and greefe, wee frame our selues most of our melancholy dreames and visions. . . . Euerie one shapes hys owne fortune as he lists. . . . Euerie one shapes his owne feares and fancies as he list" (1:377). In his desperate torment Romeo unwisely reasons: "O, what more favour can I do thee [Tybalt] / Then with that hand that cut thy youth in twain / To sunder his that was thine enemy" (5.3.98–100). But there is no friendly hand present this time to stay his own.

Romeo's second dream, this time with the contents specifically relayed to the audience, also fulfills Shakespeare's paradoxical perspective and complements the dramatic structure, where "all things change them to the contrary" (1.4.90), from "ordained festival" to "black funeral" (4.5.84–85). Romeo's dream, unlike his first one, is joyful so that despite his concern again about "the flattering truth of sleep," his dream uplifts him "with cheerful thoughts" that "some joyful news [is] at hand" (5.1.1–11). Given the popular superstition described by Nashe, this dream should foreshadow misfortune. Nashe warns: "He that dreams merily is like a boy new breetcht, who leapes and daunceth for joy his pain is past: but

long that joy stays not with him, for presently after his master the
day, seeing him so iocund and pleasant, comes and dooes as much
for him againe, whereby his hell is renued" (1:356). Right on cue
Balthasar enters with the tragic news of Juliet's death that initiates
Romeo's defiance of the stars. Because Balthasar is described in
the stage direction of the first quarto as "booted,"[19] he has apparently left Verona in such great haste, once he saw Juliet laid low,
that he must not have gone to Friar Lawrence to obtain the promised correspondence of "every good hap" that the Friar and Romeo
had agreed would be carried between them by Balthasar
(3.3.169–71).

To underscore the paradoxical significance of Romeo's dream,
Shakespeare changes the role of Romeo's servant in the sources
by having Friar Lawrence prudently assign him the function of
letter-bearer and go-between.[20] Romeo asks Balthasar for such letters twice, once before and surprisingly once after he hears Balthasar's tragic news. But Balthasar, curiously, never explains his hasty
departure from Verona. The audience might expect Romeo's first
inquiry, but his second intelligent one, "Hast thou no letters to me
from the Friar?" (5.1.31), intensifies the tragic tension because the
audience knows Friar Lawrence sent "with speed" the important
letters to Romeo by means of a fellow friar (4.1.122–24); the friar
could not risk waiting for Balthasar's return to Verona once he
and Juliet had decided on their desperate plan with the potion,
intended to achieve Romeo's secret rescue of Juliet for their sojourn together in Mantua (4.1.105–17). But the plague unexpectedly delays Friar John, and Lord Capulet's joyful resolve to hasten
the intended wedding day from Thursday to Wednesday, the very
next morning, also complicates this desperately hopeful plan.[21] On
his way to Friar Lawrence, Balthasar sees the funeral and returns
swiftly instead to Romeo. Had Balthasar consulted Friar Lawrence
as originally planned, he would have returned with the good news
that would rightly interpret the meaning of Romeo's joyful dream.

In Romeo's dream the life and death positions of Juliet and himself appear to be reversed from what ultimately will happen, but
Nashe reminds us that the nature of dreams is chaotic and "a
Dreame is nothing els but the Eccho of our conceipts in the day"
(1:356). However, despite apparent contradiction, Romeo's happy
dream would prove true if he had not resolved upon suicide when
he received Balthasar's unwittingly false news. Juliet would have
revived the spirits of "a dead man" (5.1.7; 5.3.87), such as he
describes himself when he is without her, and she would breathe
"such life with kisses in [his] lips" (5.1.8) that he would triumph

like "an emperor" in his sweet possession of love (5.1.10–11). Shakespeare's puns make Romeo's expectations and Balthasar's news all the more painful for the knowing audience: "Nothing can be ill if she be well" (5.1.17), and she is well in fact because Balthasar, speaking more truly than he knows, reminds us that her body only "sleeps in Capels' monument" (5.1.18). Instead, Romeo's "misadventure" (5.1.29) as "a desp'rate man" (5.3.59) leaves Juliet to find him literally dead. Her kisses cannot restore him to physical life, but if "some poison yet doth hang on" Romeo's lips, her kiss or "restorative" will enable her to die and lie with Romeo (5.3.165– 66). "Thy lips are warm" (5.1.167) may be the most tragic utterance in the play as Juliet realizes how close has been the *hamartia* of tragedy.

Because the audience has just witnessed the deadly duel between Romeo and Paris, Balthasar's lines on his dream might seem superfluous:

> As I did sleep under this yew tree here,
> I dreamt my master and another fought,
> And that my master slew him.
>
> (5.3.137–39)

Nashe explains that noises that a dreamer subconsciously hears can inspire a dream: "one Eccho borrowes of another: so our dreames (the Ecchoes of the day) borrow of anie noyse we heare in the night" (1:356). But that does not explain Shakespeare's choice of the yew tree, which for Elizabethans could symbolize death. As John Gerard's *Herball* clarifies, the yew tree is common in many countries, including Italy and England, but it "is of a venemous qualitie, and against mans nature . . . and that if any do sleepe under the shadow thereof, it causeth sicknes, and oftentimes death."[22] While not prophetic, Balthasar's dream is nontheless true. He is probably inspired by the noise of the duel between Paris and Romeo to dream things true; his master did indeed fight and slay another. Thus Shakespeare allows for the truth, as well as the delusion, of what may or may not be an illusion.

If we grant any of these arguments, then we should also grant that Shakespeare's imaginative power of unifying into a more complex whole that which he finds separate or scattered in his source materials helps to demonstrate that he is very much an artist of Renaissance temperament. His ingenious use of sources favors the Renaissance ideal of "imitatio," whereby the combination of old material with new is expressed in an original manner. According to Renaissance critical theory regarding the operation of the poetic imagination, the imagination's transforming or "feigning" power is guided by reason to create art: the poetic feigning of images is described in the sixteenth century as a process of severing and joining things real to form things imagined.[23] As O. B. Hardison argues, "Shakespeare seems to have known what he was doing," deriving his "sense of artistry . . . from the experience of writing plays."[24] Romeo and Juliet, Hardison reminds us, are "among the most poignantly charming characters [Shakespeare] ever created."[25] And they are so attractive partly in relation to their dramatic world, which derives partly and complexly from Shakespeare's strikingly original use of Nashe. For the intricately unified world of his play, Shakespeare imaginatively transmutes and integrates various ideas, images, and intentions from Nashe's work on demons and dreams. Shakespeare's range of invention broadens our more limited sense of "source" because he mines the literary convention of "sources" in such unconventional ways. In dramatizing the story of Romeo and Juliet as only he can, Shakespeare's imaginative art takes us "past the size of dreaming" (Ant 5.2.97) so that when we leave the theater and wake from the suspension of our disbelief in the imaginative act we have just experienced, like Caliban, we wake only to cry "to dream again" (Tem 3.2.143).

Notes

1. See Katherine A. Briggs, *The Fairies in Tradition and Literature* (London: Routledge & Kegan Paul, 1967), 6–7; *The Anatomy of Puck* (London: Routledge & Kegan Paul, 1959), 18, 44, 56–70; *An Encyclopedia of Fairies* (New York: Pantheon Books, 1976), 120–21, 275, 295, 368–69. See also Harold F. Brooks, ed., *A Midsummer Night's Dream,* Arden Shakespeare (London: Methuen, 1979), lxxii and n.; R. A. Foakes, ed., *A Midsummer Night's Dream,* New Cambridge Shakespeare (Cambridge: Cambridge University Press, 1984), 6–7.

2. See John Lyly, *Endimion,* in *The Dramatic Works of John Lyly,* ed. R. Warwick Bond (Oxford: Clarendon Press, 1967), 3:4.3.166; cf. 4.3.132. See also Lyly's *Gallathea* 3.2.5–7, where no specific size is indicated. Lyly does not directly connect fairies and dreams, nor does he use extreme diminution or the detailed and fanciful description that appears in both Shakespeare's *Dream* and *Romeo.*

3. Briggs praises *Dream* as "our greatest fairy poem," especially its "shining unity of so many different materials." See Briggs, *Puck,* 44; cf. 45–50. But curiously overlooked is the new connection between fairy and dream in *Dream* and even more directly in *Romeo.* In her *Encyclopedia* Briggs hypothetically attempts to connect diminutive fairies from medieval tradition with a sleeper's dreams, based on the fairies' connection with the dead (not the living) and the idea of the sleeper's soul as a tiny creature whose extracorporeal "adventures are the

sleeper's dreams" (98–99). This hypothesis does not relate to Shakespeare's presentation of diminutive fairy and dream in either *Dream* or *Romeo*. For different interpretations of dream in *Romeo and Juliet,* see Warren D. Smith, "Romeo's Final Dream," *MLR* 62 (1967): 579–83, and Marjorie B. Garber, *Dream in Shakespeare: From Metaphor to Metamorphosis* (New Haven and London: Yale University Press, 1974), 35–47.

4. All quotations are from *Romeo and Juliet,* ed. G. Blakemore Evans, New Cambridge Shakespeare (Cambridge: Cambridge University Press, 1984). Quotations from other plays are from The Riverside Shakespeare, ed. Evans.

5. See Briggs, *Encyclopedia,* 296–98.

6. See Nashe, *The Works of Thomas Nashe,* ed. Ronald B. McKerrow, 5 vols. (1904–10; reprint, Oxford: Basil Blackwell, 1958), 1:339–86. References to volume and page are cited parenthetically.

7. See ibid., 1:227–39.

8. All references to Brooke's poem are documented parenthetically in my text and refer to Geoffrey Bullough, *Narrative and Dramatic Sources of Shakespeare* (London: Routledge and Kegan Paul, 1957), 1:284–363.

9. For critical commentary on Mercutio's Queen Mab speech, see H. H. Furness, ed., *Romeo and Juliet,* Variorum Shakespeare (Philadelphia: J. B. Lippincott, 1899), 61–67; Brian Gibbons, ed., *Romeo and Juliet,* Arden Shakespeare (London: Methuen, 1980), 67; 1.4.53–54n; Evans, 21–22, 1.4.53–54n, 199 and note on 1.4.53; Joseph A. Porter, *Shakespeare's Mercutio: His History and Drama* (Chapel Hill: University of North Carolina Press, 1988), 104–5, 121, 124, 156, 245, n. 5 and passim. For arguments discussing Nashe's influence on Shakespeare, see Evans, 3–6; Kenneth Muir, *The Sources of Shakespeare's Plays* (London: Methuen, 1977), 9, 93, 67, 75.

10. See McGinn, *Thomas Nashe* (Boston: Twayne Publishers, 1981), 63.

11. It seems likely that Nashe's dream lore would draw on some popular traditions; he himself dismisses other authors on dreams, such as Artemidorus, Synesius, and Cardan, whom he has not had "the plodding patience to reade" (1:361). Reginald Scot, whose *Discoverie of Witchcraft* Nashe admits he has read (1:351), is cited by McKerrow for mentioning the proverb in England that dreams prove contrary. See McKerrow, 4:204. 32n. But even if we could identify all the popular traditions behind Nashe's lore, not just this particular one, we can not underestimate Nashe's collection of all these theories and his combination of them with the subject of diminutive spirits, dreams, and melancholy, as well as the sportive tone that characterizes Shakespeare's Mercutio.

12. Briggs, *Puck,* 23. But Briggs does suggest that Nashe's playful granting of a spirit to all things, including mustard, may provide a hint for Shakespeare's naming of "Mustardseed" (23).

13. See Hibbard, *Thomas Nashe: A Critical Introduction* (Cambridge: Harvard University Press, 1962), 12, 115, 117, and 118.

14. Regarding the inspiration of Nashe for Shakespeare's characterization of Mercutio, see my essay "Nashe as 'Monarch of Witt' and Shakespeare's *Romeo and Juliet,*" *Texas Studies in Literature and Language* 37 (1995): 314–43.

15. Evans cites verbal borrowings from Nashe (4, 169, 173, 203).

16. Hibbard, *Nashe,* 114–15.

17. Cf. Nashe's *Pierce Pennilesse* regarding the power of prayer as the only sure way to prevail against evil spirits (1:238–39).

18. For gentlemanly behavior in the honorable duello, see my essays "Shakespeare's Duello Rhetoric and Ethic: Saviolo Versus Segar," *ELN* 31 (1993): 10–22,

and "'Draw, if you be men': Saviolo's Significance for *Romeo and Juliet*," *Shakespeare Quarterly* 45 (1994): 163–89.

19. For the servant's hasty departure in the sources, see Brooke: "(Alas) too soone, with heavy newes he hyed away in post" (1. 2532); see Painter: Pietro "incontinently tooke poste horse." For Painter, see William Painter, trans., *The Palace of Pleasure,* ed. Joseph Jacobs (1890; reprint, New York: Dover Publications, 1966), 115.

20. In Brooke (1. 2529) and in Painter (114), it is Romeo who originates the idea to have this man (Peter/Pietro) be a spy for him in Verona and to do his father, Lord Montague, service.

21. See Evans, 4.2.23n, p. 203. Shakespeare contracts time (that is, he moves up the wedding date) and adds details to heighten tragic timing, eliciting more sympathy from well-intentioned characters caught in time's juggernaut. Friar Lawrence, for example, takes precious time to write again to Romeo to communicate "these accidents" (5.2.26–30), given Friar John's mishap, even though Juliet will awaken "within these three hours" (5.2.25). The Friar arrives before she awakens, but a "full half an hour" (5.3.130) after Romeo has entered the vault.

22. See Gerard, *The Herball or Generall Historie of Plantes* (London: John Norton, 1597), 1188. Cf. Shakespeare's other references to the fatal yew: *Tit* 2.3.207; *R2* 3.2.117; *TN* 2.4.55; and *Mac* 4.1.27.

23. For Renaissance critical theory, see William Rossky, "Imagination in the English Renaissance: Psychology and Poetic," *Studies in the Renaissance* 5 (1958): 49–73, esp. 58–59. Cf. also, Sir Philip Sidney, *A Defence of Poetry,* ed. J. H. Van Dorsten (Oxford: Oxford University Press, 1966), 24, 32, 36; John Milton, *Paradise Lost,* ed. Merritt Y. Hughes (New York: Odyssey Press, 1962), 5. 100–21.

24. Hardison, "Shakespearean Tragedy: The Mind in Search of the World," *The Upstart Crow* 6 (1986): 80.

25. Ibid., 79.

"Of Government": Theme and Action in *Measure for Measure*

Louis L. Martz

Two recent editions of *Measure for Measure,* one from Cambridge, edited by Brian Gibbons, and the other from Oxford, edited by N. W. Bawcutt, represent a confluence of recent views: both are reluctant to see the work as religious allegory, parable, or morality play.[1] Reaction against the excesses of religious interpretation has led both editors to underplay the didactic overtones of the work and to find solutions to the play's many problems in tragicomedy's ways of manipulating audience response or in wholly secular views of the complex workings of "law." So deep is the reaction against the point of workings of "law." So deep is the reaction against the point of view represented by G. Wilson Knight's once-famous essay "*Measure for Measure* and the Gospels,"[2] that the Oxford editor makes no mention of it and limits discussion of the gospel implications of the title to a curt statement that "the title is ultimately biblical (Matt. 7:2)" (42). The Cambridge editor is more generous: he opens his introduction by giving full attention to the title's evocation of the Sermon on the Mount and its shorter counterpart in the Gospel of Luke, but he makes little use of these allusions in his subsequent commentary. Indeed, the acknowledgment is strangely guarded: "The passages from St Matthew and St Luke," says the Cambridge editor, "would have been so well known to most Elizabethans that very probably they would have taken the play's title to refer in the first place to those Gospels" (1). Could we not be bolder? Could we not say that to every Elizabethan likely to watch this play, these passages from the Gospels would have been instantly and constantly relevant, since they resounded from every pulpit in the land and indeed formed the core of every child's Christian education?

I am not about to argue that we should read the play in terms of the presumed response of Shakespeare's audience. But the play's title may alert us to the importance of recognizing the Gos-

pels as an essential element in the play's fabric, just as we recognize the significance of the *Odyssey* in reading Joyce's *Ulysses.*
Both works, by their titles, insist upon the recognition of an indis-
pensable subtext. *Measure for Measure* is unique among Shakespeare's plays in presenting an abstract theme in its title. And it is
unique in another way: it is the only one of Shakespeare's plays
that can be said to present its theme directly in its opening line:
"Of government the properties to unfold. . . ." The point is made
more emphatically in the old spelling and punctuation of the Folio:
"Of Government, the properties to unfold." "Of Government"—
the phrase may suggest something like Bacon's "Of Judicature" or
Cicero's *De Officiis* or *De Legibus.* From the outset, then, we have
an indication that this play will have a didactic aim: the demonstration, or exploration, or revelation of the qualities that make up
"government." And it soon appears that the play means "government" in more than a political sense. It means self-government as
well, self-control, as we watch the loss of self-government in three
of the central characters: Angelo, as he loses control of his
"blood"; Claudio, as he succumbs to his terror of death; and Isabella, as she makes her hysterical denunciation of her brother. As
the Duke suspects, and as "governor" Angelo proves, a just political government is impossible without self-government.

   The abstract issues of the play are enforced throughout by the
persistent repetition of certain key words. First, there is *law,* usually in the phrase "the Law," with the word consistently capitalized
in the Folio so that its twenty-five repetitions convey the presence
of an abstract power, the repressive presence of what Angelo calls
"the all-binding law"—or, as the Folio reads, "the all-building-
Law" (2.4.94).[3] On the stage the same effect could be created by
an actor who gives the word a grim and threatening emphasis. The
word *law,* as the Oxford editor points out, occurs in this play more
often than in any other work by Shakespeare. The same is true of
the word *justice,* also consistently capitalized ("Iustice") in the
Folio. As a little research in Spevack's *Concordance* will show,[4] it
occurs no fewer than twenty-six times, reaching a climax in the
final scene, where the word is repeated eight times within the space
of fifteen lines, as Isabella cries:

> Justice, oh royal Duke! Vail your regard
> Upon a wronged—I would fain have said a maid.
> Oh worthy prince, dishonour not your eye
> By throwing it on any other object
> Till you have heard me in my true complaint

And given me Justice, Justice, Justice, Justice!

(5.1.20–25)[5]

The word *mercy* also occurs here more frequently than in any other work by Shakespeare: sixteen times. Even *The Merchant of Venice* uses the word only thirteen times, and eleven of these are concentrated in one great scene (4.1), whereas in *Measure for Measure* the word runs throughout, beginning with the powerful emphasis in the opening scene: "Mortality and Mercy in Vienna / Live in thy tongue and heart" (1.1.44–45). Other words, less frequently used, but still persistent, combine to reinforce the theme of law: *judge, judgment, condemn, condemned, authority.* Still another word, an essential counterforce to "the Law," is introduced jestingly but prominently, four times, in the second scene of the play, as Lucio declares, "I thinke thou never was't where Grace was said" and adds, "Grace, is Grace, despight of all controversie: as for example; Thou thy selfe art a wicked villaine, despight of all Grace" (1.2.16, 21–22; I give the Folio typography here; the word is not consistently capitalized hereafter). The word *grace* appears no fewer than twenty-three times, usually as a term of respect: "your grace." But on at least ten occasions the word carries a theological meaning or overtone, as in Lucio's allusion to current controversy over the action of grace, or when he says to Isabella, "All hope is gone / Unless you have the grace by your fair prayer / To soften Angelo" (1.4.68–70). This overtone is also present when the Duke says to Isabella: "but grace, being the soul of your complexion, shall keep the body of it ever fair" (3.1.178–79), or when Angelo, admitting his guilt, confesses, "Alack, when once our grace we have forgot, / Nothing goes right" (4.4.31–32). Finally the two meanings of the word, the courtly and the theological, converge in Angelo's realization:

> Oh, my dread lord,
> I should be guiltier than my guiltiness
> To think I can be undiscernible
> When I perceive your grace, like power divine,
> Hath looked upon my passes.

(5.1.359–63)

The word "passes" here seems to evoke the best-known portion of the Sermon on the Mount, in the prayer book version: "Forgive us our trespasses, as we forgive those who trespass against us."

Underlying and affiliating all these thematic words is the word of the title, *measure,* used in several senses. First is *measure* in

the sense of proportion, proper limit. "Lord Angelo is precise"
(1.3.51), a puritan; his life of "stricture and firm abstinence"
(1.3.13) is carried beyond proper measure and the repression of
"blood" provokes an opposite extreme. Meanwhile, he seeks to
control unmeasured sexual license in the city by excessively severe
legal measures. Isabella similarly seeks to control herself by the
"stricture and firm abstinence" of a nun, with this unmeasured
result: "More than our brother is our chastity" (2.4.186).

But at the heart of the word's meaning in the play is the gospel
reference to the Sermon on the Mount (Matthew 5–7) and the
shorter version in Luke (6), which every scholar of the play (except
the recent Oxford editor) has fully recognized, and which the play
itself enforces at the close, especially in the typography of the
Folio:

> The very mercy of the Law cries out
> Most audible, even from his proper tongue.
> An *Angelo* for *Claudio,* death for death:
> Haste still paies haste, and leasure, answers leasure;
> Like doth quit like, and *Measure* still for *Measure:*
>
> (5.1.408–12)

> Judge not, that ye be not judged. For with what judgment ye judge,
> ye shall be judged: and with what measure ye mete, it shall be measured
> to you again. (Matthew 7:1)

The underlying allusion of course is to the Law of the Old Testament, as set forth in Leviticus 24:17–20:

> And he that killeth any man shall surely be put to death. And he
> that killeth a beast shall make it good; beast for beast. And if a man
> cause a blemish in his neighbour; as he hath done, so shall it be done
> to him; Breach for breach, eye for eye, tooth for tooth.

This is the text referred to in Matthew's version of the Sermon,
as Christ goes on to declare how the old Law is modified by the
new Gospel:

> Ye have heard that it hath been said, An eye for an eye, and a tooth
> for a tooth: But I say unto you, That ye resist not evil: but whosoever
> shall smite thee on thy right cheek, turn to him the other also. . . . Ye
> have heard that it hath been said, Thou shalt love thy neighbour, and
> hate thine enemy. But I say unto you, Love your enemies, bless them
> that curse you, do good to them that hate you, and pray for them which
> despitefully use you, and persecute you; That ye may be the children

of your Father which is in heaven: for he maketh his sun to rise on the evil and on the good, and sendeth rain on the just and on the unjust. (Matthew 5:38–39, 43–45)

This is the passage that lies behind the general forgiveness at the drama's close and especially behind the prayer of Isabella for remission of Angelo's penalty. The sermon in Luke casts further illumination upon this final scene and upon the meaning of "measure":

> Be ye therefore merciful, as your Father also is merciful. Judge not, and ye shall not be judged: condemn not, and ye shall not be condemned: forgive, and ye shall be forgiven: Give, and it shall be given unto you; good measure, pressed down, and shaken together, and running over, shall men give into your bosom. For with the same measure that ye mete withal it shall be measured to you again. (6:36–38)

"Good measure" goes abundantly beyond the "mercy of the Law" as defined by Angelo in his answer to Isabella's plea, "Yet show some pity":

> I show it most of all when I show Justice;
> For then I pity those I do not know,
> Which a dismissed offence would after gall,
> And do him right, that answering one foul wrong
> Lives not to act another.
>
> (2.2.103–7)

The overflowing measure of mercy in the Gospels is the fulfillment of the Law promised near the beginning of the Sermon on the Mount (Matthew 5:17): "Think not that I am come to destroy the law, or the prophets: I am not come to destroy, but to fulfil."

One should note that immediately before this verse the Sermon gives the passage that the Duke himself echoes at the outset of the play, when he urges Angelo not to conceal his virtues:

> Heaven doth with us as we with Torches do,
> Not light them for themselves: for if our virtues
> Did not go forth of us, 'twere all alike
> As if we had them not.
>
> (1.1.32–35)

> Neither do men light a candle, and put it under a bushel, but on a candlestick; and it giveth light unto all that are in the house. Let your

light so shine before men, that they may see your good works, and
glorify your Father which is in heaven. (Matthew 5:15–16)

And only five verses after this we come upon a passage that may
seem to condemn the violent outburst of Isabella against her
brother:

> Oh, you beast!
> Oh faithless Coward, oh dishonest wretch!
> Wilt thou be made a man out of my vice?
> . . . .
> Die, perish. Might but my bending down
> Reprieve thee from thy fate, it should proceed.
> I'll pray a thousand prayers for thy death,
> No word to save thee.
>
> (3.1.137–39, 144–47)

Ye have heard that it was said by them of old time, Thou shalt not
kill; and whosoever shall kill shall be in danger of the judgment: But I
say unto you, That whosoever is angry with his brother without a cause
shall be in danger of the judgment: and whosoever shall say to his
brother, Raca, shall be in danger of the council: but whosoever shall
say, Thou fool, shall be in danger of hell fire. Therefore if thou bring
thy gift to the altar, and there rememberest that thy brother hath aught
against thee; Leave there thy gift before the altar, and go thy way;
first be reconciled to thy brother, and then come and offer thy gift.
(Matthew 5:21–24)

Isabella, of course, has some "cause" to be angry, but her violence
may seem to bring her "in danger of the judgment."

So from the beginning to the end of the play, the Sermon on the
Mount rings its changes, as Wilson Knight pointed out more than
sixty years ago. We need to read, or reread, his classic essay, for
although his tone is evangelical and his argument in places over-
stated (as in his treatment of the Duke's role), his view that the
Gospels are essential to interpretation of the play is still valid. And
more than the Sermon on the Mount is involved. Louise Schleiner,
in an essay of 1982, has pointed out the importance of certain
gospel parables for an understanding of the Duke's role in the play:

The Duke's decision to delegate his rule and disappear . . . has as
its primary model the parables of the synoptic gospels that state or
imply that a man planning a journey or absence called in servants and
gave them responsibilities. These are the parables of the wicked vine-

yard tenants (e.g., Matt. 21:33–43); the wicked steward (e.g., Matt. 24:45–51); the traveler and his doorkeeper (Mark 13:33–37); the master absent at a wedding (Luke 12:35–39); and the talents or pounds (e.g., Luke 19:11–27). A departing ruler or land owner gives responsibility to his servants, who will be called to an accounting on his return, for which they are to be constantly ready. The master's destination or motives abroad are of no importance; the servants are to be tested and later rewarded.[6]

With this analogy in mind one is, I think, bound to feel some elements of parable in *Measure for Measure.*

Yet the recent editors are right to insist that the play cannot be regarded in terms of any simple mode of didacticism; the full complexity of the play requires more complicated interpretation. The basic clue to such an interpretation lies in the play's clear division into two parts—an aspect of the play stressed by the Oxford editor, who gives a subtle and acute analysis (50–52) of the ways in which Shakespeare manages a transition into different styles at the crucial turning point of act 3 (1.153). Here the Duke intervenes at the peak of the emotional conflict between Isabella and her brother, introducing a prose style that is "mannered and artificial," "even faintly ritualistic." And this, as the Oxford editor goes on to note, "is only the first of several transitions in Act 3." After the Duke's courtly conversation with Isabella, we find "Enter Elbow, Clowne, Officers," at line 250, without any scene division. Modern editors usually introduce a new scene here (3.2), but the Oxford editor wisely allows act 3 to consist of only one long scene, displaying a "sequence of rapid modulations."

> The structure of the scene could be described as operatic: the Duke remains continuously present while two trios of characters—first Elbow, Pompey, and Lucio, then Escalus, the Provost, and Mistress Overdone—appear to him in turn. After each trio he has a verse-soliloquy of response. . . . There are considerable fluctuations of tone and style. . . . There is even a reversion, at lines 478–514, to the gnomic, formal style of the Duke's discussion with Isabella; for a brief while Escalus speaks in this manner, though he does not do so normally. . . . (51–52)

This long central act concludes with the Duke's choruslike soliloquy in gnomic tetrameter couplets, the only use of this form in the play. This is immediately followed by the only lyric moment

in the play, the song for Mariana, after which Mariana and the
Duke converse in formal couplets:

> Let me excuse me, and believe me so,
> My mirth it much displeased, but pleased my woe.
> 'Tis good; though music oft hath such a charm
> To make bad good and good provoke to harm.
>
> (4.1.12–15)

Shakespere's technique of transition here is strikingly similar to
the way in which he manages the transition from Greece to Bohemia in *The Winter's Tale,* where the Bohemian scene opens with
blank verse, then shifts to peasant prose, moves to the pentameter
couplets of the Chorus, and finally offers courtly prose. The result,
as I have argued elsewhere, is to create a drama in three parts, a
sort of trilogy in three different modes. (Others of course have
seen *The Winter's Tale* as a drama in two parts.) In much the same
way, the variations of style in the third act of *Measure for Measure*
mark a drastic shift in dramatic mode: from the action of full-
bodied characterization that we call "Shakespearean" to the much-
thinner action of didactic drama. The Duke's choric speech at the
close of act 3 explicitly signals the didactic mode, but of course
that mode has been implied earlier, at the very outset of this act,
in the Duke's didactic advice to Claudio: "Be absolute for death."
The act is thus encapsulated within two of the Duke's longest
speeches. This gnomic quality has been present throughout the
first half of the play, in moderation. Angelo recognizes the manner
when he asks Isabella: "Why do you put these sayings upon me?"
(2.2.134). Angelo himself sometimes uses the gnomic mode, as does
Escalus; the frivolous Lucio can also strike the tone: "Our doubts
are traitors / And make us lose the good we oft might win / By
fearing to attempt" (1.4.77–79). And even Pompey falls into the
vein: "Whip me? No, no, let Carman whip his Jade, / The valiant
heart's not shipped out of his trade" (2.1.218–19). But from the
middle of the third act the incidence of these "sayings" is enormously increased, especially in the Duke's versified epigrams scattered throughout the prose, high and low, of the third act, and
almost ludicrously evident in the six-line speech by the Duke
(4.1.56–61) with which Shakespeare covers the amount of time
supposedly required for Isabella to explain to Mariana the complicated device by which Angelo will be outwitted. It is as though
the dramatist were winking at the audience and saying: forget
about the realistic timing; the important thing is to swing the plot

forward into the mythical realm of the blended folk-tales upon which the play is based: the tale of the disguised ruler, the tale of the corrupt judge (the villainous bargain), and the tale of the substitute bedmate.

From the moment in the middle of act 3 when the Duke reveals to Isabella, in his courtly prose, that he knows all about the unjust action of Angelo against Mariana, his role changes from that of spectator to that of manipulator. He can no longer be regarded as a "character" in the normal Shakespearean mode: he becomes the agent of the plot in which the various characters are to be tested by the absent master on his return. He becomes now the manipulator of a morality play by which Shakespeare suggests the folly of attempting to cure the excesses of frail humanity by measures of extreme severity.

The atmosphere of the morality play is enhanced by the use of type-names for many of the characters: Angelo (meant ironically), Lucio ("light" in the sense of "frivolous"), Escalus (perhaps suggesting the scales of justice), Master Froth, Constable Elbow (not the arm, but the elbow of the law: "I do lean upon Justice" [2.1.46]). This effect is further developed for the reader by the Folio's consistent use of "Bawd" and "Clowne" in the stage directions and speech headings, instead of "Mistress Overdone" and "Pompey," as in most modern editions. These are unjustifiable emendations, I think, for they to some extent deflect the reader from the play's tendency to create types. For the viewer of the play on the stage, the "Bawd" is first called "Madame Mitigation" and later "Mistress Overdone"—"Overdone by the last" (2.1.173) of her nine husbands—another way of stressing the type, as "Mistress Kate Keepdown" identifies her type. As for "Clowne," the name gives the clue to his comic role as a low-life character since he is called "Thomas Tapster" by the "Bawd" but identified as "Pompey Bum" by himself. The Duke himself has no name in the text, only in the cast of characters at the end of the Folio printing: he is "Duke" as others are "Bawd" or "Clowne." This motif is brought to a head in the second part of the play with the long list of type-names set forth by Pompey in act 4 (3.1–16): young Master Rash, Master Caper, Master Threepile the mercer, young Dizie, Young Master Deepvow, Master Copperspur, Master Starvelackey, "young Dropheir that killed lusty Pudding," and so on. This list moves overtly into the mode of the morality play, a long announcement of the change in the basic action of the play that has been going on since the middle of act 3. But much earlier, in the comic interrogation of Elbow and Pompey by Escalus, a movement toward the personified abstractions of the morality play has been hinted by the amused and patient exclamation of Escalus, where the Folio typography stresses the abstraction by italics: "Which is the wiser here; *Iustice* or *Iniquitie*?" (2.1.148). And again, much later, Escalus makes a similar abstraction when he says of Angelo: "my brother Justice have I found so severe that he hath forced me to tell him he is indeed Justice" (3.1.508–9: Oxford; 3.2.215–17: Cambridge).

All these type-names and abstractions work together to universalize the setting, as in Shakespeare's pastoral of Bohemia. The setting is explicitly Vienna, as twice announced in the opening scene, but all the names are Italian, English, or Latin—a point almost comically brought out near the close, in preparation for the scene of the "trumpets" at the "gate," when we meet a sudden flurry of Latin names, with one incongruous "Rowland" in the midst:

> Go call at Flavius' house
> And tell him where I stay; give the like notice
> To Valencius, Rowland, and to Crassus,
> And bid them bring the Trumpets to the gate.
> But send me Flavius first.
>
> (4.5.6–9)

Then Varrius enters, his name twice repeated:

> I thank thee, Varrius, thou hast made good haste.
> Come, we will walk, there's other of our friends
> Will greet us here anon, my gentle Varrius.
>
> (4.5.11–13)

Are we in ancient Rome or modern Vienna? We are everywhere and nowhere, as with the seacoast of Bohemia, while the ceremony of testing and complete forgiveness is performed, in accordance with the Sermon on the Mount.

Measure for Measure, then, is a drama in two parts, the first half a vital drama in the full Shakespearean way, the second part a surprising excursion into the mode of the morality play, using folktales to produce the effect of parable. The two parts (or plays) are tightly woven together by the presence of the Duke, by the frequently gnomic manner, by the type-names, by the biblical motif of the master who tests his servants, and above all, by the Sermon on the Mount, which undergirds the drama from its title to the full revelation of that title's meaning in the final act. That revelation has been foreshadowed long before, in a much lower and cruder way, when Escalus asks Pompey whether being a bawd is a lawful trade (2.1.194–200):

Clo.   If the Law would allow it, sir.

Esc.   But the Law will not allow it, *Pompey*; nor it shall not be allowed in *Vienna*.

Clo.   Do's your Worship meane to geld and splay all the youth of the City?

Esc.   No, *Pompey*.

Clo.   Truely, Sir, in my poore opinion they will too't then. . . .

The Duke's foregiveness in the final scene suggests that he sees the truth of Pompey's opinion.

Notes

1. William Shakespeare, *Measure for Measure,* ed. Brian Gibbons, New Cambridge Shakespeare (Cambridge: Cambridge University Press, 1991); and idem, *Measure for Measure,* ed. N. W. Bawcutt, Oxford Shakespeare (Oxford: Clarendon Press, 1991). Editorial comments are cited parenthetically by page number.

2. In G. Wilson Knight's *Wheel of Fire* (London: Oxford University Press, 1930).

3. I recognize the erratic nature of capitalization in Elizabethan texts, and that the capitals may be the work of a printer or a scribe, but the persistent capitalization of key words in *Measure for Measure* seems to carry special significance.

4. Marvin Spevack, *A Complete and Systematic Concordance to the Works of Shakespeare,* 9 vols. (Hildesheim: George Olm, 1968–80).

5. In general I follow the modernized text of the recent Cambridge edition, but have restored capitalization wherever the Folio gives capitals.

6. Louise Schleiner, "Providential Improvisation in *Measure for Measure,*" *PMLA* 97 (1982): 227–28.

Second Chances: Milton's Eve and the Law

Jason P. Rosenblatt

THE beginning and end of John Milton's theological writings and the main doctrinal outlines of his great epic are marked by a Pauline absolutism that will not compound with human weakness as an inevitable condition lying within the bounds of divine forgiveness. His first published prose trace, *Of Reformation* (1641), begins by tracing the decline of the Church from the perfect pattern of Scripture clearly revealed, "backslid[ing] one way into the Jewish beggery, of old cast rudiments, and stumbl[ing] forward another way into the new-vomited Paganisme of sensuall Idolatry."[1] Milton's mission in his early antiprelatical tracts is to recover the pristine original of the gospel by removing layers of ecclesiastical accretion, to rebuild the Church according to that pattern stamped in religion's golden age, and to prepare for the Second Coming, "when thou the Eternall and shortly-expected King shalt open the Clouds to judge the severall Kingdomes of the World" (*YP*, 1:616). Those who assist that mission "shall receive, above the inferiour *Orders* of the *Blessed,* the *Regal* addition of *Principalities, Legions,* and *Thrones* in their glorious Titles, and in supereminence of *beatifick Vision* progressing the *datelesse* and *irrevoluble* Circle of *Eternity* shall clasp inseparable Hands with *joy,* and *blisse* in over measure for ever" (1:616). Those who attempt to thwart the mission "shall be thrown downe eternally into the *darkest* and *deepest Gulfe* of HELL, where . . . they shall remaine . . . for ever, the *basest,* the *lowermost,* the *most dejected,* most *underfoot* and *downe trodden Vassals* of *Perdition*" (1:617).

Although Milton in *De doctrina Christiana* (ca. 1658–ca. 1660) distributes rewards and punishments with less fiery zeal, his most radically Pauline chapters continue and even extend the ethos of the antiprelatical tracts. Preaching death to the Mosaic law and redemption in Christ, Milton maintains distinctions between regenerate Christians and other human beings (Jews and pagans). Where *Of Reformation* rejects the Jewish ceremonial law, *De doctrina* rejects the moral and judicial laws as well: "If you do no good unless you obey the law in every detail, and if it is absolutely impossible to obey it in every detail, then it is ridiculous to obey it at all" (*YP*, 6:531). Milton's rejection of the entire Mosaic law, including the decalogue, and his insistence on salvation by death to the world in Christ presuppose profound and unforgivable human weakness. Any attempt to achieve salvation unmediated by Christ's own act of self-annihilation is both futile and perversely opposed to the divine redemptive mission. If anyone wants to keep the Mosaic law in any sense whatsoever, for that person Christ died in vain (Gal. 2:21; *YP*, 6:488).

The Hebraic polity of paradise in Milton's great epic is in some ways antithetical to Pauline soteriology. Existing before and apart from the New Testament, our sinless first parents need no mediatorial prophet, priest, and king because they are themselves good, holy, and just. But even Milton's paradise before the Fall exploits Paul's view of the law as a single indissoluble entity. Adam and Eve keep the entire law by obeying the terms of a single prohibition described as a benign, proto-Mosaic law. When they transgress, the white light of the prohibition breaks up into countless refractive prohibitions of every color, a spectrum of offenses, and they become "manifold in sin."[2] There is no point in keeping sinful Adam and Eve under the dominion of a law that they violated in their perfect state, especially since sin has already proliferated uncontrollably and since their ability to perform "good works" (*PL*, 9.234) has obviously become impaired. Both God the Father and his Son describe them as bankrupt, "Indebted and undone" (3.235). Human helplessness causes law to yield to gospel. The Son in his role as priestly mediator, figuring forth his ultimate priestly sacrifice of self-obliteration, pleads with the Father: "all [humankind's] works on mee / Good or not good ingraft, my Merit those / Shall perfet, and for these my Death shall pay" (ll. 34–36). To live transplanted in Christ is to obliterate one's identity as a human being with even the smallest capacity for unmediated achievement. Any apparent good on humankind's part consists entirely of God's "motions in him; longer than they move, / His heart I know, how variable and vain / Self-left" (ll. 91–93).

In reading Milton's prose chronologically, there is no way to prepare for the differences between the last antiprelatical tract (April 1642) and the first divorce tract (July 1643). Scholars and biographers have found in *Doctrine and Discipline of Divorce* traces of the bitter disappointment most likely caused by young Mary Powell's refusal to leave her family and rejoin her new husband. Far more profound, though less immediately noticeable than the occasional bitter tone, are transformations in Milton's theology, philosophy, and politics, and in his attitude toward human weakness. In the great prose tracts of 1643–45—including the four treatises on divorce, *Of Education,* and the *Areopagitica*—a Pauline absolutist confronts with compassion a life of mistake and the inseparability of good and evil in this imperfect world. If Milton's prose provides the doctrinal underpinnings of his greatest poetry, then his first marriage and separation constitute a major correlative of the Fall: like the prohibition, marriage is a "mysterious Law" (4.750) instituted in paradise (Gen. 2:18), whose subjects find it at first easy to keep, then discover tragically that it has become impossible.

Missing from these tracts are the essential tenets of Christian liberty, death to the law, and redemption in Christ. Milton argues instead, against the "common expositors" of the Pauline renaissance, that divorce is a permanent moral and judicial Mosaic law and not a temporary dispensation based on the Jews' hardheartedness (*YP,* 2:285, 354). Most interpreters of the New Testament hold that on one occasion only Jesus dissociated himself directly from a regulation of the Torah: when, in defiance of pharisaic interrogation, he rejected explicitly and categorically the Deuteronomic right of divorce (compare Deut. 24:1–2 and Matt. 19:3–9). But in the divorce tracts Milton forces Christ's words into compliance with that Deuteronomic right and thus becomes in effect a defender of the entire Mosaic law. Of the relation between Christ's words and the Mosaic law, Milton reverses the motion of typology by insisting, "If we examine over all [Christ's] sayings, we shall find him not so much interpreting the Law with his words, as referring his owne words to be interpreted by the Law" (*YP,* 2:301).

The Christ of the divorce tracts is not a redeemer but a charitable interpreter who ratified the moral law of Moses and who "never gave a judicial law" (*YP,* 2:334). On the issue of divorce, the law is clear and charitable, the gospel obscure, apparently severe ("What . . . God hath joined together, let not man put asunder" [Matt. 19:6]), and therefore in need of radical reinterpretation. In the *Areopagitica* (1644), "a good Book is the pretious life-blood of a master spirit, imbalm'd and treasur'd up on purpose to a life beyond life" (*YP,* 2:493) and the New Testament is the good book that contains the essence of Christ, the master spirit whose lifeblood was spilled on the cross and whom Joseph of Arimathea entombed with myrrh and aloes. Jesus is portrayed in this tract as a victim whose sad followers perform acts of charity to keep his memory alive. Although Truth herself is only his servant, few can read of her "mangl'd body" (549) and of "our obsequies to the torn body of our martyr'd Saint" (550) without recalling the crucifixion.

Milton's famous definition of the purpose of education, which his editors have referred to Platonic, New Testament, and Reformation sources, is also Hebraic:

> The end then of learning is to repair the ruins of our first parents by regaining to know God aright, and out of that knowledge to love him, to imitate him, to be like him, as we may the neerest by possessing our souls of true vertue, which being united to the heavenly grace of faith makes up the highest perfection. (*Of Education* [1644], *YP*, 2:366–67)

Like the primal covenant in paradise between humankind and God, requiring a "Pledge of thy Obedience and thy Faith" (*PL*, 8:325), *imitatio Dei* requires both the "true vertue" of human beings responsible for their own actions and "the heavenly grace of faith." Virtue and faith, joined in the Torah, were first torn asunder by Paul, who created in Galatians 3 a contradiction between Deuteronomy 27:26 (the imperative of performing the law) and Habakkuk 2:4 (the imperative of faith). For the converted Paul, faith based on spiritual absorption into the risen Christ replaced observance of Torah, thus removing "true vertue" as a possibility for humankind. This entirely new duality is repeated in Romans 10, when Paul contrasts the righteousness of Torah (Lev. 18:5) with the righteousness of faith (Deut. 30:12–14), thus setting up a contradiction that would never have occurred to a believing Jew, for whom both passages would have applied to Torah as revealed on Mount Sinai. In *Of Education,* as in Miltons' paradise, obedience to two or more kinds of righteousness are set alongside each other, not, as they will be after the Fall and in the Pauline chapters of *De doctrina,* played off against each other.

Where *Of Reformation* and the Pauline chapters of *De doctrina* segregate pagans or Jews from Christians, nature or law from gospel, Old Testament from New, the monist spirit of the 1643–45 tracts emphasizes congruity and inclusiveness. Urging Parliament to make the Mosaic law of divorce part of English civil law, these tracts shade into Erastianism. They treat as compatible the natural rights of all human beings as reasonable creatures, the rights of biblical Israel as members of a holy community, and the individual privilege of the regenerate Christian saint. The higher includes the lower without any sort of turning away or disparagement and without the surrender of individuality. Regarding the relationship among pagans, Jews, and Christians, Milton emphasizes the gospel's perfect correspondence with Mosaic law "grounded on [the] morall reason" of natural law (*YP*, 2:264). In these tracts, as in paradise before the Fall, "God and Nature bid the same" (*PL*, 6.176), and Milton speaks of "the fundamentall law book of nature; which *Moses* never thwarts but reverences" (*YP*, 2:272):

> mariage, unlesse it mean a fit and tolerable mariage, is not inseparable neither by nature nor institution. Not my nature[,] for then those Mosaick divorces had bin against nature, if separable and inseparable be contraries, as who doubts they be: and what is against nature is against Law, if soundest Philosophy abuse us not: by this reckning *Moses* should be most unmosaick, that is, most illegal, not to say most unnaturall. Nor is it inseparable by the first institution: for then no second institution in the same Law for so many causes could dissolve it: it being most unworthy a human (as *Plato*'s judgement is in the fourth book of his Lawes) much more a divine Law-giver to write two several decrees upon the same thing. (309–10)

The Mosaic law must always be in accord with nature; and Moses the author-lawgiver, in "the same Law" of Genesis and Deuteronomy, has instituted both marriage and divorce as laws in harmony with each other. Although the institution of marriage in paradise (Gen. 1:27, 2:18, 23–24) is part of the primary law of Moses, and the Deuteronomic "second institution," divorce, is part of the secondary law of Moses, edifying footpaths connect the laws of paradise and the fallen world, which are part of "the same Law" and the same Pentateuchal text. (Although *deuteronomy* means "second law" and Milton's central Pentateuchal texts are often Deuteronomic, Milton seems to mean by secondary law the entire Torah except for the slender prelapsarian chapters of Genesis.)

In *Tetrachordon* (1645), Milton maintains that in our fallen world the "second institution" of divorce, part of the secondary law of Moses, is actually more compassionate than marriage, part of the primary law that originates in paradise. Moreover, he associates Christianity with the mistaken belief that we can recover the perfection of the primary law. He cannot accept the plain sense of Matthew 19:8, Christ's abolition of divorce and establishment of permanent marriage modeled upon that of Adam and Eve "in the beginning":

> In the beginning, had men continu'd perfet, it had bin just that all things should have remain'd, as they began to *Adam & Eve*. But after that the sons of men grew violent and injurious, it alter'd the lore of

justice, and put the government of things into a new frame. While man and woman were both perfet to each other, there needed no divorce; but when they both degenerated to imperfection, & oft times grew to be an intolerable evil each to other, then law *more justly* [emphasis added] did permit the alienating of that evil which mistake made proper, then it did the appropriating of that good which Nature at first made common. For if the absence of outward good be not so bad as the presence of a close evil, & that propriety, whether by cov'nant or possession, be but the attainment of some outward good, it is more natural & righteous that the law should sever us from an intimat evil, then appropriate any outward good to us from the community of nature. The Gospel indeed tending ever to that which is perfetest, aim'd at the restoration of all things, as they were in the beginning. And therefore all things were in common to those primitive Christians in the Acts, which *Ananias & Sapphira* dearly felt. . . . But who will be the man shall introduce this kind of common wealth, as christianity now goes? (*YP,* 2:665–66)

Milton distinguishes between the primary Mosaic law of marriage and the secondary Mosaic law of divorce. The Mosaic law as promulgated in Genesis, transcending natural law, permits "the appropriating of that good which Nature at first made common." The Edenic law of marriage is founded on the privilege and exclusivity of private property ("sole propriety") in a world where all else is held in common. Misuse of the primary law, with its requirement of perfection from Eden's perfect inhabitants, caused a change in human nature, and it then became impossible to fulfill it. Milton clearly regards both Genesis and Deuteronomy as part of the same law, but the law that eventually governs the Edenic books of *Paradise Lost* interests him less in this excerpt than the Deuteronomic divorce law, accommodated to fallen human nature, which "more justly did permit the alienating of that evil which mistake made proper." If marriage is a Mosaic law of possession superseding the wholly communal relationships of natural law, then the secondary Mosaic law of divorce is founded on the relinquishing of proprietorship for the sake of common household peace. In a sense, the secondary law of divorce returns from privilege to the wholly communal relationships of nature.

To demand perfection under either the primary Mosaic law of Genesis or the gospel is to condemn imperfect human beings to death: even Adam and Eve fell, and they were perfect. Ananias and Sapphira, good and bad like all of us, donating some of their profit and holding back some, fell down dead (Acts 5:1–10). The primary law, once benign, applies standards impossible for ordinary human beings to maintain. "If then mariage must be as in the beginning, the persons that marry must be such as then were, the institution must make good, in som tolerable sort, what it promises to either party. If not, it is but madnes to drag this one ordinance back to the beginning" (666). Concessions to weakness were unnecessary in paradise, and the perfection required was absolute. But in the fallen world, the secondary law of Moses is more natural, righteous, and just.

Milton's exposition of a Mosaic law for fallen humankind comprises some of his most mature and passionate prose. We hear in other Miltonic treatises the accent of judgment in relation to frail, erring humanity, but in the prose tracts of 1643–45 we hear the accent of sympathy as well. Where Christ rejects divorce for the Jews as a temporary concession to *"the hardnesse of your hearts"* (Matt. 19:8, *YP,* 2:660), Milton interprets hardheartedness as a universal condition: "when it is in a good man taken for infirmity and imperfection, which was in all the Apostles, whose weaknesse only, not utter want of beleef is call'd hardnes of heart" (661). The Fall hardens all hearts, not only among the Jews, and therefore God permitted divorce "partly for this hardnesse of heart, the imperfection and decay of man from original righteousnesse" (661). "If nothing now must be suffer'd for hardnes of heart, I say the very prosecution of our right by way of civil justice can no more bee suffer'd among Christians, for the hardnes of heart wherwith most men persue it. . . . But if it be plaine that the whole juridical law and civil power is only suffer'd under the Gospel, for the hardnes of our hearts, then wherefore should not that which *Moses* suffer'd, be suffer'd still by the same reason" (662).

Whereas the antiprelatical tracts apotheosize the spiritual aristocrats of the Reformation and anathematize the bishops and their supporters, the treatises on divorce, more than any other Miltonic works, emphasize commonality. In these tracts, Milton regards Christians as superior in faith but not in virtue: "Wee find . . . by experience that the Spirit of God in the Gospel hath been alwaies more effectual in the illumination of our minds to the gift of faith, then in the moving of our wills to any excellence of vertue, either above the *Jews* or the Heathen" (303). Christians unhappily matched should not presume upon the superior refinement of patience and suffering but should instead accept the relief divorce affords them: "If wee bee wors [than the Jews], or but as bad, which lamentable examples confirm wee are, then have wee more, or at least as much need of this permitted law, as they to whom God therfore gave it under a harsher covenant" (354).

The ethos of a secondary Mosaic law, more humane in its contemporary application to fallen humankind than the perfect primary Mosaic law of prelapsarian paradise, extends into other Miltonic tracts that emphasize the need for second chances. In the divorce tracts, God is not the stern judge who demands the sacrifice of earthly pleasures, but a force of mercy who offers us, through divine law, the freedom from misery that custom in the form of canon law would prevent us from exercising (222–27). This view of the world as imperfect but improvable carries over into the *Areopagitica,* where parliamentary legislation takes the place of the Mosaic law: "For this is not the liberty which wee can hope, that no grievance ever should arise in the Commonwealth, that let no man in this World expect; but when complaints are freely heard, deeply consider'd, and speedily reform'd, then is the utmost bound of civill liberty attain'd, that wise men look for" (487).

People can repent of their choice of ruler, just as they can repent of their choice of mate, and Milton uses the state as a model for the family: "He who marries, intends as little to conspire his own ruine, as he that swears Allegiance: and as a whole people is in proportion to an ill Government, so is one man to an mariage" (229). Later, in 1650, Milton will underscore the Hebraic ethos of a political tract, *The Tenure of Kings and Magistrates,* by citing as a central text the secondary Mosaic law limiting royal prerogative: "the Law of *Moses* was to the King expresly, *Deut.* 17. not to think so highly of himself above his Brethren" (*YP,* 3:205). In these tracts, treating as choice what others before him had treated as necessity, Milton exhorts radical change for the improvement of the human condition and thus asserts faith in human beings as agents capable in some measure of controlling their lives. The secondary Mosaic laws permitting divorce and limiting the king's privileges are a gift from a benign God who pities our misery and wants us to achieve happiness. The theology of the divorce tracts bears upon Milton's paradise in his great epic, which combines the primary Mosaic law (Gen. 1–3) with some aspects of the postlapsarian secondary Mosaic law, as when Adam and Eve enter directly into covenant with God, work hard, make mistakes, and know pain.

I should now like to concentrate not on the considerable influence of the secondary Mosaic law on Milton's poetry and prose, but rather on the suppression of that law both within contemporary Milton scholarship and within *Paradise Lost.* When Milton, writing on divorce in one of the non-Pauline chapters of *De doctrina,* refers to "numerous rabbinical texts ("multis Rabbinorum testimoniis"), the translator, Sumner, elides the phrase's central term so that it becomes only "numerous testimonies."[3] The fate of the Mosaic law of divorce, at which Milton repines ("an ancient and most necessary, most charitable, and yet most injur'd statute of *Moses* . . . thrown aide with much inconsiderat neglect" [224]), is also the fate of the secondary Mosaic law in contemporary scholarship. The 1643–45 tracts appeal to the harmonies within natural law, the Mosaic law, and the gospel. Arthur Barker, whose *Milton and the Puritan Dilemma* remains the most influential book ever written on Milton's prose,[4] consistently elides the central term. Although his book indexes eleven different sorts of law, neither he nor anyone else writing on Milton's prose ever mentions a secondary Mosaic law. When the Mosaic law occupies a positive central position in Milton's works, as it does in the divorce tracts, Barker dissolves it, assimilating it to what he calls "the secondary law of nature," a term with a very different meaning for Milton.[5] Barker looks at the 1643–45 tracts through the distorting lens of Milton's radically Pauline chapters in *De doctrina*. He identifies the Mosaic law with repressive ecclesiastical and civil authorities and sets against it a universal natural law and a gospel preaching freedom for the regenerate. Attempting to graft a democratic conception of natural liberty upon Milton's exclusivist Pauline conception of Christian liberty, Barker would create a single entity of nature and grace, all of humankind and the regenerate. Barker wants to associate Milton with "the extreme Puritan revolutionaries."[6] But there is no place at all for nature in the Pauline chapters of *De doctrina*, which presuppose distinctions between nature and grace and between Christians and other human beings.

Commenting on the long passage from *Tetrachordon* (665–66), cited above, that finds the secondary Mosaic law more just in a fallen world than either the gospel or the law of paradise, Barker concludes:

> The law of fallen human nature is clearly an impossible foundation for Christian liberty. . . . [T]hat law is incompatible with the Gospel, which tends to restore things to their original perfection. Moreover, it can hardly be by this imperfect law that we are to interpret Christ's statement [on divorce]. . . . It is therefore with the primary not the secondary law of nature that the Gospel accords. . . .[7]

Except for the fact that Milton does indeed interpret Christ's statement on divorce by the light of the Deuteronomic permission, there is nothing wrong with any of Barker's assertions taken separately. Barker simply cannot imagine the possibility that Milton might ever actually prefer the secondary Mosaic law, which Barker can only designate here as the "law of fallen human nature." Milton asserts that it is better to be single than to be unhappily married, and that after the Fall the Mosaic law of divorce may be accommodated "more justly" to human nature than marriage instituted in paradise and made inescapable in the gospels: "If any therefore demand, which is now most perfection, to ease an extremity by divorce, or to enrage and fester it by the greevous observance of a miserable wedloc, I am not destitute to say which is most perfection" (666). Milton presents Deuteronomy as a second law, not merely summarizing but altering, from a more humane and compromising position, moral, ritual, and judicial laws previously set down in the Pentateuch. Of course, Milton's selective view of a humane secondary law requires that one avert one's gaze from apparent cruelties in the Mosaic law, just as his heterodox conception of Christian liberty requires a gaze averted from the potential cruelties of antinomianism and from the doctrine's classic, Lutheran formulation, in which it coexists with repressive regimes. The common ground between law and gospel *as interpreted by Milton* is freedom from institutional coercion.

Barker, recognizing that the "law of fallen human nature is clearly an impossible foundation for Christian liberty," interprets it as second best, "imperfect," especially when compared with the Pauline "liberty which is Milton's real concern."[8] Certainly the secondary law of Moses has no assigned place in the doctrine of the last books of *Paradise Lost*. There is in paradise a perfect primary law of Moses, often mixed with the secondary law—hence the coexistence of innocence and experience in Milton's Eden. After the Fall, the law is devalued in Pauline terms as a minister of death and condemnation, impossible to keep, and the postlapsarian books of the epic replace poetry with doctrine and law with gospel, preaching nothing but Christ crucified (1 Cor. 1:23). By replacing the Mosaic law of paradise with Christian liberty, the last books of the epic assert discontinuity rather than continuity between dispensations. Fallen Adam, sometimes with the help of the angel Michael, frequently reinterprets the literal judgment on the serpent (Gen. 3:15) as an evangelical promise of Christ (10.1028–36; ll. 153–58; 12.233–35, 383–896). But when he projects marital disaster that will afflict his progeny ("He never shall find out fit Mate, but such / As some misfortune brings him, or mistake" [10.899–900]), there is no hint that the secondary law will one day provide succor.

Although the Miltonic bard excludes the Pauline scheme of redemption from paradise, he includes Paul's pronouncements on the subordination of women (1 Cor. 11:3–9 and *PL,* 4.299–308; 1 Cor. 14:35, 1 Tim. 2:11–12, and *PL,* 8.48–56). This makes paradise, even in a state of perfection, less perfect for Eve than it was for Adam. Worried about whether she can keep up, she will take no pleasure from unearned leisure (9.225). After the Fall, in subtle counterpoint to the surgings of doctrinal piety, Eve occasionally records the muffled vibrations of the secondary Mosaic law that accommodates legal imperatives to the postlapsarian human condition. This law of fallen human nature, found only in the interstices of the epic's Christian doctrine, offers the prospect of continuing life without Christ's sacrificial redemption. Compassion for fallen Adam, "afflicted" (10.863), prompts Eve to apply "Soft words to his fierce passion" (865). Her primary concern is neither salvation nor the kingdom of heaven but common household peace, however brief: "While yet we live, scarce one short hour perhaps, / Between us two let there be peace" (10.923–24). Adam understands, as Eve cannot, that there can be no peace without Christ (10.1028–38), and he overcomes her poetry with his doctrine. Later Eve will accept sleeplessness, sweat, and nature's indifference. Her one request applies literally to the garden but also perhaps to the law of ultimate human sufficiency: "Here let us live, though in fall'n state, content" (180). And of course no one—God the Father or the Son, fate, the angel Michael, Adam—listens to her: "So spake, so wish'd much humbl'd *Eve,* but Fate / Subscrib'd not" (ll. 181–82).

In both *The Doctrine and Discipline of Divorce* and the *Areopagitica,* Milton singles out for praise "the chief of learned men reputed in this Land, Mr. [John] *Selden*" (*YP,* 2:350, 513). Selden, the major source of Milton's rabbinic learning, translated at length Talmudic and midrashic accounts of postlapsarian Adam's righteousness.

Adam, the first man, was greatly virtuous ("Adam, primus homo, valde erat pius"). When he saw that through him death was ordained as a punishment, he spent a hundred and thirty years in fasting, severed connections with his wife for a hundred and thirty years ("ab uxore item separatus fuerit annos 130"), and wore clothes of fig leaves on his body for a hundred and thirty years.[9]

Adam spoke in the presence of God: Lord of all worlds! I beseech you to remove my sin from me and accept my repentance, so that all the generations to come will learn that there is such a thing as repentance and that you support penitents who return to you. Then God put forth his right hand, and removed his sin from him, and accepted his repentance. "I acknowledged my sin unto thee, and mine iniquity I have not hid" [Ps. 32:5].[10]

Michael Drayton, whose *Poly-Olbion* John Selden annotated and young Milton imitated in his *At a Vacation Exercise,* describes "Moses, his Birth and Miracles" in *The Muses Elizium.* Jochebed, the future mother of Moses, proposes to her husband, Amram, that they abstain from sexual relations to prevent the conception of children doomed by Pharaoh's decree to death by drowning:

> Though her chast bosome that faire Altar were,
> Where Loves pure vowes he dutifully pay'd,
> His Armes to her a Sanctuary deare,
> Yet they so much his tyranny obay'd,
> By free consent to separate their bed,
> Better at all no Children yet to have,
> Then their dear love should procreate the dead,
> Untimely issue for a timelesse grave.[11]

Fallen Eve in *Paradise Lost,* echoing the Talmud's Adam a well as Drayton's Jochebed, proposes to atone without a mediator for her sin and Adam's and to defeat death by sexual abstinence. She tells Adam:

> both have sinn'd, but thou
> Against God only, I against God and thee,
> And to the place of judgment will return,
> There with my cries importune Heav'n, that all
> The sentence from thy head remov'd may light
> On me, sole cause to thee of all this woe,
> Mee mee only just object of his ire.
>
> (10.930–36)

> If care of our descent perplex us most,
> Which must be born to certain woe, devour'd
> By Death at last, and miserable it is
> To be to others cause of misery,
> Our own begott'n, and of our Loins to bring
> Into this cursed World a woeful Race,
> That after wretched Life must be at last
> Food for so foul a Monster, in thy power
> It lies, yet ere Conception to prevent
> The Race unblest, to being yet unbegot.
> Childless thou art, Childless remain: So Death

Shall be deciv'd his glut, and with us two
Be forc'd to satisfy his Rav'nous Maw.

(10.979–91)

Adam rejects decisively both of Eve's suggestions. There is no trace of Milton's Arminianism in the final books of his great epic. Salvation is the result not of free human choice but of Christ's atonement. The prayers of our first parents would never have reached heaven if the Son, in his role as priestly intercessor, had not presented them in his golden censer, mixed with incense (ll. 14–44). A Hebraic conception of merely human atonement capable of moving God to extend his hand, remove sin, and accept repentance is alien to the final books of *Paradise Lost*.

And yet Eve—rebuked, corrected, patronized—achieves a privilege kept from Adam. The radically Pauline theology of the last books systematically devalues Adam. The angel Michael strips him of the privilege of genetic transmission as father of the human race: his sin transmits only death (Rom. 5:14, 1 Cor. 15:22), and the distinction between the children of loins and of faith (*PL*, 12.446–50; Rom. 9:6–8) makes believing Christians the children of Abraham's seed and sinners the progeny of Adam. Adam, like the Jews, is of the devil's seed (*PL*, 12.394–95; John 8:44), and his progeny, in turn, are the evildoers of every generation, like those who perished in Noah's flood ("all thy offspring" [ll. 755]). Typology, with its tendency toward generalization and de-individualization, requires Adam to remove the tokens of his identity in order to be saved. The old Adam must be fully absorbed in the second Adam, just as the Church requires the absorption of Judaism in Christianity, the second Israel. But as the angel Michael frequently insists, the redeemer is of the woman's weed. Eve never wholly relinquishes her identity or the privilege of genetic transmission. In the very last words exchanged between our first parents, she proclaims the continuity of her love for her husband and the supreme value of their life together. Poetically, though not doctrinally, Adam the unworthy becomes worthy, not through a complex system of mediation that requires his own loss of identity and his redeemer's crucifixion, but simply and immediately through the transforming power of Eve's love for him. Eve, far from living transplanted in Christ, brings the redeemer into the world, his mother just as she is ours: "By mee the Promis'd Seed shall all restore" (12.623). Taking Adam's hand to leave the garden, she may find consolation for exile in the renewal of desire. Adam, indoctrinated, knows that he is happier than he feels. Eve never completely surrenders Hebraic poetry to Pauline doctrine.

Notes

1. *The Complete Prose Works of John Milton,* gen. ed. Don M. Wolfe (New Haven: Yale University Press, 1953–82), 1:520. Parenthetic volume and page references to Milton's prose are to this Yale edition, cited hereafter as *YP.*

2. *Paradise Lost,* 10.15, in *John Milton: Complete Poems and Major Prose,* ed. Merritt Y. Hughes (New York: Odyssey, 1957), 424. All further references to Milton's poetry will be to this edition and will be included in parentheses in the text.

3. *De doctrina Christiana,* in *The Works of John Milton,* gen. ed. Frank Allen Patterson (New York: Columbia University Press, 1931–38), 15:171.

4. See, for example, the long introductory note to 1:xxvii of *De doctrina* in the Yale edition, whose editors follow Barker in tracing Milton's doctrine of Christian liberty to the divorce tracts (*YP,* 6:521–22, n. 1). Those are precisely the tracts that assert the contemporary applicability of the Mosaic statute on divorce.

5. Milton refers in *Tetrachordon* to "that which by Civilians [i.e., authorities on civil law] is term'd the *secondary law of nature and of nations*" (2:661), associating it not with moral law but rather with "juridical law and civil power" (662). John Selden was Milton's principal civilian, whose *De Jure Naturali et Gentium* (London, 1640) identifies the primary, universal natural law with the seven Noachide commandments found in the Talmud and Maimonides. Although Barker and other scholars have noted Selden's influence on Milton, none has mentioned that the works in question are thoroughly rabbinical.

6. Arthur E. Barker, *Milton and the Puritan Dilemma 1641–1660* (Toronto: University of Toronto Press, 1942), 324.

7. Ibid., 116.

8. Ibid., 117.

9. John Selden, *De Synedriis* [1650], in *Opera Omnia,* ed. David Wilkins (London, 1726), I, ii, col. 1025. Selden quotes tractate *Erubin* 18b, as well as additional midrashic accounts of tribulations undergone by a penitent Adam.

10. Ibid., col. 1025. Selden cites "Pirki R. Eliaezer cap. 20. unde R. Abraham Zacuth in *Juchasin.* fol. 5.a": "Dixit Adam coram Deo . . . Domine universi mundi, transeat, quaeso, peccatum meum a me, & recipe poenitentiam meam, ut discant omnes aetates (tota posteritas) quod sit resipiscentia, & quod suscipias tu resipiscentiam convertentium se. Tunc autem Deus extendit dexteram suam, atque removit ab illo peccatum ejus, & recepit conversionem ejus . . . peccatum meum tibi notum feci, & iniquitatem meam te non celavi. . . ."

11. Michael Drayton, *The Muses Elizium* (London, 1630), 124.

Rhymes and Reasons

EDWARD R. WEISMILLER

In 1668, the year after *Paradise Lost* was first published, a second issue of the poem appeared, enlarged by several pages of introductory material. Most of these pages are taken up with a series of Arguments—that is, concise prose summaries of the poem's ten books. But the Arguments were prefaced, and followed, by two statements of more than passing interest. The first was headed "The Printer to the Reader," and was signed "S. [for Samuel] Simmons":

> *Courteous Reader,* There was no Argument at first intended to the Book, but for the satisfaction of many that have desired it, I have procured it, and withal a reason of that which stumbled many others, why the Poem Rimes not.[1]

Dear Samuel Simmons. One likes to think of delegations—nay, hordes—of readers waiting upon him, their approach halting, to body forth the stumbling of their wits, their purpose unswerving nonetheless, and Simmons like a good father procuring for them what in such numbers they desired. But if a kind of contented benignity informs the words of Mr. Simmons, the same cannot be said for the words he "procured" from John Milton, the words articulating the "reason . . . why the Poem Rimes not." Even today, reading Milton's statement on "The Verse" of *Paradise Lost* is a little like getting a wasp by the tail:

> The measure is *English* Heroic Verse without Rime, as that of *Homer* in *Greek,* and of *Virgil* in *Latin;* Rime being no necessary Adjunct or true Ornament of Poem or good Verse, in longer Works especially, but the Invention of a barbarous Age, to set off wretched matter and lame Meter; grac't indeed since by the use of some famous modern Poets, carried away by Custom, but much to thir own vexation, hindrance, and constraint to express many things otherwise, and for the most part worse than else they would have exprest them. Not without cause therefore some both *Italian* and *Spanish* Poets of prime note have

236

rejected Rime both in longer and shorter Works, as have also long since our best *English* Tragedies, as a thing of itself, to all judicious ears, trivial and of no true musical delight; which consists only in apt Numbers, fit quantity of Syllables, and the sense variously drawn out from one Verse into another, not in the jingling sound of like endings, a fault avoided by the learned Ancients both in Poetry and all good Oratory. This neglect then of Rime so little is to be taken for a defect, though it may seem so perhaps to vulgar Readers, that it rather is to be esteem'd an example set, the first in *English,* of ancient liberty recover'd to Heroic Poem from the troublesome and modern bondage of Riming.

No one who knows the course my own studies have taken will doubt for a moment my admiration of *Paradise Lost,* and therefore of its writer; yet the tone of this statement has always astonished and troubled me. If Milton had simply had the gout when he wrote it, surely he would have softened its wording in some subsequent reprinting or reedition of the poem. Since he did not, must we for our part be so mean-spirited as to suspect that Milton was simply no good at rhyme, and that in abandoning it he was trying to claim an austere grandeur of virtue incommensurate with the desert of the mere prudence which had in fact prompted his decision? Pressed to adduce evidence—evidence, at least, that Milton's natural abilities did not extend to the writing of graceful rhyme—we might quote *Samson Agonistes* 1519–20, a nerveless couplet displaying the only rhyme in dozens of lines, in which Samson's father, Manoa, hearing at a distance the collapse of the Temple of Dagon upon the heads of the Philistines, and the "universal groan / As if the whole inhabitation perish'd," says,

> Some dismal accident it needs must be;
> What shall we do, stay here or run and see?

Well, you may say, if the temple collapses, why not Manoa? And it is a generous thought, which I cannot but commend. Still I hope to convince you before I have done that Milton was in fact a genius at rhyming, though capable no doubt of the occasional foolishness; and so I must try to find some other way out of the dilemma. We shall not resolve the problem wholly, since if Milton has the skill I say he has, he is clearly speaking contemptuously in his statement on "The Verse" of a device, a technique, a form he could scarcely have failed to understand profoundly and to admire. But if we cannot clear up the mystery altogether, we can perhaps introduce some ray of light into its dark recesses.

As they are phrased, Milton's remarks on the absence of rhyme from *Paradise Lost* constitute, as it were, an explanation to those who ought not to have had to ask, and a reprimand to "vulgar Readers." But who are the vulgar? The uninitiated, of course; the uneducated—or those who, having had, at one time, access to the Truth, have slackly let it go. And what is the Truth? Suddenly a door into the English past yawns open, and we go back through it to a time forty years before Milton's birth, and to the beginning of a controversy over what form English verse, just then recommencing to be written, ought to take. When Roger Asham wrote *The Scholemaster*[2]—even when that work was published, posthumously, in 1570—no major poet had appeared to shape the English of the time into art; the triumphs of Spenser, of Sidney, of Marlowe, of Shakespeare, and of the other great Elizabethans were in the future still, if not far in the future. Wyatt and Surrey had done what they could, and there were other names, other practitioners. But where was greatness? Had it not failed to come, perhaps, because of the inadequacies of the *form* of English verse?

Centuries before, the poets of Rome, dissatisfied with the clumsiness, the rudimentary nature of the verse forms that had thus far evolved naturally in Latin, had imported into their language and superimposed upon it the quantitative measures of the earlier, and undeniably brilliant, poetry of Greece: and soon enough a golden age had arrived, the Augustan Age of Latin poetry. Dissatisfied with the inadequacies of English sixteenth-century verse, could not English poets undertake a comparable task, and with equal hope?

Educated poets they would have to be, for the rules of quantitative verse (which depended on a complex patterning of durations conventionally ascribed, syllables judged to be long in intricate combination with others judged to be short—those rules were elaborate and difficult to learn. English schoolboys learned them by rote as they applied to Latin verse; it would take an advanced learning to apply them to an English poetry that might be worth being called poetry.

What, on the other hand, was the alternative? An unballasted verse, the lines of which seemed to have no meter at all, only movement. "Rhythms" they might be called—no better. And so ill were these lines made, so lightly and unevenly were they worked, that rhyme had been pressed upon them only to give them a little more shape and identity—if nothing else, to mark their endings, which might otherwise go unrecognized. In the classical poetries of Greece and Rome, in which every syllable of every line was carefully disposed and patterned, rhyme had been unnecessary;

indeed, it had been thought excessive, a blemish. That it was needed in a less-accomplished verse was no great argument in its favor. Only "rhymes" had need of rhyme; any verse that rhymed was overwhelmingly likely to be a mere "rhythm." So indissolubly linked were the two concepts, we are told, that the words for "rhythm" and "rhyme" are etymologically the same word—barely differentiated decedents of the Greek *rithmos*.

"As *Virgil* and *Horace* were not wedded to follow the faultes of former fathers," Ascham says in *The Scholemaster*, ". . . but by right *Imitation* of the perfit Grecians had brought Poetrie to perfitnesse also in the Latin tong, [it might be wished]

that we Englishmen likewise would acknowledge and understand rightfully our rude beggerly ryming, brought first into Italie by *Gothes* and *Hunnes,* when all good verses and all good learning to were destroyed by them, and after caryed into France and Germanie, and at last receyved into England by men of excellent wit in deede, but of small learning and lesse judgement in that behalfe.

But now, when men know the difference, and have the examples, both of the best and of the worst, surelie to follow rather the *Gothes* in Ryming than the *Greekes* in trew versifying were even to eate ackornes with swyne, when we may freely eate wheate bread emonges men. In deede, *Chauser, Th. Norton* of Bristow, my L. of Surrey, *M. Wiat, Th. Phaer,* and other Ientlemen, in translating *Ovide, Palingenius,* and *Seneca,* have gonne as farre to their great praise as the copie they followed could cary them; but, if soch good wittes and forward diligence had bene directed to follow the best examples, and not have been caryed by tyme and custome to content themselves with that barbarous and rude Ryming, emonges their other worthy praises, which they have justly deserved, this had not bene the least, to be counted emonges men of learning and skill more like unto the Grecians than unto the Gothians in handling of their verse.[3]

I should point out that Ascham's version of the origins of rhyme among the barbarians, however commonly it was accepted, was not the only version available; there were and are others who hold that the use of rhyme originated in the medieval (and therefore Roman Catholic) church, as a mnemonic device designed to give the teachings of the Fathers in verse a greater hold upon the minds of those who were being taught. If you know what Elizabethan England thought of the Roman Catholic church, you will not suppose that this version of the story bestowed upon rhyme a prestige greater than that conferred by the other. Simple poets may have found it "natural" to use rhyme, but neither simplicity nor naturalness seemed necessarily to be—as, ironically, both would very much be today—a recommendation.

And so the lines were laid down: "trew versifying" required the utmost skill, the highest and most impressive kind of learning; rhyming was "rude," "beggerly," "barbarous"—and the taste that enjoyed it (as Milton would remark so much later) common, "vulgar." During the last thirty years of the reign of Elizabeth, the controversy involved some of the greatest poets and critics in England, most of them specifically taking the side we should now suppose to be the sensible one. For whatever "trew versifying" is "trew" to, it is not true to the genius of English; and with the most ardent and ingenious support, the fashion for writing quantitative verse in English—even though Spenser and Sidney themselves, among others, tried their hands at such verse—scarcely survived the end of the sixteenth century. The last major critical espousal of the already lost cause was Thomas Campion's "Observations in the Art of English Poesie" (1602)[4]; Samuel Daniel's eminently sensible retort to it, "A Defense of Ryme" (1603)[5], articulated a position that had already, in effect, triumphed. So simplicity and naturalness had won out, after all.

And Milton, sixty-five years later? He was not, of course, advocating the writing of quantitative verse, even though he tells us that "fit quantity of syllables" is one of the elements of "true musical delight" in poetry. He was merely harking back, for the sake of convenience, to the traditional attack on rhyme, which the educated had continued half-heartedly to press even after the "rithmes" of the great Elizabethan and Jacobean poets had established accentual-syllabic verse in English as an achieved form unparalleled in the wealth and magnificence of its possibilities. *Paradise Lost* is written in accentual-syllabic verse. Milton simply did not wish to use in it, *regularly,* the end rhyme that then-current practice would have suggested he use.

Milton castigates rhyme as "trivial"; he speaks of "the jingling sound of like endings; he admits that the use of rhyme has been "grac't . . . by . . . some famous modern Poets," but goes on to say that they were "carried away by Custom," and "much to thir own vexation, hindrance, and constraint to express many things otherwise, and for the most part worse than else they would have exprest them." Where the earlier criticism of rhyme is explicit its arguments are much the same. Sidney, in his "Apologie for Poetrie" (1583/1595)[6], complains that few English poems "have poeticall sinewes in them"; most are "a confused masse of words, with a tingling sound of ryme, barely accompanied with reason."[7] Rhyme

is superficial, external; too often the "honny-flowing Matron Eloquence" is "apparelled, or rather disguised, in a Curtizan-like
painted affection."[8] The fault here extends to the overuse of alliteration; and poets who depend too much on musical patterning,
including rhyme, are "like those Indians, not content to weare eare-
rings at the fit and naturall place of the eares, but they will thrust
jewels through their nose and lippes, because they will be sure to
be fine."[9] One is reminded of Aldous Huxley's complaints about
Poe, who, he says, uses meter and rhyme so exorbitantly that
his verse is as bedizened as someone wearing "diamond rings on
every finger."[10]

Rhyme, then, is a mere verse mechanism, a marker signaling the
end of a line; or it is an aid to memorization; or it is decoration,
the manner of its application unspecified and its use too often overdone. It betrays the writer into saying "otherwise, and for the
most part worse," what he wishes to say; or, as Campion remarks
morosely, "it in forceth a man oftentimes to abjure his matter and
extend a short conceit beyond all bounds of arte."[11] Is there nothing good about rhyme? To be sure, there is. It has a sweetness of
its own, says the gentle Sidney, gently[12]; and if we recall that for
Sidney, as for most classical critics, the function of poetry is,
through delight, to teach, we will understand that sweetness is no
idle attribute. Finally, all defenders of rhyme remark that it seems
natural to English, that verse writers are familiar with it, accustomed to it; that there is an ease in its use. This would seem to
contradict Milton's criticism that it makes poets express themselves otherwise than they would without it, but never mind that.
If rhyme comes easily to the poet, that fact too can be turned
against it: "the facilitie and popularitie of Rime," says Campion,
"creates as many Poets as a hot sommer flies."[13]

What fascinates me most as I look back on this controversy is
the very general phrasing of the arguments on both sides. Certain
of the critics of rhyme give examples of bad or imperfect rhyme,
but no one tells us why good rhyme is good. Puttenham speaks of
"our concordes, or tunable consentes in the latter end of our
verses,"[14] and his language tells us something: "concord" and
"consent" are terms at once literal and figurative, and, like their
sister term "harmony," they lead poetry into the worlds of music
and philosophy simultaneously. Concord is better than discord, we
all know; and harmony is heavenly. All these words breathe to us
a sense of the shaped, the ordered, the exactly wrought; the fulfilled. And that which is ordered is comprehensible and pleasing,

as chaos is not. It does not matter today that those who supported the "trew versifying" against rhyme believed that they were exponents of a more complex and satisfying order than rhyme could confer. What matters is that English poets themselves found rhyme—and assonance and alliteration and musical patterning of all kinds—at their best magnificent in effect.

What *are* the delights of rhyme? What, indeed, *does* it do? If the poets will not tell us, we must examine their work and find out for ourselves. Delight, after all, is, as a *concept* general, but the experience of it is specific. Let us begin with a quick definition: rhyme as we ordinarily speak of it is the identity of the vowels of two stressed syllables, an identity extending to everything that follows the vowels in the same syllables, if anything does. Thus "owe" rhymes with "go," "own" with "tone," "old" and "told" with "bold." Note that where consonants *precede* the stressed vowel in rhyme, these differ: what begins by differing, then, ends by being the same. There is a kind of pleasure, perhaps, in that thought itself. The turn toward concord may surprise us, or it may come precisely when we expect it to; the setting up, and then the satisfying of expectation—perhaps with some subtle difference we had not expected—is central to the creation of all form in art and to our experience of it. Let us listen to the effect in couplet rhyme:

> Let *Sporus* tremble—A. What? that thing of silk,
> *Sporus,* that mere white curd of Ass's milk?
> Satire or sense, alas! can *Sporus* feel?
> Who breaks a butterfly upon a wheel?
> P. Yet let me flap this bug with gilded wings,
> This painted child of dirt, that stinks and stings;
> Whose buzz the witty and the fair annoys,
> Yet wit ne'er tastes, and beauty ne'er enjoys:
> So well-bred spaniels civilly delight
> In mumbling of the game they dare not bite.
> Eternal smiles his emptiness betray,
> As shallow streams run dimpling all the way.
> Whether in florid impotence he speaks,
> And, as the prompter breathes, the puppet squeaks;
> Or at the ear of *Eve,* familiar Toad,
> Half froth, half venom, spits himself abroad,
> In puns, or politics, or tales, or lies,
> Or spite, or smut, or rhymes, or blasphemies,
> His wit all see-saw, between *that* and *this,*
> Now high, now low, now master up, now miss,
> And he himself one vile Antithesis.
> Amphibious thing! that acting either part,

The trifling head or the corrupted heart,
Fop at the toilet, flatt'rer at the board,
Now trips a Lady, and now struts a Lord.
Eve's tempter thus the Rabbins have exprest,
A Cherub's face, a reptile all the rest;
Beauty that shocks you, parts that none will trust;
Wit that can creep, and pride that licks the dust.[15]

Now of course it is far more than rhyme in this that delights us. But notice that the requirements upon rhyme are insistent and severe, and that Pope—the passage is from his *Epistle to Dr. Arbuthnot,* lines 305–333—meets them with a firmness, a command, that is a part of the effect of the passage: his authority over his verse becomes confidence in his own judgments, and his obvious control begets a like confidence in us.

Note in addition that the first line of a couplet, or of any rhymed structure, is (so to speak) blank until we reach the line, and the syllable, that completes it. The completion is a corroboration; we identify, usually at the moment we expected to do so, a sound we have heard before, and for a split second our ears—and our minds—take us back to the word that carried that earlier sound, now being repeated. With poetry as with prose, to make sense of what we are reading we read straight forward, sentence by sentence, with a need to finish sentences so that we will understand them. But in poetry, forward movement is, here and there—sometimes at regular intervals, sometimes not—and of course in part only, countered by recognitions and returns, identifications of structures of sound. The tendencies are opposite, and produce a kind of fruitful tension that leads to a deliberateness of reading, a fullness and ordered multiplicity of response characteristic of poetry—of verse, if you will. The tension between movement and structure can exist without rhyme, but it is very much heightened by rhyme, its ordered effects made appreciable to the receiving consciousness.

The first two lines of Gerard Manley Hopkins's "The Leaden Echo and the Golden Echo" illustrate superbly, it seems to me, the effect rhyme has of holding us back even as we must go forward. Hopkins is of course using not merely the kind of rhyme I have defined, but alliteration, assonance, half-rhyme (as in "brooch" and "latch") and full rhyme in endlessly and astonishingly varied combinations; and he is using these effects throughout his lines, not merely at mathematically determined line ends. It will, however, already have become clear that what is ordinarily

called rhyme is part of a continuum that embraces sound patterning of all kinds. (Of mathematics I will have more to say in a
moment.) Here are the lines from Hopkins: he is asking, as so
many poets had asked before him, whether there is any way in
which mortal beauty can be preserved, held onto:

> How to kéep—is there ány any, is there none such, nowhere
>   known some, bow or brooch or braid or brace, láce,
>   latch or catch or key to keep
> Back beauty, keep it, beauty, beauty, beauty, . . .
>   from vanishing away?[16]

Note how frantically the sounds, by repetition, grasp at one another, how the words clutch at parts of one another, and are pulled
loose by some counterseizure, some further unexpected conso-
nance (in a series of words that name, miraculously, our useless
means of restraining, holding, keeping what we have), until the
means are exhausted, the desperate attempt failed, and "beauty,
beauty, beauty," held by sheer force those moments longer, "van-
ishes away" in words that run like water, and rhyme with nothing.

It is a brilliant effect, but it comes late, we are likely to think,
in the history of rhyme, whereas the use of rhyme clearly defined
to support meter, to fix attention upon the mathematical proportions of measured verse, is perhaps the first true delight it afforded
the writer—and the reader—of accentual-syllabic verse. We have
heard, in the passage from Pope, rhyme returning inexorably ten
syllables by ten syllables, in an *aa, bb, cc* pattern capable of even
continuation as long as the wit and the invention of the poet held.
Comparable effects could be illustrated from Chaucer—who would
also show us that there are differences in effect when the end of a
sentence coincides with the completion of a rhyme structure, and
when the sentence goes on through, though the rhyme is made,
done, over with. If the sense overflows a rhyme structure by only
a syllable or two, the effect of this will in turn be different—more
shocking—than if it flows forward far enough to participate in the
inception, and perhaps even in the completion, of a new rhyme
structure.

So the relationship between rhyme and syntax is important. An
ear expecting rhyme, momentarily defrauded of it by the fact that
a sentence ends in midline, may feel a discomfort it will transfer
to its sense of what is being said. Witness these lines from *Lycidas,*

in which Milton is lamenting the abrupt and meaningless end of a life designed to have meaning:

> *Fame* is the spur that the clear spirit doth raise
> (That last infirmity of Noble mind)
> To scorn delights, and live laborious days;
> But the fair Guerdon when we hope to find,
> And think to burst out into sudden blaze,
> Comes the blind *Fury* with th'abhorred shears,
> And slits the thin-spun life. (70–76)

After lines of rhyme, "shears" is not rhymed, and "life" cuts off the sentence midway in its line and is of course left dangling.

> "But not the praise,"
> *Phoebus* repli'd, and touch'd my trembling ears
>
> (76–77)

And so something goes on beyond the end of the life, completes thus an enlarged structure of thought, goes on to another line that provides a rhyme for "shears," goes on, completing and (so to speak) making sense of interrupted movement and apparently shattered structure. . . . All this is true, and it all works. And still we do not forget—and we are meant not to forget—the horror of that incompletion, forever frozen in time—"And slits the thin-spun life."

Do I seem to praise Milton in his management of rhyme? Let me abandon pretense and continue to praise him. I have touched lightly on the mathematics of measured verse; let me speak now, briefly, of stanza. (*Lycidas* is written not in stanzas but in irregular *canzoni,* a form adapted from the Italian.) Without rhyme, as Samuel Daniel seems at least to imply,[17] stanza would be impossible, for rhyme defines the components of stanza and gives them their relationship. This is particularly true of, and important to say about, stanzas in which the lines are of different lengths; in blank verse all lines are of the same length, and we may train our ears to recognize that length, but continual change, unmarked, would defeat us. Here is a stanza from Milton's *Nativity Ode,* one of the finest stanzas of the seventeenth century: it is about the song of the angels at the birth of the Christ child, and it is about the music of the spheres.

> For if such holy Song
> Enwrap our fancy long,
>   Time will run back, and fetch the age of gold,

And speckl'd vanity
Will sicken soon and die,
    And leprous sin will melt from earthly mold,
And Hell itself will pass away,
And leave her dolorous mansions to the peering day.

(133–40)

There is a sense of amplitude, of fulfillment, in moving from a shorter line to a longer one; in moving from longer to shorter there is a return to concision, or perhaps to the tentative, the partial, the incomplete. Milton's *Nativity Ode* stanza provides us first with the equality of six syllables with six syllables, then with a series of increases and dwindlings, variously but exactly proportioned. Six syllables are in clear proportion to ten, ten to eight, eight to twelve; the relationships please in themselves and compound the meaning of what is being said. Six-syllables lines, being brief, are not commonly divided by pauses. Ten-syllable lines, however, often break four and six (as do those in the stanza quoted); an eight-syllable line is a *double* four, a twelve-syllable line a *double* six. The stanza is complex, but it is made of simplicities. It is a very beautiful invention. And the beauty is in the service, not of itself, but of what the poetry says.

Let me quote Daniel:

> The body of our imagination being as an unformed *Chaos* without fashion, without day, if by the divine power of the spirit it be wrought into an Orbe of order and forme, is it not more pleasing to Nature, that desires a certaintie and comports not with that which is infinite, to have these clozes, rather than not to know where to end, or how farre to goe, especially seeing our passions are often without measure?[18]

So measured verse provides an ordering for what is least ordered in us, makes available to us what might be called a mathematics of the emotions. In all this, rhyme plays a central part. Is it artificial? What is art, or artifice, when—as Daniel points out—order is agreeable to nature?

"In longer works especially," it might seem that the possibilities of rhyme would at length be exhausted and its use become monotonous; indeed, how much variety in rhyme does the language afford? The "tuneful fools" Pope complains of in Part 2 of *An Essay on Criticism* are, after all, mere caricatures of a recognizable face,

While they ring round the same unvaried chimes,
With sure returns of still expected rhymes;

Where'er you find "the cooling western breeze,"
In the next line, it "whispers through the trees:"
If crystal streams "with pleasing murmurs creep,"
The reader's threatened (not in vain) with "sleep:"

(348–53)

If fulfillment of expectation is one of the ways in which rhyme contents us, we would probably, with Pope, wish the expectation of rhyme to be fulfilled at times through *words* we did not expect. All the same, I must point out that, marvelous as the stanza quoted from Milton is, "Song" and "long," "gold" and "mold," "away" and "day" are not remarkable rhymes, and the rhyme of "vanity" with "die" is to modern readers uncomfortable, whether they say "vanitee" or (as the early seventeenth-century reader might have done) "vanit[a^i]." One might almost judge all the rhymes in the stanza to be trivial, and, in themselves, of no true musical delight. It is the proportions they open to us, fixed in appropriate and beautiful utterance, and successively and dazzlingly then changed, that delight us. Perhaps rhyme need not be overinventive, as it should not be underinventive; perhaps only if what is said *in* rhyme is foolish will the rhyme seem foolish. Only occasionally, it may be, can rhyme afford in itself to be imaginatively stimulating; if it were so more often, it might compete with, rather than complement, what is being said.

And yet the meaningful coupling of words by sound, across the top of the syntax, is familiar enough, and at times very powerful as an effect: think of "blaze" and "blind" in the lines quoted from *Lycidas;* where, as commonly happens with alliteration, words that start out to be the same end in difference. It is meaning, of course, that makes that difference sweet or bitter. We might be pardoned, then, for supposing that end-rhyme ought logically to provide similar couplings independent of syntax, and perhaps even greater excellences, more meaningful connections. Indeed it can do so. Here is Milton's Sonnet 19, sometimes titled "On His Blindness":

When I consider how my light is spent,
　Ere half my days, in this dark world and wide,
　And that one Talent which is death to hide,
　Lodg'd with me useless, though my Soul more bent
To serve therewith my Maker, and present
　My true account, lest he returning chide;
　"Doth God exact day-labor, light denied,"
　I fondly ask; But patience to prevent
That murmur, soon replies, "God doth not need

Either man's work or his own gifts; who best
Bear his mild yoke, they serve him best; his State
Is Kingly. Thousands at his bidding speed
And post o'er Land and Ocean without rest:
They also serve who only stand and wait."

I am sure I am not the only reader who has noted that this sonnet ends with more than a simple rhyme. "His State / Is Kingly" is a regal phrase, brief as it is, and yet divided across the end of a line. Further, the initial consonants and the rhyme portion of "State" are divided between "*st*and" and "*w*ait" in the poem's conclusion. What have "stand" and "wait" to do with "State"? For one thing, the word "State" derives from the past participle of the Latin word for "stand." So there is a kind of state even in the simplest standing—and waiting. And since the agitated rhythms, the broken lines of the earlier, rebellious part of the poem are resolved in the one-line comprehension with which it closes, we feel that the poem's speaker has achieved at the end a control and a dignity as appropriate to him as is the kingly state to God—that these dignities are in fact somehow connected. And they are, and that is what the poem says. But we could afford to find such richness, I think, in no more than one of its rhymes, and that the final one.

If Milton was so skilled in the use of rhyme, why then does he fulminate against it in the statement prefixed to *Paradise Lost*? It is the last question we have to answer here. It is also a question that could inaugurate long explorations and explanations, but I must be very brief. In the first place, *Paradise Lost* is over ten thousand lines in length, and (in spite of the example of the *Faerie Queene*, longer still and rhymed in a complex stanza) the kind of rhyme that would have been expected in it would have been couplet rhyme. Whether or not the horror of that thought informs the scathing phrase "the jingling sound of like endings," we must remember the compass of the couplet, its scope; even if Milton had been able to produce five thousand miniatures as fully perfect as those of Pope, how could he have achieved in couplets the vastness required of him by his subject, the flexibility, the range he achieves in the blank-verse paragraph?

Yet unrhymed verse that is not quantitative—Milton speaks only for "*fit* quantity" (my italics), syllables appropriately heavy or appropriately light, where the sense asks for heaviness or lightness—must be lacking a formidably important element of structure: how can mere "rithmes" subsist without rhyme? Dramatic blank verse even at its more highly wrought is meant, after all, to strike us as sufficiently like speech, so that we expect it to pass from our awareness, to leave us, as speech—however eloquent—does. But nondramatic verse must exhibit complex shapes of thought that will require us to return to certain passages again and again, for contemplation, for study. How can such passages hold together without rhyme?

The answer is that *Paradise Lost is* rhymed, generously, plentifully; it is simply not rhymed regularly. It even displays, at times, conventional end-rhyme, but this is swallowed up in a musical patterning so pervasive that its presence, where it is detected, may seem almost accidental. It is not. Milton intended to "rhyme"; he intended to brocade his poem with continuously evolving patterns of sound that would support the verse without seeming to confine it. These patterns are emergent associations and dissociations of alliteration, assonance, half-rhyme and full rhyme, such patterns occurring sometimes at line-end but involving any stressed syllable of any sequence of lines, one part of a pattern dissolving into silence as another comes into being, single patterns seldom so clearly defined that they seem unmixed with others. Divisions like that of "state" between "stand" and "wait" take place commonly:

> *H*esperus that led
> The *st*arry *Host,* rode brighte*st*
>
> *(PL:* 4.605–6)

Recombinations take place:

> All *pa*th of M*a*n or Bea*st* that *past* th*a*t way.
>
> *(PL* 4.177)

Sometimes so much happens that it is as if we were in one of those snow scenes in overturned paperweights, imprisoned with sound instead of snow settling into its myriad combinations around us:

> though from off the *boughs* each Morn
> We *b*rush mellifluous De*w*s, and fi*n*d the *ground*
> Cover'd with pearly *g*rain.
>
> (PL 5.428–30)

I have arrested these movements for inspection, but you will find them in the original still unfixed, except as they are intended to help define the shape of a phrase, a line, a sentence, a thought, a verse paragraph. The effect is of what might be called progressive rhyme, and Milton's invention of it was an extraordinary act of the imagination. He uses it sometimes within lines, sometimes at line ends; sometimes to produce effects almost stanzaic. Here is Beelzebub speaking in *Paradise Lost* 2:

> Well have ye judg'd, well ended long deb*ate*,
> Synod of Gods, and like to what ye are,
> Gr*eat* things resolv'd, which from the lowest d*eep*
> Will once more lift us u*p*, in spite of F*ate*,
> Nearer our ancient S*eat*
>
> (*PL* 2.390–94)

If the organization of sound causes us to remember the passage, we will be the better off when, two books later, Satan admits:

> Which way I fly is Hell; myself am Hell;
> And in *the lowest deep* a lower deep
> Still threat'ning to devour me opens wide,
> To which the Hell I suffer seems a Heav'n.
>
> (*PL* 4.75–78)

When we read *Paradise Lost* the concept of rhyme seems slowly to enlarge itself, to grow, to come to include all forms of repetition and interconnection. Thus it becomes possible to say that in this extraordinary poem Milton rhymes rhythms. When Satan and Death first encounter one another,

>   Éach át thĕ Héad
> Lével'd hĭs déadly aim,
>
> (*PL* 2.711–12)

and the rhyme is more than mere rhyme—though we must not forget that the repetition of a pattern of accents is quite literally a part of rhyme conventionally understood.

When after the Fall Adam struggles to explain to Eve what Death is, or may be, he says that

> thís dáy's Déath denounc't, if aught I see,
> Will próve nó súddĕn, but ă sló-pác't évil,
> Ă lóng dáy's dýing to augment our pain
>
> (*PL* 10.962–64)

Whitman would rhyme rhythms in this way; and who is to say that he did not learn the strange skill from Milton?

In the very first book of *Paradise Lost* we read,

> So stretcht out huge in length the Arch-fiend lay
> Chain'd on the burning Lake, nor ever thence
> Had ris'n or heav'd his head, but that the will
> And high permission of all-ruling Heaven
> Left him at large to his own dark designs,
> That with reiterated crimes he might
> Heap on himself damnation, while he sought
> Evil to others, and enrag'd might see
> How all his malice serv'd but to bring forth
> Infinite goodness, grace and mercy shown
> On Man by him seduc't, but on himself
> Treble confusion, wrath and vengeance pour'd.
>
> (*PL* 1.209–20)

"Évil tŏ óthĕrs" prepares us for "Ínfĭnĭte góodnĕss." The lines beginning "Ínfĭnĭte góodnĕss" and "Trébl̆e cŏfúsĭon" in their entirety contrast what humankind is to expect, and what the devil's lot will be. The two lines echo one another syllable by syllable, word by word, syntactically and rhythmically. Milton trains us so carefully to hear such echoes that when Raphael descends to Paradise in Book 5 of *Pardise Lost* to warn Adam and Eve of their danger, making his way

> through Groves of Myrrh
> And flow'ring Odours, Cassia, Nard, and Balm;
> A Wilderness of sweets
>
> (*PL* 5.292–94),

we are taken back to the climax of Milton's description of Hell in Book 2,

> Rocks, Caves, Lakes, Fens, Bogs, Dens, and shades of death,
> A Universe of death
>
> (*PL* 2.621–22)

"Ă Wíldĕernĕss ŏf swéets": "Ă Únĭvĕrse ŏf déath." Utterly opposite; uncannily like. Almost they rhyme: as *almost* do the courses taken by Satan on the one hand and Adam and Eve on the other. The seed of the whole poem sleeps in that echo.

I have pointed out that Milton trains us, in *Paradise Lost*, to hear effects of repetition across great distances. Let me return to rhyme itself, rhyme anyone would call rhyme. It is everywhere in the poem, present at varying distances, giving sinew to a passage here, closing a verse paragraph there, playing its part, over and over, in providing a texture of sound. But I want to go now to the end of the poem. Michael has shown the future of the world to Adam; Eve has been asleep. They return to wake her, but find her waked. She says:

> Whence thou return'st, and whither went'st, I know;
> For God is also in sleep, and Dreams advise,
> Which he hath sent propitious, some great good
> Presaging, since with sorrow and heart's distress
> Wearied I fell asleep: but now lead on;
> In mee is no delay; with thee to go,
> Is to stay here; without thee here to stay,
> Is to go hence unwilling; thou to mee
> Art all things under Heav'n, all places thou,
> Who for my wilful crime art banisht hence.
> This further consolation yet secure
> I carry hence; though all by mee is lost,
> Such favor I unworthy am voutsaf't,
> By mee the Promis'd Seed shall all restore.
> So spake our Mother *Eve,* and *Adam* heard
> Well pleas'd, but answer'd not; for now too nigh
> Th' Arch-Angel stood, and from the other Hill
> To thir fixt Station, all in bright array
> The Cherubim descended; on the ground
> Gliding meteorous, as Ev'ning Mist
> Ris'n from a River o'er the marish glides,
> And gathers ground fast at the Laborer's heel
> Homeward returning. High in Front advanc't,
> The brandisht Sword of God before them blaz'd
> Fierce as a Comet; which with torrid heat,
> And vapor as the *Libyan* air adust,
> Began to parch that temperate Clime; whereat
> In either hand the hast'ning Angel caught
> Our ling'ring Parents, and to th' Eastern Gate
> Led them direct, and down the Cliff as fast
> To the subjected Plain; then disappear'd.
> They looking back, all th' Eastern side beheld
> Of Paradise, so late thir happy seat,
> Wav'd over by that flaming Brand, the Gate
> With dreadful Faces throng'd and fiery Arms:
> Some natural tears they dropp'd, but wip'd them soon;
> The World was all before them, where to choose

Thir place of rest, and Providence thir guide:
They hand in hand with wand'ring steps and slow,
Through *Eden* took thir solitary way.

(*PL* 12.610–49)

"In mee is no delay; with thee to go" / Is to stay here; without thee here to stay, / Is to go hence unwilling" (*PL* 12.615–17). No delay. To stay: to go. To go: to stay.

They hand in hand with wand'ring steps and slow,
Through Eden took their solitary way.

(*PL* 12.648–49)

So ends, with two rhymes heard across more than thirty lines, the greatest unrhymed poem in the history of English. What would the imposition of couplet rhyme on *Paradise Lost* have done to that effect—to any of the effects I have described here, effects designed to give structure to vastness?

Perhaps Milton did not know himself quite what he was doing in *Paradise Lost,* though I think he did know. What I have shown here is only a little of what is in the poem to be found. But what poet likes to be asked to discuss his method, especially when the answer, to make any sense, would have to run to many pages? "Read the poem," we all say. "It's all there. Read the poem."

Paradise Lost changed English poetry forever; its influence is felt in the non-metrical poetry of the twentieth century as it was felt, intensely, in the metrical poetries of the eighteenth and nineteenth centuries. Perhaps it is felt in our very lives: in the lives, even, of those who have never read it, in the lives of children. I am only half serious, of course. But I remember a moment in the childhood of my son Peter, a moment when he, my wife and I were approaching the locked door of our house—we had been away—and Peter wanted to be the one to unlock the door. At the same moment my wife and I gave him our keys. He laid one upon the other, and regarded them with wonder. Then he looked up blissfully. "They rhyme," he said.

Peter could not have known that it was, in part at least, Milton's expansion of the idea of rhyme that made his own perception so apt. Certainly he knew nothing of *Paradise Lost,* or of how, in Book 2, Sin—portress of Hell Gate—reminds Satan that she is his daughter, and fell with him and the other rebel angels from heaven,

. . .at which time [she says] this powerful Key
Into my hand was giv'n, with charge to keep
These Gates for ever shut

(*PL* 2.774–76)

"This . . . *Key* . . . with charge *to keep*"—Hopkins's "key to keep"
lies atop Milton's, a small, shining duplicate. With other such echoes of Milton in Hopkins and other poets, it constitutes a kind of
rhyme across the centuries, giving what almost seems, at times, a
ghostly structure to what is indeed vastness.

Rhyme—I now use the term in its largest sense—is itself a key,
and a powerful one. A way of making connections, it can be a
source of meaning, and so a key to meaning. It is a source of form,
and so a key to keep forever closed the gates that give on Chaos.
It may even be—for me, it is—a "key to keep / back beauty," a
"braid or brace, lace, latch or catch or key to keep" one valued
kind of beauty, at least, "from vanishing away."

Notes

1. This note and the quotations from Milton following in this essay I present
as they appear in *John·Milton, Complete Poems and Major Prose,* ed. Merritt Y.
Hughes (New York: Odyssey Press, 1957).
2. Reprinted in part in *Elizabethan Critical Essays* (hereafter *ECE*), ed. G.
Gregory Smith, 2 vols. (London: Oxford University Press, 1904), 1.1–45.
3. *ECE*, 1.29–30.
4. *ECE*, 2.327–355.
5. *ECE*, 2.356–384.
6. *ECE*, 1.148–207.
7. *ECE*, 1.196.
8. *ECE*, 1.202.
9. *ECE*, 1.202.
10. "Vulgarity in Literature," *Music at Night and Other Essays,* (New York:
Harper and Brothers, 1930); reprinted 1970 by Books for Libraries Press in Freeport, New York. The essays occupies pp. 243–303 of the reprint; the phrase quoted
in the text is to be found on p. 269.
11. *ECE*, 2.331.
12. *ECE*, 1.204.
13. *ECE*, 2.330.
14. *ECE*, 2.81.
15. Quotations from Pope are presented as they appear in *The Best of Pope,*
ed. George Sherburn (New York: Thomas Nelson and Sons, 1929).
16. The lines quoted are as they appear in *Poems of Gerard Manley Hopkins,*
3rd ed. (Oxford: Oxford University Press, 1948).
17. *ECE*, 2.366, 382–83.
18. *ECE*, 2.366.

Part 4
The Postmodern Age

The Splendor of Truth

F. X. MURPHY, C.S.S.R.

AMID the clash of empires at the close of the sixth century, with Rome subject to barbarian control, Pope Gregory the Great, who reigned as pope for fourteen years (590–604), formulated a pastoral theology that served the Church for centuries. His "Pastoral Rule" *(Liber regulae pastoralis),* written for bishops, laid down a way of life that allowed priests and people to practice their faith in a fashion suitable to the primitive spiritual, social, and economic conditions of the age. In so doing, he reduced the cerebral theology of Augustine of Hippo to the mindset of the newly converted barbarians and insisted that the primary task of priests and prelates was the care of souls.

Thirteen centuries later, at a critical moment in world history, Gregory's successor John Paul II laid out a series of moral considerations that in their fashion depend upon Augustine, but reflect the moral concerns of the contemporary world. This pope's intention seems to be not so much the salvation of souls as the safeguarding of the "law of God."

Like Gregory's *"Pastoral Rule,"* the new encyclical letter, *The Splendor of Truth (Veritatis Splendor,* Editrice Vaticana, 5 October 1993), is addressed to the bishops rather than to the clergy or laity, providing them with a prescriptive moral code whose primary concern is to establish the fact that there are absolutes in the moral order whose violation is always and everywhere *(semper et pro semper)* a great evil.

More precisely John Paul insists that the negative precepts of the Ten Commandments—do not kill, steal, lie, fornicate, or calumniate or envy your neighbor's spouse or goods—are paranetic absolutes, absolutes of moral law, admitting of no exceptions. Whereas Gregory's moral admonitions and directives were basically humane and sympathetic, John Paul's perspectives are absolute and seemingly severe.

There can be no doubt that had O. B. Hardison been confronted with Pope John Paul's encyclical *Veritatis Splendor* he would have rejoiced at the high-minded intent of the Roman pontiff in asserting the existence of ethical absolutes in human conduct, while caustically evaluating the pragmatic principles behind the papal prescriptions.

Open at all times to challenging arguments on an intellectual plane, Hardison would have congratulated the pope on the deep, discursive quality of the document. He would have acknowledged its pertinence in the current contretemps within both the church and secular society regarding the tumultuous moral problems constituted by scientific experimentation, particularly in the fields of genetics and bioethics. Nor would he have failed to appreciate the papal condemnation of the arms race, the pope's ambivalent stand on the possession of nuclear weapons, as well as the horrendous discrepancy between the have and have-not nations, not to mention the horrors perpetrated by leaders in pursuit of national security and ethnic cleansing. With his natural skepticism, O.B. would surely have appreciated the *agon* or contention within the church initiated by this ambiguous document.

During the course of the half-decade of its making, preliminary texts of the papal document had been pirated by unscrupulous journalists and overconcerned theologians. It was anticipated as a definitive condemnation of current sexual mores in both the church and contemporary society. In reality it was nothing of the kind. While inevitably touching on the problems of sex, the document relies on Saint Paul's Letter to the Corinthians (1 Cor.6:9–10) to enumerate the evil actions in the sexual order condemned by the church.

Reduced to its essential message, the encyclical deals with the relationship between the objective moral order, or truth, and the human conscience. It advises the church's bishops that the morality of an individual human action is determined by the nature of the act itself—thus lying, killing, stealing, fornicating, and calumniating are always sinful in themselves, no matter what the consequences resulting from their commission. Accordingly the pope condemns efforts on the part of contemporary pastors and moral theologians to alleviate guilt by introducing circumstances arising from the context, intent, consequences, or the process whereby the conscience comes to its decision. In his view the morality of a thought, word, or deed is determined by the action itself. And certain acts are always evil, hence intrinsically sinful, by their very nature and thus never justifiable.

In pursuit of the assertion that there is an inviolable objective moral order that, the pope maintains, is the constant traditional teaching of the church down the ages, John Paul introduces a series of considerations dealing with the nature of man and woman as intelligent beings endowed with conscience and free will, and oriented to the pursuit of truth in both the spiritual and the moral orders.

The Vatican's contention that Catholic teaching regarding sex and marriage has been uniform and constant from the beginning is simply not factual. Curial theologians feel that the theory of natural law that the church inherited from Stoic philosophy, buttressed by Saint Paul's reference to a "law in our inner being," has given the church a thorough understanding of human beings.

Originally based on a static concept of the universe, reflecting the mind of God as the Immobile Mover and the Eternal Now, a seemingly authentic concept of men and women and their propensities prevailed in the church's moral constructions down to the current noetic revolution centering on biology, anthropology, psychology, and psychoanalysis.

In place of the presumption of a timeless, unambiguous Catholic standard of morality, contemporary theologians have come to realize that the structure of morality built into the human heart is not a static set of regulations or commandments constituting human nature. It is rather an interior cognitive realization of a pattern of dynamic moral norms that have come from social experience in history. While its basic foundation—do good and avoid evil—is absolute, its disposition by way of reasoning in keeping with the awareness of value known as conscience becomes uncertain in its application to specific thoughts and actions.

John Paul attempts to ward off the contention that the ancient, primitive understanding of the human biological structure rendered many notions of the traditional natural law questionable, yet he does accept the contemporary realization of the need to adapt current natural law theory to the signs of the times.

The *Splendor of Truth,* John Paul's tenth encyclical, appears to be the final link in a series of theological pronouncements intended as the doctrinal heritage that he desires to leave to the church as his application of the Christological presence in the world, beginning with his concept of Jesus Christ, *Redeemer of Man,* and concluding with *Splendor of Truth,* which stresses the dignity of the individual as a temple of the Holy Spirit.

An original draft of the encyclical was prepared by a group of curial theologians connected with the Congregation for the Doctrine of the Faith (the former Holy Office). Its rigorous tenor was eventually rejected by the pope, particularly in its assertion that the prerogative of papal infallibility included judgments and decisions in the moral order. This original draft, submitted for comment to bishops and theologians outside the curial domain, was severely criticized, and the surreptitiously released to the press by dissenting theologians. The final text, revised by John Paul and several of his trusted collaborators, avoids all mention of infallibility and relies on the pope's forceful and highly complicated reasoning to be persuasive.

The epistle-to-be was first announced on 1 August 1987, the second centenary of the death of Saint Alphonsus Liguori, the eighteenth-century Italian theologian who was credited with defeating the rigorous moral theology of Jansenism—a severe moral reaction to the breakdown of ethical values after the spread of the French Enlightenment in Western Europe.

Liguori was a talented young lawyer-turned-priest and street preacher who concentrated his care on the poor and marginalized in the streets, slum areas, and peasant countryside of his native Naples. As a consequence of his experiences in dealing with the consciences of both the learned and the ignorant in daily life, he wrote a series of pamphlets and a three-volume manual of moral theology that reflected his intimate knowledge of the need for compassion in interpreting the law of God and forming consciences. As a result Liguori was not only canonized a century ago, but awarded the title "Prince of Moral Theologians," and Rome declared him to be a Doctor of the Church, one whose teaching could be followed without fear of error. While acknowledging the preeminence of Liguori as a moral theologian, John Paul's encyclical ignores his merciful orientation.

In early October 1993 *Veritatis Splendor* was presented to the Roman press by Josef Cardinal Ratzinger, the Vatican's pro-prefect of the Congregation for the Doctrine of the Faith. In elucidating the document's contents, the German cardinal made a Freudian slip that he immediately acknowledged; he referred to the complicated genesis of the encyclical as a "contestation" or dispute, rather than a "consolidation," and admitted that the first term was the more accurate.

A preliminary observation helps to explain the document's intention. Chapter 1 is an extended exegesis of the pericope in Matthew's gospel that discusses the dialogue between Jesus and the Rich Young Man in which the youth asks the Good Master and Teacher what he must do to gain eternal life (Matt. 19:16–22).

In the parable the pope pursues a dialectical analysis of the prin-

cipal ideas that constitute morality. Dissecting the nature of good-
ness, he describes truth concerning human nature and freedom of
conscience as interchangeable and the basis for the sovereignty of
human dignity, free will, and conscience. At the same time he insists that in the realm of morality there exist absolute imperatives,
the violation of which is always evil.

These imperatives become the theme of the second chapter,
which most readers will find difficult or impossible to comprehend.
It is a dense and technical excursus on contemporary tendencies
in Catholic moral teaching in which the pope indulges an intricate
theological repudiation of various contemporary tendencies in
Catholic ethical doctrine. These heresies—though he did not use
that word when in 1984 he called them "systems of ethics"—are
relativism, proportionalism, and consequentialism.

Chapter 2 also reveals what is apparently a primary intention of
the encyclical: to dissipate dissent from papal teaching among
moral theologians. As long ago as 1984 Cardinal Ratzinger had
identified the diseases of consequentialism and proportionalism in
his book, *The Ratzinger Report.* He accused American moral theologians of being infected with these aberrations, even though the
original contributors to this tendency were mostly Europeans.

Chapter 3 describes the consequences of a teleological approach
to morality. The pope rejects the idea of statistical research as a
basis for measuring moral values. Moral teaching certainly cannot
depend on the results of public opinion polls, and morality is not
established by the rules and deliberative procedures of a
democracy.

At this point the pope firmly discourages dissent or differences
of opinion within the church's moral teaching. Contention or dispute has been an integral function in theological development, from
Saint Paul's "when Peter was come to Antioch, I withstood him
to the face, because he was to be blamed" (Gal. 2:11), down to the
recently deceased Archbishop Marcel LeFebvre of France, who
defied two popes in his rejection of most of Vatican II's decrees.

Receiving a mixed reaction from Italian journalists as well as
theologians and Catholic thinkers, the document caused considerable comment during the first weeks after its promulgation. The
most savage criticism came from the sixty-six-year-old Swiss theologian Hans Kung, deprived of his title as a Catholic theologian at
Pope John Paul's suggestion for having challenged the prerogative
of papal infallibility. Kung called the encyclical a return to the
antimodernist tactics of Pope Pius X (1903–14) and the procedures

of the Spanish Inquisition. "The encyclical," Kung concluded in an interview on Swiss radio, "is a sign of papal bankruptcy."

No less shocked by the encyclical's apparent intransigence, the octogenarian Redemptorist Bernard Haring, who in the wake of World War II answered the outcry for an updating of the church's moral teaching with the 1954 publication of his *Das Gesetz Christi* (The law of Christ), proclaimed his strong personal opposition. Haring, himself a victim of forty years of conflict with the Vatican, wrote, "It is clear that the Pope and his advisors do not have a proper picture of what moral theology today is like."

Similar observations were made by outstanding moralists such as the Jesuits' Richard McCormick, Joseph Fuchs, and Bruno Schueller, each of whom deplored the fact that the document distorted their teachings. Father Charles Curran, deprived of his title and teaching position at the Catholic University of America, while admitting that he is a target of papal censure for a number of nuanced interpretations of moral prescriptions in the sexual and biomedical spheres, also maintains that the pope incorrectly characterized his approach as relativism.

The pope's critique of the fundamental option—an interior state of self-consciousness thoroughly dedicated to observing the gospel imperatives—rightly recognized the possibility that one who has dedicated his or her style of life to religious observance may feel that an individual act against one of the commandments does not destroy one's overall dedication. In describing this aberration (which may explain the phenomenon of conscientious celibate priests guilty of pedophilia), the pope failed to quote a brilliant bit of satire in which the third-century apologist Tertullian rules out all equivocation in the moral order:

> Some say, however, that God is satisfied if he be honored in heart and mind, and even though this be not done externally. Thus they sin, yet lose not faith and reverential fear. That is to say, they lose not charity and commit adultery! They lose not filial piety and poison a parent. So also they will not lose pardon and be cast down into hell, seeing that they sin and lose not religious reverence.
>
> On this principle, he who does not wish God to be offended should have no reverence for him at all, if it is fear that sponsors his offense. (*On Penitence*, 10–14)

In his condemnation of moral theologians in conflict with Roman curial teaching, the pope does not take into account their motives. A majority of the priests and pastors are reacting to the excruciating agony of their faithful, particularly the more conscientious, who are faced with nearly impossible problems of conscience. In seeking a remedy for these difficulties, the moralists have interpreted the rigid older prohibitions in a benevolent fashion.

While many Catholics of an earlier generation were shocked by the Vatican Council's achievement of change in doctrine and moral perceptions, conscientious pastors and theologians are determined to relieve their faithful of merciless burdens such as those set forth in pre-Conciliar (and now outdated) manuals of moral theology. Thus they feel that attempts to rectify traditional moral judgments by ethical mechanisms such as proportionalism and consequentialism—taking into consideration the consequences of the human act beyond the immediate observation of a commandment—are justified. It is the papal definition of these terms that has given rise to unabashed criticism, mainly on the part of Catholic moral theologians who maintain that the papal perceptions do not represent their positions. While challenging the restrictions laid on the "option for the poor" and "liberation theology" by the Roman curia, critically minded moralists do appreciate the document's recent condemnation of the sins and evils haunting illegitimate business practices, political chicanery, torture, abduction, drunken driving, environmental negligence, ethnic cleansing, and the exploitation of the poor, the marginalized, and the homeless.

There appears to be little room for compromise in the pope's approach to these evils, indicated by his contention that "It is human for the sinner to acknowledge his weakness and ask for mercy. What is unacceptable is the attitude of one who makes his weakness the criterion of the truth about the good." As regards the appeal to the freedom of the individual's conscience, the pope insists that its judgments are not infallible, and while he admits that one must follow an invincibly false conscience, he asserts that this does not make its judgments any the less erroneous.

In keeping with this contention, the pope abjures casuistry because it is "concerned only with doubtful or uncertain matters since there can be no doubt or question about intrinsically evil acts." Yet the casuistic process is not based on equivocation or spurious types of reasoning, as the pope implies. It is a systematic use of a dialectic device in search of right decisions in the realm of human conduct. It was employed by the Good Teacher in justifying his cure of the man on the Sabbath (Matt. 12:9–14) and again in explaining his position on divorce (Matt. 10:2–12). Saints Paul and Augustine frequently employed the method. Ridiculed by Blaise Pascal as a Jesuitical trivialization of human behavior, its nature and use were rescued by Liguori in his *Praxis confessarii,* or *Confessor's Handbook,* as needed for the training of spiritual directors and applying to Christ's admonition not to burden peoples' consciences unnecessarily.

While John Paul mentions the behavioral sciences and acknowledges that differences in cultural experience affect moral standards, he does not analyze the basic problems in human behavior patterns. By not using modern psychology in ferreting out the physical, mental, and psychic sources of human misbehavior, he apparently fails to acknowledge fully the complexity of human morality.

Likewise the document seems to have countermanded Paul VI's 1968 encyclical *Humanae vitae* (par. 25), which urged priests and laity not to be discouraged if at first they do not succeed in living up to the church's teaching on, for example, contraceptive evil. John Paul asserts, "it would be a serious error to conclude that the Church's teaching is essentially only an 'ideal' which must then be adapted to the limited capabilities of men and women."

The Polish pontiff's caution regarding dissent is not without some comprehension. No authority, particularly if it considers itself endowed with infallibility in some sphere of knowledge, can long tolerate a direct challenge to its decisions without losing influence—and, not unnaturally, the authority's temper.

John Paul sees a world in turmoil in which an alliance between democracy and moral relativism threatens the introduction of a new type of totalitarianism, a spiritual malaise robbing men and women of their God-given knowledge of right and wrong and the freedom to follow their conscience in pursuit of truth. Having played his own part in the overthrow of Marxism, he sees a need to warn the world of the dangers involved in social and political spheres, as well as in the breakdown of civil and religious conduct through relativism, skepticism, and individualism in the pursuit of human well-being. In this regard, the pope is only doing his duty.

In his fundamental observations, the pope maintains that martyrdom for the faith includes the refusal to violate even the least of God's commandments under any circumstance. While he pretends to tolerate differences of opinion in various theological schools and denies categorically that the Vatican has any intention of imposing any one school of thought on the church, the evidence challenging that contention is unmistakable in the encyclical's demonstration of his concept of morality in which the Roman variety predominates. Proof is supplied by the admonitions to bishops to caution the heads of Catholic institutions—seminaries, colleges and universities, hospitals and social service clinics—to conform to the papal ethical teaching or risk losing their Catholic designation.

It was his humaneness and compassion that made Pope John XXIII such a beloved figure. While attempting to emulate his benevolent predecessor, John Paul is unable to tolerate sinners, particularly theologians, who disagree with his moral absolutes. Prayerful, congenial, and compassionate as he visits the poor, the dispossessed, and the downtrodden in almost every corner of the globe, the pope possesses love for individuals of every nation, religious belief, and character. It seems incredible, then, that he should not consistently demonstrate this quality in his pastoral care of souls.

While a monument of paranetic elaboration, the encyclical has not inspired the conviction necessary to change minds and move hearts. Its tone and tenor seem to encourage bishops to pursue an adversarial vigilance in regard to the teaching of moral theologians. This may be the intention of the present heirs to the old Holy Office, where the Grand Inquisitor once ruled, but the world can only hope this is not the intention of the author of *The Splendor of Truth*.

Culture and Technology: Reflections on O. B. Hardison, Jr.'s *Disappearing through the Skylight*

CAROL DWORKOWSKI

IN an essay written in 1977 for the bicentennial of the Declaration of Independence, O. B. Hardison expressed considerable optimism regarding the competence of the American people as demonstrated in "two revolutions" that had "attempted the impossible and accomplished the unbelievable."

In his 1988 *Disappearing through the Skylight,* however, he reflects "optimism" *à rebours* as he describes the "disappearance" of culture as we have always known it, as well as the technological challenge projecting the eradication of human beings themselves.

The contrast between these two reflections seems to require an elucidation that touches on the meaning of the universe as well as on the significance of human life. In pursuing this objective, I hope to do justice to a man of modest self-awareness who contributed substantially to the intellectual development of the modern age.

In rejecting the simplistic, excessively gloomy projections that are often so appealing to the popular imagination, Hardison made the eminently sensible observation in his essay that "[w]hat does appear certain is that we are going to have to come to terms, sooner or later, with the limits that surround us, and this means finding a set of values with which to replace the frontier mentality." He wrote of Thomas Jefferson's anthropocentric philosophy that valued human beings over technology and economics, a view that "begins with man's humanity and deploys the limited resources of society and nature around humanity in the best possible manner," and of the "need to understand better than we have in the past just what is essential to American democracy and what we can surrender without changing or warping our basic values." While affirming our need for technology in the future, "probably much more of it than we have today," Hardison made the point that "we are going to need, even more than the technology itself, the wisdom to use our technology in a life-enhancing way."[1]

We shall look in vain for this wisdom in a postmodern philosophy of life that celebrates the disappearances of nature, of history, of language, of art, and of human being. It used to be that people who lost touch with concrete reality were certified insane. Now, apparently, an escape into subjective mental abstractions is considered de rigeur by many within the scientific academic community.

Few people attempt to examine consciously the epistemological presuppositions of their age and culture, but Hardison has done just that in *Disappearing through the Skylight,* and with considerable depth and perception. He begins with an examination of the fundamental epistemological question "How do we know that we know?" in light of the discoveries of postmodern science. The answer appears to be "We don't!"

A little over twenty years ago, Reformed Evangelical philosopher-theologian Francis Schaeffer, founder of L'Abri Fellowship, wrote the trilogy still in print—*Escape from Reason, The God Who Is There,* and *He Is There and He Is Not Silent*—in which he used the development of science and the fine arts to analyze the epistemological changes occurring in postmodern or, as Schaeffer termed it, "modern-modern" society.[2] There the similarity between Schaeffer and Hardison seems to end. While Schaeffer, a staunch proponent of philosophical objectivism, greets the dawning of the new postmodern age with a sense of apocryphal doom, Hardison is undauntedly optimistic. Although Hardison's book may leave the reader with more questions than answers, the questions of anyone other than a committed technophile will undoubtedly be more perceptive than they would have been.

The postmodern emphasis within the scientific community on "invisible"—micro and macro—realities that lie outside the middle distance accessible to conventional empirical testing is precipitating an epistemological crisis in contemporary Western society. Hardison likens "crossing the horizon of invisibility" to the experience of fourth-century Christians who converted from pagan to Christian culture. If widespread, this rejection of the subject as "detached observer" that permitted objectivists to claim for themselves the initiative of objectivity itself for their human truths, giving rise to a dogmatic absolutism in Western thought, means the death of rationalism as it has been expressed in the modern age.

This development is a major paradigm shift that has already begun to have far-reaching effects on Western thinking. An imme-

diate result has been the lessening of conflict, typified in the Renaissance by the Galileo affair, between religion and science, as the
proposal of speculative scientific theories had begun to replace the
proclamation of "scientific truths." Since there has been, simultaneously, a growing tolerance for intellectual pluralism within the
churches that has encouraged more openness to ideas originating
outside of the ecclesial community, perhaps we are seeing the beginning of the end to a sacred/secular dichotomy that has tended
to produce increasingly soulless sciences and mindless religions in
the West.

Considering the often-vicious polemics that have existed between scientists and religionists since the collapse of the unified
world view of medieval Christendom, it seems almost ironic to
read that Guth and Steinhardt's "inflationary theory" of creation
predisposes an openness to the suggestion that the universe originated "as a quantum fluctuation from absolutely nothing." It would
seem that *creatio ex nihilo* is no longer an exclusively theological
concept.[3]

One cannot help but wonder how many other faith/science con-
vergences may be in the offing. Influenced by a new spirit of dialogue, even a Darwinian faith in the ultimate triumph of life over
death in the natural evolutionary processes may come to be interpreted as analogous to a Christian faith in the triumph of grace
over sin and death. On the question of a Creator or Prime Mover,
postmodernist scientists are more likely to be agnostic than
atheistic.

Although the demise of modernism's objectivist absolutism is a
relief to all but the most contentious among us, is postmodern-
isms's subjectivism really an acceptable alternative? Both epistemologies have their philosophical roots in a Cartesian dualism that
presupposes a false dichotomy between the object and the subject,
making a balanced epistemology virtually impossible.

Absent from Hardison's reflections on a radically subjective
technological society are the pessimistic but nonetheless valid res-
ervations found in the analysis of our technical civilization by
French sociologist Jacques Ellul.[4] Ellul points out that "[t]he new
order [that] was meant to be a buffer between men and nature . . .
[u]nfortunately . . . evolved autonomously in such a way that man
has lost all contact with [the world of nature] and has to do only
with the organized technical intermediary which sustains relations
both with the world of life and with the world of brute matter."
Ellul writes of man "enclosed within his artificial creation," unable

to "pierce the shell of technology to find again the ancient milieu to which he was adapted for hundreds of thousands of years." The "new milieu" has its own specific laws that are not related to organic or inorganic matter, laws of which man is still largely ignorant. Ellul feels that a "new necessity" is replacing the old and, while acknowledging that "[i]t is easy to boast of victory over ancient oppression," he asks the disturbing question, "what if victory has been gained at the price of an even greater subjection to the forces of the artificial necessity of the technological society which has come to dominate our lives?"

While exuding optimism about the projected advancements in technological development, Hardison does not speculate on how we are to gain control over the "artificial necessity" of a technological environment. Surely it will take more than programming in "humanlike" error factors to put a human face on our technologies.

Perhaps a glimmer of hope can be found in the growing influence of Eastern thought forms on Western culture. In spite of Fritjof Capra's taking up the nondualistic philosophies of the East and showing their compatibility with contemporary physics, the influence of Eastern epistemologies has probably been greater among the various spiritual and ecclesial communities than within the scientific community.[5] The epistemological goal of Eastern thought forms is to transcend opposites—such as the distinctions between object and subject—so that unity of thought may be accomplished without denying or ignoring the paradoxical nature of reality/truth. Perhaps postmodernism will prove to be a transitional phase between modernism and post-modernism or a neomoderism that will take us out of the Cartesian dichotomy between object and subject into the development of a world view that, like Eastern thought forms, will "lead us beyond dualism into the realm where we recognize the interdependence of all reality."

Hardison documents, or rather celebrates, postmodernism's loss of historical consciousness. Other authors such as Harvey Cox, *Religion in the Secular City: Toward a Postmodern Theology*,[6] and Anton C. Zijderveld, *On Clichés: The Supersedure of Meaning by Function in Modernity*,[7] have noted the absence of tradition that characterizes our contemporary technological society, where the past is no longer "experienced as a meaningful component of the present," but few have welcomed its demise so enthusiastically. No one who has experienced the tyranny of a radically conservative use of "history" can doubt the latent power of the past to enslave or limit the potential for realizing present and future possibilities, but does the possible threat of a misuse of our sense of history really justify the claim increasingly made in postmodern culture that "history is bunk"?

Historical symbolism not only preserves and perpetuates the past, but it unites a people by placing them in a common concrete cultural context. "Technology ceaselessly transforms the world along abstract and artificial lines," writes Hardison. Our radically new technological culture is producing symbols no longer grounded in the solid experience of human history. Hardison claims a "universality" for postmodern symbolism. Traditionally, universalism has meant that a concept has validity for all peoples, everywhere, for all times—a shared experience, giving individual existential experiences a much larger meaning through consensual validation. Hardison's universality seems to be devoid of this quality, and is "independent of time and space." The universality of abstraction is not that of commonality, but is rather a universality so contentless that it can mean all things to all people. It supports a radically subjective individualism, rather than promoting the formation of a sense of human community. Contentless symbols arising from abstractions cannot satisfy the cravings of the human spirit for meaning. Perhaps the renewed current interest in religion and spirituality is, in part, due to a hunger for symbols rich in content, symbols that communicate a reality that goes beyond the limits of individual existential experiences.

Hardison observes in his book that "science is committed to the universal." How true that observation is after postmodern science's discovery of "randomness" is a matter for debate, but in any case technology is not, strictly speaking, "science." It is the functional application of scientific knowledge. In our capitalistic society economic principles dominated by the profit motive quickly replace scientific principles in technological development.

Hardison's example of universality, the growing global homogeneity of "architectural styles, dress styles, musical styles—even eating styles," has been artificially imposed by the economic necessities inherent in the technology of mass production. It has not arisen naturally from within the context of shared human experience.

Many Third-World peoples have been forced to endure the negative effects of Western cultural imperialism to acquire the material benefits of our technological development. A society that is failing to preserve its own cultural identity as a result of the loss of historical consciousness cannot be expected to respect the cultural identity of others. Then, too, since an economically enforced

homogeneity or external conformity is more likely to produce col-
lectivism than community, the common social and individual psychological price exacted for an increase in material prosperity has
been seen by some to be disproportionately high.

Freedom from the "judgment of history" has given our developing technological society an autonomy unprecedented in the
development of human cultures. The development of a contemporary architecture devoid of historical symbolism by technical engi-
neers for whom utility and cost-effectiveness, not cultural identity
or beauty, became the primary considerations demonstrates how
an antihistorical bias can affect human creativity. The impact on
the human psyche and quality of life when utility and efficiency
replaced beauty and the cultural memories of our society in modern architecture was not one of our technological triumphs.

A return to the use of "historical symbolism and decoration" (or
beauty) for its own sake in postmodern architecture represents a
humanizing influence on our society. The fact that the "intended
result is not history but play" does not negate its humanizing effect. The presence of playfulness reveals the survival of a childlike
primal humanity in what has become an increasingly collectivized
and deterministic, and therefore dehumanizing, cultural environment. Clean lines may be more efficient, but cleanliness carried to
extreme results in sterility. Outside of the hospital environment,
this is not a very appealing goal.

Ahistoricism has often been credited with facilitating the new
dynamism that permeates contemporary culture. A dynamic, in
contrast to a static, view of reality is experienced as vital and life-
enhancing. However, it can also engender a sense of meaning-
lessness when change is uncritically accepted for its own sake
and a loss of values when change is introduced for superficially
pragmatic or functional reasons, apart from a consideration of substantial or metaphysical realities. A science that "has shown the
insubstantiality of the world" can not provide an adequate basis
for human ethics. It can tell us what we can do, but not whether
we should or should not do it. Can we really afford to disregard
totally the lessons of history before we develop a new metaphysics
to complement our new science?[8]

Perhaps it is historicism, rather than history, that has so often
proven to be intolerably limiting. Just as it might be said that "tradition is the living faith of the dead and traditionalism is the dead
faith of the living," so we might say that history is the living experience of the dead and historicism the dead experience of the living.
The lessons that history can teach are limited. History can show

us how we got to where we are, but not where we are going. Both historical continuity and discontinuity are present in every age. Contrary to orthodox Marxist belief, the future is largely determined by human choices, not by the inexorable flow of history. It is not history, but a deterministic interpretation of history that challenges human freedom and dignity and needs to be rejected if our human potential is to be realized within the context of the challenges of contemporary life.

Authentic history in no way opposes the legitimate discontinuity with the past demanded by the challenges of new historical circumstances, but provides a context out of which to develop a creative response to new social realities without the unnecessary sacrifice of our cultural identity. Historicism rightly deserves to be consigned to the past, but the growing antihistorical bias within contemporary society, leading to a loss of our sense of cultural identity, is a serious intellectual shortcoming.

Although Hardison claims universality, as the corollary of abstraction, to be a quality associated with both modern science and modern art, it is evident from what he writes about the loss of "meaning" in its classical sense that the postmodern concept of universality is much more subjective than our traditional understanding of the term has been. Tension always exists between the universal and the particular. This is not because the universal is abstract (although it may not speak directly to the individual's existential experience) while the particular is concrete—both are rooted in an experience of solid reality—but because the universalist perspective is broad and the particularist perspective is narrow. Universalism broadens our understanding and particularism gives it depth.

What is this contemporary universality of abstraction that has been freed from concrete experience as communicated through historical tradition and the human personality of the artist? It is first a universality without any commonality based on human experiences. Its abstract images rise from the depths of the imaginations and personal experiences of individuals who have cut themselves off from the collective historical memories of their cultures. Its artistic images are created by individuals not interested in communicating what it means to be truly human at this time and in this place.

If the traditional function of art has been to interpret what exists and not to invent reality, what are we to think of "art" that expresses the purely subjective state of individual human psyches?

Surely it has ceased to play a mediating role in the apprehension of cultural realities for the viewer. Abstract symbols having no commonly recognized content leave the viewer free to fill the images of modern art with his or her own meaning. It is because these symbols can mean anything that they ultimately mean nothing—what Hardison calls "the disappearance of art." Sacrificed, too, by the move from representation to abstraction is the sacramental principle in art, the power of symbols to "effect that which they signify." Along with meaning, modern art has lost the sacramental power to unite people in commitment to a common vision. Abstract artistic images accommodate the excessive individualism, born of a radical subjectivity, that has become so characteristic of contemporary Western culture.

Hardison believes that abstract modern art complements the ideal of world unity since it is free of specific religious and national traditions. It does not, however, complement the ideal of world unity that many of us are seeking to implement. Our ideal global community will experience diversity in its unity, a diversity acknowledged and appreciated as a unique expression of our common humanity, not masked by contentless symbols having no relationship to the shared experience of human history and cultures. Hardison's concept of world unity is roughly analogous to false ecumenism, an ecclesial attempt at religious unity based on the acceptance of theological formulas so ambiguously written that they can be interpreted to mean whatever the believer wishes them to mean.

Any "unity" attempted through a withdrawal from common experience and understanding into the inner life of an individualistic subjectivity will ultimately prove to be more illusory than actual. There is no doubt that this subjective unity can reduce the chances of human conflict by producing a "live-and-let-live" individualistic universal "peace," but it cannot effect a universal concord based on the mutuality, cooperation, and recognition of the interdependence that many of us hold to be the only authentic source of global unity.

In *Disappearing through the Skylight* Hardison extols the virtues of "transparency" in abstract art, claiming that this quality should appeal equally—"at least in theory"—to people from widely differing social and cultural backgrounds. Why, then, has modern art appealed more to an esoteric elite than to the masses? Could it be that most people need images that "speak" to their experiences, providing them with validation from without?

If abstract art's origin from "spirit rather than nature" makes it "deeply and uniquely human," then it is as likely to reflect the dark, irrational, or at the very least rational side of human nature as it does the more admirable human qualities. Artistic abstractions have been known to express and give rise to nihilism on more than one occasion. Abstract symbols leave us free to impose our own meaning, give free play to self-expression, but they do not provide opportunities for self-transcendence.

Hardison quotes from an essay by Werner Heisenberg, "The Tendency to Abstraction in Modern Art and Science." An excerpt reads: "The realization of this program [universality through abstraction] has pushed the sciences on to even higher levels of abstraction, and . . . the relation of our life to the whole spiritual and social structure of the earth will also be capable of artistic presentation *only if we are ready to enter into regions more remote from life*" (emphasis mine).

Perhaps the best we can hope for from the contemporary concept of universality as it has been expressed in modern abstract art is a solution to our drug problem. With a head trip like this there is no need for chemical substances to escape the challenges and conflicts inherent in the concrete realities of contemporary life!

There seems to be considerable speculation in certain circles on how closely artificial intelligence has come to resemble human intelligence. If "ego" or self-consciousness makes us human, then machine intelligence, like that of lower life forms, can never be equated with human mental capacity. The saying that to be self-aware is to be human is probably even more true than the old maxim "to err is human. . . ." Human intelligence consists of an as-yet largely undefined relationship between mind and psyche. Artificial intelligence resembles mind, but not psyche. Although it has become possible to program a computer to assist in the psychoanalysis of a human person, when the computer malfunctions it will be served by a computer technician or programmer, not by a psychiatrist.

Since human beings are capable of, in fact even inclined toward, self-transcendence or identification with an "other," environmental objects—animate and inanimate—have a profound effect. Contemporary men and women experience themselves dynamically, more as "becoming" than as "being," and becoming takes place in relationships, not in isolation. Rather than asking if computers are capable of human thought, one might more appropriately speculate on whether human intelligence is becoming more like artificial intelligence.

Technology is not new. Every time we drive a nail with a hammer we are employing technology. What is new in contemporary culture is the degree of sophistication and pervasiveness of technological means. The relationship between humanity and technology is reciprocal: technology changes the way we experience ourselves. Although there has been no intrinsic physical change, a person with a hammer will feel more powerful than if he or she had attempted to drive a nail with a fist. We not only shape our technology, but our technology shapes the way we see ourselves. We cannot afford to ignore the "laws of necessity" inherent in the new technologies that have come to dominate modern society.

Many of the effects of these technological laws of necessity are already manifesting themselves in contemporary society. There has been a loss of cultural values as technology has focused attention on function and the immediate result, leading us away from the deeper metaphysical realities. Freed from metaphysical considerations or a recognition of the intrinsic nature of things by an abstract universality, our society acknowledges no limitations on subjective human will. All things have become permissible; nothing is prohibited. All of Hardison's "disappearances"—of nature, history, language, art, and finally human beings—can be attributed to the failure to formulate a postmodern metaphysical alternative to replace modernism's unified but inadequate metaphysical understanding. This is an intellectual compromise that guarantees that the future will be shaped by the self-sustaining momentum of technological developmental progress, rather than by informed human choices.

Instead of mediating between humanity and nature, technology has alienated us from nature, encasing us in its own "artificial environmental shell" while it objectifies and exploits nature as a source of energy to sustain its own artificial existence. Today we are experiencing an ecological crisis of massive proportions that is due only in part to an increase in population.

Mass production made possible by modern technology has not only raised our standard of living; it has also created the cultural phenomenon known as "consumerism," an obsession with the acquisition of "things" that has nothing to do with a legitimate desire for the goods necessary to provide an acceptable quality of life. Moreover, psychological instability is spreading in contemporary Western society as people feel increasingly pressured to choose between adapting to what is often experienced as impersonal or social marginalization.

The list of social ills whose origins can be traced either directly

or indirectly to an inadequately regulated proliferation of technological means seems to grow in proportion to our gains in technological "progress." For every problem "solved" by technology, a
host of others are created.

Technology increases human power, but to exercise this power
well we need "a certain faculty of criticism, discrimination, judgment, and option." It is not technology, but a lack of these "faculties" in our technicians and those who supervise them that is
responsible for the many social crises we are currently experiencing. An uncritical acceptance of the possibilities for technological
development is as unjustifiable as an uncritical rejection of it.

Hardison likened the change from modernism's philosophical
objectivism, with its unified metaphysical focus on the world of
concrete realities, to postmodernism's philosophical subjectivism,
with its focus on theoretical abstractions, to passing through a
"horizon of invisibility." True, these epistemological differences do
create a barrier between people by eliminating common understanding, but regardless of our different world views, we still share
a common humanity. Playfulness exists among people on either
side of the barrier as an encouraging sign that in spite of dehumanizing tendencies, which have always existed in one form or another
in all ages and cultures, the human spirit has not been extinguished
by either modernism or postmodernism.

Apparently Hardison feels that the philosophical subjectivism
that undergirds postmodern thought is preferable to the philosophical objectivism that has shaped modern Western thinking. He has
completely overlooked a growing number of people who, judging
this kind of radical epistemological dualism to be inadequate for
the formation of a satisfactory contemporary world view, have for-
saken entirely the Cartesian philosophical categories and are looking instead to the East for nondualistic philosophical perspectives.

Unfortunately Hardison's analysis of culture and technology in
the twentieth century in *Disappearing through the Skylight* lacks
the sensible insight expressed so eloquently in his 1977 essay: "we
may be asked to surrender a great deal, and saving what is important will demand all the intelligence, all the resourcefulness and
all the passionate commitment that we can muster."

Contemporary men and women need a new epistemology incorporating the valid insights, without the exaggerated emphases, of
both objectivism and subjectivism to formulate an adequate and
more balanced world view. Then they will be able to make responsible choices about the development and employment of techno-

logical means with a view to the long-term betterment of the quality of life for the human family.

Notes

1. Robert Penn Warren et al., eds., *A Time to Hear and Answer: Essays for the Bicentennial Season* (Tuscaloosa: University of Alabama Press, 1977), 55–56.

2. Francis Schaeffer's *Escape from Reason* (1968); *The God Who Is There* (1968); and *He Is There and He Is Not Silent* (1972) were all published by Inter-varsity Press in Downer's Grove, Illinois.

3. Alan H. Guth and Paul J. Steinhardt, "The Inflationary Universe," *Scientific American* 250 (1984): 116–39.

4. Jacques Ellul, *The Technological Society* (New York: Vintage, 1964), 428.

5 Cf. B. Bruteau, *Cross Currents* 35 (1985): 205.

6. (New York: Simon and Schuster, 1984), 68.

7. (London: Routledge and Kegan Paul, 1979), 39.

8. Some contemporary theologians feel that a "relational" metaphysics is more compatible with the postmodern dynamic world view than the modern "substantial" or "essential" metaphysics. See Walter Kasper, *Theology and Church* (New York: Crossroad, 1989).

The Creative Brain

RICHARD M. RESTAK

Ask someone "What are the five personal qualities you most desire for yourself?," and the response "creativity—the ability to be creative" is almost as certain to turn up on the list as health, good looks, charm, and sexual prowess. One of the reasons many people wish to be creative is their recognition that creativity can help them attain almost any other goal they set for themselves.

Attempts at understanding and nourishing creativity traditionally concentrate on social, psychological, and cultural contributions. Unfortunately these bypass the ultimate determinant of creativity: the human brain. Recent research reveals that various aspects of creativity are mediated and nourished by specific organizational patterns within the brain. This finding is not the same as saying that creativity can be explained on a strictly neurological basis—a form of reductionism Arthur Koestler rightly criticized as "nothing buttery"—but it does suggest that some understanding of the brain may contribute toward the desire for personal creativity.

When the two brain hemispheres are compared, the right side seems particularly important in the visual and performing arts. Numerous studies on normals, neurosurgical patients, and brain-injured people reveal that the right hemisphere is generally dominant for recognizing and identifying natural and nonverbal sounds. It is better at appreciating depth perception; maintaining a sense of body image; producing dreams during light sleep; and appreciating and expressing the emotion aroused by music and the visual arts. Finally, the right hemisphere specializes in perceiving emotional expression in others and generating it in oneself.

Damage to the right hemisphere results in distortions in the appreciation of music and natural sounds. In addition, a host of neuropsychiatric expressions—all of them germane to activity—may arise. These include indifference and loss of "drive," depression, manic excitement, euphoria, impulsivity, delusions, and perceptual distortions in regard to the body.

"The right hemisphere maintains a highly developed social-emotional mental system and can independently perceive, recall and act on certain memories and experiences without the aid or active reflective participation of the left hemisphere," writes R. Joseph of the Neurobehavioral Center in Santa Clara, California.[1] He is describing on the neurological level what every creative person experiences regularly; creative ideas and images seem to spring "out of the blue," which might be characterized more accurately as out of the right hemisphere. "Of the truly creative no one is ever master; it must be left to go its own way," Goethe wrote on the serendipitous ways of creativity.

In all instances personal insight into the source of one's own creativity is hampered by the fact that

> We know more than we can say: we live
> in waves and feelings of awareness
> where images unfold and grow
> along the leafwork of our nerves and
> veins. . . .

as poet Peter Meinke describes the process in his poem "Azaleas."

With writers and other creative individuals who work with words, the right hemisphere's contribution is undoubtedly much different. Since language and verbal centers are in the left hemisphere, writers are capable, at least in theory, of continuing to be creative in the event of right-brain damage. What usually stops them is one or more of the emotional sequelae of right-brain damage mentioned above.

Split-brain patients provide an unusual opportunity to explore the mutual interactions between brain organization and creativity. These patients—referred to as split-brain because of a surgically created separation of the right and left hemispheres—behave normally in ordinary social situations. Despite their apparent normality, however, they show little creativity as measured by tests of language, thinking, and emotional expression. They lack the ability to transform the imagery and symbols generated by the right hemisphere into creative verbalizations.

Dr. Klaus D. Hoppe, a psychiatrist at the Hacker Clinic in Los Angeles, believes that the absence of creativity in split-brain patients is similar to what is observed in people suffering from alexithymia, a term taken from the Greek meaning "without words for feelings." People with alexithymia have great difficulty in identifying and verbalizing their feelings. And although the term is rarely encountered, alexithymics are far from rare. They appear frequently in medical clinics and doctors' offices. Typically they experience and express emotional stress by developing physical symptoms. Insight into the psychological origin of their distress eludes them. Moreover, they vigorously deny inner feelings and seem to inhabit a robotic inner life devoid of the finer shades of emotional experience. As a result they are oblivious to suggestions that "stress" or other emotional factors may be playing a role in their illness. Needless to say, alexithymics are difficult and frustrating patients to treat.[2]

Creativity is the opposite of alexithymia. As a rule creative individuals are "in touch" with their feelings and express them through their creative productions. At the neurological level this involves an enriched communication between the hemispheres—bisociation—rather than the hemisphere dissociation typical of the split-brain patient. The more creative one is, the more likely the two sides of the brain are in easy communication with each other. Supporting this theory are EEG studies carried out by Hoppe and associates: they found greater coherence and communication between the two hemispheres in creative people.

According to UCLA neurosurgeon Joseph E. Bogen, who carried out early research on split-brain operations in humans, "It is now certain that the corpus callosum can transfer high-level information from one hemisphere to another."[3] Bogen suggests that the neurological underpinnings of creativity may require not only good communication between the hemispheres but "a partial (and transiently reversible) hemispheric independence" whereby one hemisphere may for a time independently engage in creative production outside of immediate conscious awareness. This could explain the "ah ha!" response: "the illumination that precedes subsequent deliberate verification," says Bogen. Anticipating such developments years ago, neuroscientist Frederick Bremer wrote that the corpus callosum, by uniting the activities of the two hemispheres, makes possible "the highest and most elaborate activities of the brain"—and what can fit this description better than creativity?

A good model of the creative process is suggested by Arthur Rothenberg, clinical professor of psychiatry at Harvard Medical School. He speaks of homospatial thinking as "actively conceiving two or more discrete entities occupying the same space."[4] To test this hypothesis Rothenberg showed forty-three artists three sets of slide photographs (each set consisted of two different slides: for example, five racehorses rounding the turn paired with a separate slide of five nuns walking together in Vatican Square). Some of the artists were shown the slides aligned side by side on the projection screen, while others viewed them superimposed on each other. Each artist was then asked to create a pastel drawing stimulated by each of the three pairs of slides. In evaluating the drawings two internationally prominent artists judged drawings stimulated by the superimposed slides as significantly more creative than those resulting from the separated slides.

Nor is homospatial thinking limited to drawing and the visual arts. Rothenberg believes creative people in literature, music, science, and mathematics excel in their ability to intermingle and superimpose elements from many different spatial and temporal dimensions. He calls this *janusian* thinking, or actively conceiving two or more opposites or antitheses simultaneously during the course of the creative process. These internal conceptions can be opposite or antithetical words, ideas, or images. After clarification and definition, they are either conceptualized side by side and/or as coexisting simultaneously. Finally, they are modified, transformed, or otherwise employed in creative productions in the arts, sciences, or other fields.

In a test of janusian thinking Rothenberg administered timed word-association tests to twelve creative Nobel Laureates, eighteen hospitalized patients, and 113 college students divided into categories of high and low creativity. The Nobel Laureates gave the highest proportion of opposite (unusual) responses. They also furnished these opposite responses at significantly faster rates than those of common responses. Indeed, their average speed of opposite response was fast enough to indicate that conceptualizing the opposites could have been simultaneous. Rothenberg thinks of these highly creative people as engaging in a "translogical process."

Homospatial and janusian thinking correspond in neurological terms to the actions of the frontal and prefrontal lobes. Thanks to these brain areas, which are more evolved in the human brain than in the brain of any other creature, we can mentally access information and keep it online (that is, in mind) until it is integrated into one's ongoing plans. Thanks to this ability to bind time we are able to hold online real or imaginal ideas that form the basis for creativity. We can internally rehearse and anticipate the consequences of our actions, and introduce innovative and novel responses. We know this because after frontal and prefrontal damage the injured person is reduced to living in a here-and-now world in which future consequence and possibilities exert little influence on present behavior and preoccupations. Such persons have great difficulty managing new situations or demands and almost never initiate innovative activities on their own. The victim of frontal-lobe damage is at the opposite end of the spectrum from the creative person.

A high degree of cortical arousal (heightened responsiveness to the events and people in one's environment) is also a prerequisite for creativity. Since introverts characteristically show high cortical arousal, it is not surprising that, in general, creativity comes easier to introverts and those with emotionally responsive dispositions. "Creativity is a problem-solving response by intelligent, very active, highly emotional and extremely introverted persons," writes Dr. L. M. Bachtold, who since 1985 has concentrated on understanding the neurophysiological basis of creativity. His findings suggest to me that if there is a neurological basis for creativity, a single distinguished trait separating the creative from others, it will be discovered within the frontal and prefrontal areas. According to Bachtold, "Subjected to a vast array of disorganized perceptual data and strongly feeling the inconsistencies, the active and intelligent individual forms new perceptual relationships to develop feelings of consistency and harmony."[5]

But there is a hazard in deriving one's neurological concepts about creativity strictly on the basis of observing the effects of deficits resulting from brain damage. It is always possible that the injured brain area may be only a small contributor to creativity, important enough to stymie the creative process, but not at all its major impetus. Furthermore, there are rare instances on record where brain damage enhanced creativity.

An artisan in his midtwenties began to experience attacks marked by the feeling that he was floating helplessly in space. During these episodes, in which "waves" engulfed him, he would begin drawing impulsively. This behavior was all the more remarkable since he had never previously expressed any interest in drawing or artistic activity. An electroencephalogram showed epileptic seizure discharges within the frontal and temporal lobes on the left. Additional tests measuring brain-activity levels yielded more evidence of dysfunction in the anterior regions of the left hemisphere.

Although a certain amount of speculation is always involved in explaining strange phenomena like this, and equally qualified observers may hold in good faith differing opinions about what is going on, I tend to agree with the opinion of the neurologists who cared for the patient. They speculated that the impulses toward artistic expression resulted from the release, as a result of damage to the left hemisphere, of the complex visual and spatial skills of the right hemisphere. It is as if blockage of this man's customary expressive powers, brought on by left-hemisphere injury, led to an unusual and unpredictable form of artistic expression.

But despite the fascination engendered by this patient, it is necessary to remind oneself that this case is unique, the only example so far of enhanced artistic creation resulting from brain damage. Every other example I have personally encountered or read about in case reports confirms that brain damage produces a failing, usually serious, in creative expression.

For example, brain injury to either hemisphere interferes with drawing ability in specific ways. If the right hemisphere is damaged, the drawings lack features on the left side of the picture. This is because right-brain damage results in neglect of persons and objects in the left visual field, which is mediated by the right hemisphere. Spatial relationships are also distorted. Left-brain damage, in contrast, results in overly simplified childlike productions marked by conceptual rather than spatial errors (a drawing of a table setting for one may show three forks).

Probably the most feared form of brain damage results from Alzheimer's disease. And although the cause of this devastating degenerative brain disorder has so far eluded the efforts of neuroscientists around the world, more is known about its effects on creativity.

Over a two-year period an elderly artist underwent a dramatic deterioration in painting skills and intellectual ability. His artistic skills, however, deteriorated more slowly than his other mental functions. In fact, until late in his illness his artistic talents suffered only because of decline in motivation, memory, and organizational skills. In normal aging such deteriorations fail to occur.

A study of seventy-year-olds carried out at the University of Gothenburg in 1989 showed that creativity did not decline over a thirteen-year follow-up period. The study was obviously unusual since it involved tracking for more than a decade individuals already at an advanced age. Unusual measures of reactivity were employed: the interpretation of ink blots coded for three components of creativity, fluency, flexibility, and originality.

Rather than declining with age, creativity in the older person may change according to the special circumstances of aging. For instance, self-expression for its own sake or as a sublimation for sexual or aggressive urges plays a smaller role. Like it or not, most

of us really do mellow with age; even the most ambitious eventually
share to some degree the ancient wisdom that recognizes, even in
the face of fame and creative accomplishment, the transitoriness
of all things. In addition, stylistic and thematic concerns are likely
to change in the older creative artist in response to interests different from his younger counterpart. Picasso was an excellent example of the creative artist who retained an ever-evolving creative
sense despite the ravages of time and aging.

Creative persons of varying ages may also differ in the ways
they artificially boost their creativity. For centuries people have
relied on chemical aids to spur their creativity. These chemicals
include perfectly legal substances like tea (Balzac drank quarts of
it during marathon writing sessions), alcohol (Faulkner and Ker-
ouac drank heavily while in the process of composition), and nicotine (innumerable writers have attested to nicotine's power to
enhance concentration and focus); also included are other chemicals that are either illegal or available only by prescription (am-
phetamine, cocaine, or LSD). The real question is, of course, do
these chemical aids really stimulate creativity, or are the users only
fooling themselves?

In 1989 psychiatrists from the University of California in Irvine
reported on a unique experiment carried out thirty years earlier
on the effects of LSD on creativity. Artists were asked to draw
and paint a Kachina doll. They then took LSD and drew a second
doll. When they were finished a professor of art history analyzed
and compared the two productions.

The most significant changes occurred in the works of those
artists with representational or abstract styles. Under LSD the
paintings were more expressionistic or nonobjective. In almost all
cases the artists saw this as "fashioning new meanings to an emergent world." Indicators of this change included relative size expansion, movement, alteration of boundaries and figure/ground
relations, greater intensity of color and light, oversimplification,
fragmentation, disorganization, and the symbolic and abstract rendering of people and objects. In short, there seems little reason to
doubt that the creative produce was different, but was it better?

Of course this perfectly reasonable question is difficult to answer
because of the highly subjective nature of art appreciation. Evaluating whether or not an artist is more creative as a result of taking
LSD or other drugs is not as easy as deciding whether a scientist
is more creative under the influence of psychoactive chemicals.
With the scientist one can perform experiments or check such
variables as the number of papers written and the frequency of

their citation by other scientists. But what type of measure does one employ for evaluating whether an LSD-influenced work is better than the artist's usual production? One point is certain: no artist that I am aware of has created under the powers of LSD an acclaimed body of work over an extended period of time. Moreover, I cannot help wondering if the artist's claims for the creativity-stimulating effects of LSD are not a variation of what we refer to in medicine as the placebo effect, where such psychological factors as expectations and hopes play an inordinately important role.

When it comes to psychological factors, the creative person must possess what psychologists refer to as ego-autonomy. And various neurologic and psychiatric illnesses can impair this sense of autonomy. Obsession and compulsions interfere with spontaneity and the flexibility that is a requirement for creative breakthroughs. Frontal-lobe disease, as mentioned earlier, disrupts programming, novel associations, and persistence. And any disease or malfunction that interferes with smooth communication from one hemisphere to another prevents the integration and expression that forms the basis of creativity.

But not all emotional and neurological illnesses are incompatible with creativity. Writers have a high prevalence of depression and bipolar disorder (manic-depression). Since alcohol is the most commonly employed self-prescribed medication for depression, it comes as no surprise that alcoholism is also common among writers given to depression. It will be interesting to see if this pattern of alcohol abuse among creative writers will change in response to the current emphasis on health and the mild but persistent social stigma attached to alcohol use. Also playing a factor in determining this change will be the increasing acceptance of mood disorders as illnesses rather than character flaws and the associated willingness of writers, artists, and other creative persons to seek help. As things now stand, some creative people refuse to take medication such as lithium for bipolar disorder; they claim the drug blunts their sensibilities and lessens their creative powers.

Associations between neuropsychiatric illness and creativity have prompted some psychiatrists to conclude that a touch of madness may enhance creativity. While this is possible in the individual instance, the vast number of studies conclude that in general creative individuals are most productive when their moods, thoughts, and behavior are under control. Certainly untreated mental illness or brain disease can be expected to interfere with one quality for creativity identified by former world chess champion Max Euwe:

"the ability to distinguish with certainty that infinitesimal dividing
line between the inspired and the unsound."

Rather than being connected to brain and emotional disorders,
creativity seems to be linked with what Freud referred to as ordinary human unhappiness. In describing the psychological demands
made on the creative individual, Proust wrote: "We enjoy lovely
music, beautiful paintings, a thousand intellectual delicacies, but
we have no idea of their cost, to those who invented them, in
sleepless nights, tears, spasmodic laugher, rashes, asthmas, epilep-
sies, and the fear of death, which is worse than all the rest."

One final point can be made about writers. When thirty writers
were administered psychological tests, they were found to have
above-average IQs but failed to do any better than matched controls in any subtest other than vocabulary. This finding further
confirms the everyday observation that intelligence and creativity
are independent mental abilities. It is possible to be creative although not exceptionally intelligent; the majority of highly intelligent people are not conspicuously creative.

Future research on creativity is likely to dispel another common
assertion: that creativity is more likely to be found in the arts
rather than the sciences. Such distinctions are illogical and wrongheaded. A mathematical formula can be as creative as a sonnet.
And the application of medical knowledge and skill in the service of
arriving at a life-saving diagnosis of a serious but treatable illness is
the most marvelous creative expression of all: the rescue of life,
from which all creativity emerges, from the implacable clutches of
death and oblivion. In my own professional life—divided between
writing and the practice of neuropsychiatry—I have experienced
in these two very different disciplines the joys attendant on creative expression.

No, creativity does not play favorites; it espouses the arts no
more nor less than the sciences. Thus it is likely future knowledge
about the brain will shed light on the creativity of both the physicist
and the dancer, the chemist and the playwright. And why should
we expect it to be otherwise, given that the human brain is the
progenitor of all creativity?

Arthur Koestler has said, "Einstein's space is no closer to reality
than Van Gogh's sky. The glory of science is not in a truth more
absolute than the truth of Bach or Tolstoy, but in the act of creation
itself. The scientist's discoveries impose his own order on chaos,
as the composer or painter imposes his—an order that always refers to limited aspects of reality, and is biased by the observer's

frame of reference, which differs from period to period, as a Rembrandt nude differs from a nude by Manet."[6]

Notes

1. R. Joseph "The Right Cerebral Hemisphere: Emotion, Music, Visual-Spatial Skills, Body-Image, Dreams, and Awareness," *Journal of Clinical Psychology,* 44 (1988): 630–73.

2. W. D. TenHouten, Ph.D., K. D. Hoppe, M.D., J. E. Bogen, M.D. and D. O. Walter, Ph.D., "Alexithymia: An Experimental Study of Cerebral Commissurotomy Patients and Normal Control Subjects," *American Journal of Psychiatry,* (March, 1986): 143:3.

3. J. E. Bogen and G. M. Bogen, "Creativity and the Corpus Callosum," *Psychiatric Clinics of North America,* 11 (1988): 293–301.

4. A. Rothenberg and R. S. Sobel, "Adaptation and Cognition. II. Experimental Study of the Homospatial Process in Artistic Creativity," *Journal of Nervous & Mental Disease,* 169 (1981): 417–23.

5. L. M. Bachtold, "Speculation on a Theory of Creativity: A Physiological Basis," *Perceptual & Motor Skills,* 50 (1980): 699–702.

6. A. Koestler, "The Act of Creation," London: PAN, 1970.

Invisible Evolution in the Works of O. B. Hardison, Jr. and His Contemporaries

E. J. APPLEWHITE

> Our part in the universe may possibly in some distant way be analogous to that of the cells in an organized body, and our personalities may be the transient but essential elements of an immortal and cosmic mind.
> —Francis Galton, *Inquiries into Human Faculty and Its Development (1883)*

THE title of this essay may sound like a doctoral dissertation, but it captures for me a particular thread of the legacy of O. B. Hardison. All of us sharing the posthumous celebration of his career might ponder at times what we would like to talk to O.B. about if we could have the gift of just one more conversation, the grace of just one more encounter before he died at midcareer burgeoning into grandfatherhood. What I would want to pursue is the notion of invisible evolution.

I would like to start with his highly charged metaphor and title of his valedictory book, "disappearing through the skylight." What is it that we are supposed to see disappearing through the skylight? What is disappearing, he says, what is destined to slip from our grasp forever, is the very idea of *what it means to be human.*[1] What Hardison proposes is nothing less than the profane and subversive notion that humanity's claim to uniqueness—our sense of the past and the comfort of our identity—is all going up the chimney like smoke. The sacrifice of our humanity to a computerized world of artificial life appears to be inevitable, irreversible, and even oblivious of all the pronouns—the *us, we,* and *I*—who were the agents of its manufacture.

Omnipotent silicon devices may pursue their own destiny in a universe of space and time where the role of humans is reduced to a vestigial genetic function, like so many honeybees spreading pollen. He writes, "The idea of humanity is changing so rapidly that it, too, can legitimately and without any exaggeration be said to be disappearing. . . . man is in the process of disappearing into the machine he has created."[2] It is a millenarian vista devoid of religious redemption but tempered by an aesthetic sensibility.

A future world of silicon machines may or may not work out a symbiotic accommodation with organic carbon life in which humans might survive as evolutionary remnants—as canaries were to coal miners or as eventual stowaways on Starship Enterprise. It is this prospect that ordains the most apocalyptic conjecture of Hardison's *Disappearing through the Skylight;* "To admit that meaning can be separated from language seems to surrender an anchor holding man to the earth."[3]

Silicon machines suggest that we can have information (at least of a binary sort) without language. In some mysterious way, can we relinquish our language and still hope to retain our humanity? The evolutionary biologist Dobhzhansky said that "Darwin supplied the keystone of the arch connecting our understanding of the destiny of the atom with that of the destiny of man."[4] How could there be greater irony—to the point of blasphemy—than the notion that our unique love affair with destiny could be shared with the lowly atom? And that language be put out of business altogether?

In nature, only the genotype and germ line are in principle immortal. Postbiology is technological. The prospective transformation of consciousness from the vessel of the organic human body to the computer program of organometallic artifice renders immortality of the individual irrelevant—poignant, but irrelevant. On the day when we make ourselves immortal we make ourselves extinct.[5]

The prospect for the survival of life in the far future has now become a respectable area of study and concern within the established physical sciences. Orthodox journals publish papers in this new field of "physical eschatology," speculating on the future of intelligent beings consistent with the recognized laws of physics and computer theory.[6]

Two physicists, John D. Barrow from the University of Sussex in England and Frank J. Tipler from Tulane University in Louisiana have written a consummate work entitled *The Anthropic Cosmological Principle.* They forecast a migration of humanity from the organic to the inorganic:

We may even say that a human being is a program designed to run on particular hardware called a human body, coding its data in very special types of data storage devices called DNA molecules and nerve cells. The essence of a human being is not the body but the program which controls the body; we might even identify the program which controls the body with the religious notion of a *soul,* for both are defined to be nonmaterial entities which are the essence of a human personality. In fact, defining the soul to be a type of program has much in common with Aristotle and Aquinas' definition of the soul as "the form of activity of the body." A living human being is a representation of a definite program rather than the program itself. In principle, the program corresponding to a human being could be stored in many different forms— in books, on computer disks, in RAM—and not just in the brain of a particular human body.[7]

The meaning of life in our culture may be disappearing through Hardison's skylight, but the essence of personality lingers on. In a lengthy footnote to the passage from Barrows and Tipler quoted above, they argue that a soul is immortal because it is abstract in the manner that a number is abstract. For them, the very word *information* is derived from the Aristotle-Aquinas notion of form, and that even semantically the information theory of the soul is the same as Aquinas's theory.[8]

From different premises, J. D. Bernal, a physicist and crystallographer at the University of London, wrote in 1929 (the year of O. B. Hardison's first birthday) an earlier prescient picture of the supersession of man by machine. In his formulation the identity of the individual is transformed to a composite entity subsumed in a sort of community or group consciousness:

> Men will not be content to manufacture life; they will want to improve upon it. . . . Living and organized material will be as much at the call of the mechanized or compound man as metals are today, and gradually this living material will come to substitute more and more for such inferior functions of the brain as memory, reflex actions, etc., in the compound man himself; for bodies at this time would be left far behind. . . . Even the replacement of a previously organic brain-cell by a synthetic apparatus would not destroy the continuity of consciousness.
> Bit by bit the heritage in the direct line of mankind . . . would dwindle, and in the end disappear. . . .
> Finally, consciousness itself may end or vanish in a humanity that has become completely etherialized, losing the close-knit organism, becoming masses of atoms in space communicating by radiation, and ultimately perhaps resolving itself entirely into light. That may be an end or a beginning, but from here it is out of sight.[9]

Our human bodies left far behind and out of sight, indeed; or as Hardison has said more explicitly, invisible.

Another physicist, Freeman Dyson, has written of the future of life in space without reference to the survival of any individual self or soul, but with a rather generalized view of information organizing itself in an inanimate but evolving environment of invisible circuitry.

> . . . it is not absurd to think of redesigning terrestrial creatures so as to make them viable in space or on other celestial bodies. . . . The move of life from air to vacuum is as fundamental and as liberating as the move which our ancestors made from water to air half a billion years ago. . . . Life is capable of making itself at home in every corner of the universe.
>
> My argument will be based on a fundamental assumption concerning the nature of life, that life resides in organization rather than in substance. I am assuming that my consciousness is inherent in the way the molecules in my head are organized, not in the substance of the molecules themselves. If this assumption is true, that life is organization rather than substance, then it makes sense to imagine life detached from flesh and blood and embodied in networks of superconducting circuitry or in interstellar dust clouds.[10]

These are not the words of a vitalist or New Age spiritualist but of a physicist at the Princeton Institute for Advanced Studies. He envisions the transformation of life from its ancient organic abode to a new inorganic home on the cosmic range—where the processes of evolution will continue to function, but not in a way that would be visible to creatures such as we are now, any more than ancient microbes and fish could imagine how we look now. For that matter, we humans are completely invisible to the ants who greatly outnumber us on earth today.[11] In Dyson's future the culture and technology of the twentieth century will be left far behind, as predicted in Hardison's book.

This argument finds an echo in Buckminster Fuller's concept of ephemeralization concerning the application of technology of industry, with its ever more exquisite refinement from structures of compression of those of tension. (In his preface to *Disappearing through the Skylight* Hardison acknowledges that Fuller—his and his wife's friend of many years—gave him an insight into the relationship between design and the efficient use of materials.) Fuller's view is implicitly utopian:

> The Stone Age logic said that the wider and heavier the walls, the more happily secure would be the inhabitants. The advent of metal alloys in the twentieth century has brought an abrupt change from the advantage of structural ponderousness to the advantage of structural lightness.

This is at the heart of all ephemeralization: that is the dymaxion principle of doing ever more with ever less weight, time, and ergs per each given level of functional performance. With an average recycling rate for all metals of 22 years, and with comparable design improvements in performance per pound, ephemeralization means that ever more people are being served at ever higher standards with the same old metals.[12]

Doing vastly more with vastly and invisibly less is known technically as *ephemeralization*. The mass production of electronic controls inaugurated automation. With automation has come—just now—a dawning awareness of the invisible avalanche of ephemeralization. . . . A key part of ephemeraliation's acceleration has been played by the return of approximately all the world's metallic scrap into complete reuse. This scrap recirculation released by progressive obsolescence of earlier inventions by newer more efficient ones . . . constitutes a fundamental factor in the doing-more-with-less process.[13]

And even earlier Fuller foresaw an industrial trend from the material to the abstract:

The very character of simple arithmetic of mathematics indicates that all progressions are from material to abstract, by which we mean intangibility, nonsensoriality, ephemeralization.[14]

The most appealing aspect of Hardison's vision is that he approached it as a teacher and poet whose entire career—academic and creative—had been totally devoted to the life of the mind as expressed in the humanities: the rationale for humanism was central to his *raison d'être*. Hardison writes of the technological imperatives that corrosively subvert an ideal in which our highest values attach to the dignity of the individual. Biological individuation has reached its peak in *homo sapiens* among the mammals. The astronomer Eric Chaisson describes the brevity of our role in any universal accounting of time and space:

. . .we are now nearly beyond the realm of *biological* evolution and much of the realm of cultural evolution, just as the specific atoms in our bodies have already passed through particle, galactic, stellar, planetary and chemical evolution.[15]

The poet and scientist seem to be converging in their consensus that the arena for the next stage of evolution is inevitably technological.

I do not suggest that any of the writers cited here were (except as noted) an influence on Hardison and his book. As far as I know, Fuller was the only one whose work he had read, and—in the last conversation I ever had with O.B. (on a break at the Georgetown University colloquium "Individuality and Cooperative Action" on 4 April 1989)—I asked him if he saw any connection between the arguments in his last book and Fuller's concept of "ephemeralization and trends to invisibility," and he said he saw none. But I think it is a tribute to *Disappearing through the Skylight* that his and Yeats's vision of humanity's eventual supersession by machine was anticipated by even more researchers than he was able to cite in the book's quotations and references. It only adds luster to his intuition that those whose careers were devoted to science and technology shared—not without similar misgivings—his bleak, arresting perception of our denouement in a secular and technological millennium.

Notes

1. O. B. Hardison, *Disappearing through the Skylight: Culture and Technology in the Twentieth Century* (New York: Viking, 1989), 5.

2. Ibid., 347.

3. Ibid., 4.

4. Theodosius Dobzhansky, *Mankind Evolving: The Evolution of the Human Species* (New Haven: Yale University Press, 1962), 4.

5. E. J. Applewhite, *Paradise Mislaid: Birth, Death, and the Human Predicament of Being Biological* (New York: St. Martin's Press, 1991), 251.

6. John D. Barrow and Frank J. Tipler, *The Anthropic Cosmological Principle* (Oxford: Clarendon Press, 1986), 658.

7. Ibid., 659.

8. Ibid., 680.

9. J. D. Bernal, *The World, the Flesh, and the Devil* (1969; reprint, Bloomington: Indiana University Press, 1929), 45–47.

10. Freeman Dyson, *Infinite in All Directions* (New York: Harper & Row, 1988), 104–7.

11. Hardison, *Disappearing,* 341.

12. R. Buckminster Fuller, *Synergetics 2* (New York: Macmillan, 1979), sec. 792.52.

13. R. Buckminster Fuller, *Utopia or Oblivion: The Prospects for Humanity* (New York: Bantam Books, 1969), 184–86.

14. R. Buckminser Fuller, *Nine Chains to the Moon* (Philadelphia: J. B. Lippincott, 1938), 256.

15. Eric Chaisson, *Th Life Era: Cosmic Selection and Conscious Evolution* (New York: Atlantic Monthly Press, 1987), 218.

Selected Works by O. B. Hardison, Jr.

Books

Lyrics and Elegies. New York: Charles Scribner's Sons, 1958. (Poetry)

The Enduring Monument: The Idea of Praise in Renaissance Literary Theory and Practice. Chapel Hill: University of North Carolina Press, 1962. (Reprinted 1973)

Modern Continental Literary Criticism. New York: Appleton-Century-Crofts, 1962. (Reprinted London: Peter Owen, 1964) (Editor)

English Literary Criticism: The Renaissance. New York: Appleton-Century-Crofts, 1963. (Editor)

Christian Rite and Christian Drama in the Middle Ages. Baltimore: Johns Hopkins Press, 1965. (Reprinted 1983)

The Princeton Encyclopedia of Poetry and Poetics. Princeton: Princeton University Press, 1965. (Associate editor, with Alex Preminger and Frank Warnke)

Medieval and Renaissance Studies No. 1. Proceedings of the First (1965) Session of the Southeastern Institute of Medieval and Renaissance Studies. Chapel Hill: University of North Carolina Press, 1966. (Editor)

Practical Rhetoric. New York: Appleton-Century-Crofts, 1966. (Textbook)

Aristotle's Poetics for Students of Literature. Englewood Cliffs, N.J.: Prentice-Hall, 1968. (Translation of *Poetics* by Leon Golden with Commentary by O. B. Hardison, Jr. Reprinted 1981, 1990, Tallahassee: Florida State University Press)

A Facsimile Edition of the Examination and Tryal of Old Father Christmas. Boston: G. K. Hall, 1971. (Editor)

Film Scripts I. II, III, IV, 4 vols. New York: Appleton-Century-Crofts, 1971. (Editor, with George Garrett and Jane Gelfman)

Instructor's Manual for Film Scripts I and II. New York: Appleton-Century-Crofts, 1971. (With George Garrett)

Medieval and Renaissance Studies No. 5. Proceedings of the Fifth (1970) Session of the Southeastern Institute of Medieval and Renaissance Studies. Chapel Hill: University of North Carolina Press, 1971. (Editor)

The Quest for Imagination: Essays in Twentieth-Century Aesthetic Criticism. Cleveland: Case Western Reserve University Press, 1971. (Editor)

The Forms of Imagination. New York: Prentice-Hall, 1972. (Editor, with Jerry Mills)

Toward Freedom and Dignity: The Humanities and the Idea of Humanity. Baltimore: Johns Hopkins Press, 1972.

Classical and Medieval Literary Criticism. New York: Frederick Ungar, 1974. (Translations and introductions, edited with Leon Golden)

Pro Musical Antiqua. Baton Rouge: Louisiana State University Press, 1977. (Poetry)

Entering the Maze: Change and Identity in Modern Culture. New York: Oxford University Press, 1982.

Medieval Literary Criticism: Translations and Interpretations. New York: Frederick Ungar, 1985. (Editor)

The Princeton Handbook of Poetry and Poetics. Princeton: Princeton University Press, 1986. (Editor, with Alex Preminger and Frank Warnke.)

Disappearing through the Skylight: Culture and Technology in the Twentieth Century. New York: Viking/Penguin, 1989.

Prosody and Purpose in the English Renaissance. Baltimore: Johns Hopkins University Press, 1989.

The New Princeton Encyclopedia of Poetry and Poetics. Princeton: Princeton University Press, 1993. (Associate editor, with Alex Preminger, T. V. F. Brogan, Frank J. Warnke, and Earl Miner)

Horace's "Ars Poetica" for Students of Literature. Jacksonville: University Press of Florida, 1995. (Translation of *Ars Poetica* by Leon Golden with Commentary by O. B. Hardison, Jr.)

Series Editor

Goldentree Bibliographies. New York: Appleton-Century-Croft and Chicago: Harlan Davidson, 1966–90.

Crofts Classics. New York: Appleton-Century-Crofts and Chicago: Harlan Davidson, 1967–90.

Editorial Boards

Studies in Philology, 1966–69.

Milton Studies, 1967–90.

English Literary Renaissance, 1969–90.

The Film Journal, 1970–75.

Journal of Medieval and Renaissance Studies, 1970–90.

The Collected Works of Erasmus, 1980–90.

Film

The Mystery of Elche. Color/sound film of the only medieval play to survive to the present day in performance. 110 minutes. Made in 1978, released in 1979. Shown nationally on PBS Television; in Europe, on BBC Television in England and on television in Germany, Ireland, and Belgium. (Executive producer)

Essays

"The Decorum of *Lamia.*" *Modern Language Quarterly* 19 (1958): 33–42.

"The Dramatic Triad in *Hamlet.*" *Studies in Philology* 57 (1960): 144–64.

"Criticism and the Search for Pattern." *Thought* 36 (1961): 215–30.

"The Scholastic Backgrounds of Milton's Poem 'On Time.'" *Texas Studies in Language and Literature* 3 (1961): 107–22.

"Robert Lowell: The Poet and the World's Body." *Shenandoah* 14 (1963): 24–32.

"Symbol and Myth: More Questions than Answers." *Bucknell Review* (12 (1964): 17–28.

"*Poetics*, Chapter I: The Way of Nature." *Yearbook of Comparative Literature* 16 (1967): 5–15.

"The Rhetoric of Alfred Hitchcock's Thrillers." In *Man and the Movies*, ed. W. R. Robinson, 137–52. Baton Rouge: Louisiana State University Press, 1967.

"The Case Against Activism." *PMLA* 83 (1968): 985–87.

"Three Kinds of Renaissance Catharsis." *Renaissance Drama*, n.s., 2 (1968): 3–22.

"Independent Research Libraries Association." In *Encyclopedia of Library and Information Science*, Vol. 2. (1986) New York: M. Decker,

"Gregorian Easter Vespers and Early Liturgical Drama." In *The Medieval Drama and Its Claudeliam Revival*, 27–39. Washington, D.C.: Catholic University Press, 1970.

"The Place of Averroes' Comentary on the *Poetics* in the History of Medieval Criticism." In *Medieval and Renaissance Studies No. 4*, edited by John Livesay, 57–81. Durham: Duke University Press, 1970.

"Teaching the Humanities." In *Effective College Teaching*, edited by William H. Morris, 56–65. Washington, D.C.: American Council for Higher Education, 1970.

"The Orator and the Poet: The Dilemma of Humanist Literature." *Journal of Medieval and Renaissance Studies* 1 (1971): 33–44.

"Spenser's 'Amoretti' and the Dolce Stil Novo." *English Literary Renaissance* 2 (1972): 208–16.

"The Two Voices of Sidney's *Apology for Poetry*." *English Literary Renaissance* 2 (1972): 83–99. (Reprinted in *Sir Philip Sidney: Essential Articles*, edited by Arthur F. Kinney, 73–90, Hamden, Conn.: Archon Books, 1986; and *Sidney in Retrospect*, edited by Arthur F. Kinney and the Editors of *ELR*, 45–61. Amherst: University of Massachusetts Press, 1988.

"Culture and Openness." *Ohio Review* (Spring 1973): 5–14.

"The Future of the Independent Research Library." *The Athenaeum Annals*, Annual Address, February 1973.

"The Promises of Humanistic Education: Can They Be Kept?" In *What Is Humanistic Education?* 9–19. Washington, D.C., 1973.

"Catharsis in *Samson Agonistes*." *Classical Journal* (1974).

"Shakespeare: Was He Shakespeare?" *Washington Post*, 11 December 1974, B-3.

"Myth and History in *King Lear*." *Shakespeare Quarterly* 26 (1975): 227–42.

"Politics and Beauty." *Soundings* 58, no. 1 (1975): 1–13.

"Attempting the Impossible and Accomplishing the Unbelievable: Thoughts on Two American Revolutions." In *A Time to Hear and Answer: Essays for the Bicentennial Season*. The Franklin Lectures in the Sciences and Humanities. Fourth Series, 39–58. Tuscaloosa: University of Alabama Press, 1976.

"No Póssum, No Sop, No Tates: Or, a Lack of Cash and a Failure of Nerve." Reprinted from *Toward Freedom and Dignity* (1972) in *Challenge and Choice in Contemporary Education*, edited by Christopher Lucas. New York: Macmillan, 1976.

"Toward a History of Medieval Literary Criticism." *Medievalia et Humanistica*, 1–12. Cambridge: Cambridge University Press, 1976.

"The Vital Center: Higher Education and the Liberal Arts." Written for the Inauguration of Reverend C. D. Sherrer, King's College, Wilkes-Barre, Pennsylvania. Privately published, 1976.

"Petrarch and Modern Lyric Poetry." In *Studies in the Continental Background of Renaissance English Literature*, 24–41. Durham: Duke University Press, 1977.

"Famine or Feast: The Humanities in Contemporary American Society." In *The Humanities: Perceptions, Purposes, Prospects*, 33–41. October 1978.

"George Washington in Marble." *CCA-NS Journal* 2 (1978): 16–29.

"Shakespeare on Film: The Developing Canon." In *Twelfth Annual Comparative Literature Symposium*. Lubbock: Texas Tech University, 1979.

"The Ivory Tower in the Arena: Research Libraries and Public Outreach." *Wilson Library Bulletin* (1979): 384–91.

"Cultural Funding in the United States." UNESCO *Cultures* (Paris) 7, no. 3 (1980): 62–78. (In English, French, and Spanish)

"Logic vs. the Slovenly World of Shakespearean Comedy." *Shakespeare Quarterly* 31 (1980): 311–22.

"Shakespeare's Political World." In *Politics, Power and Shakespeare*, edited by France McNeely Leonard. Arlington: Texas Humanities Resource Center, 1981.

"Administration and Scholarship." *Communicator* 14, no. 5 (1982): 1, 10–11.

"Teaching Literature to Undergraduates." *ADE Bulletin* 73 (1982): 38–40.

"The De-Meaning of Meaning." *Sewanee Revire* 91 (1983): 397–405.

"*In Media Res* in *Paradise Lost*." *Milton Studies* 17 (1983): 27–42.

"Speaking the Speech: Shakespearean Dialogue." *Shakespeare Quarterly* 34 (1983): 133–46.

"Virtues of Necessity: New Connections for the Humanities." *Communicator* 17 (1984): 1, 4–5.

"Model Teachers: A Dissenting Opinion." *NYCEA Newsletter* 7 (1983–84): 1–3.

"Blank Verse Before Milton." *Studies in Philology* 81 (1984): 253–74.

"Dada, the Poetry of Nothing, and the Modern World." *Sewanee Review* 92 (1984): 372–96.

"The Hard Core Curriculum: *Realpolitik* for the Liberal Arts." In *Politics, Society, and the Liberal Arts*, edited by Reed Sanderlin and Craig Barrow, 55–62. Chattanooga, Tenn.: Southern Humanities Press, 1984.

"Conversion and Poetry in the Fourth Century." *Sewanee Mediaeval Colloqium Occasional Papers* 2 (1985): 45–65.

"Education for Utopia." In *High Technology & Human Freedom*, edited by Lewis H. Lapham, 41–48. Washington, D.C.: Smithsonian Institution Press, 1985.

"The Future of the Literal Arts: A Humanist's View." *Georgia Review* 39 (1985): 576–85.

"Liturgy and the Emergence of Christian Reality." *Sewanee Mediaeval Colloquium Occasional Papers* 2 (1985): 67–80.

"The Poetry of Nothing" (with comments). In *Science and Literature: A Conference,* 41–82, 135–70. Washington, D.C.: Library of Congress, 1985.

"Virginia, the Humanities, and the Schools." *Newsletter of the Virginia Foundation for the Humanities and Pubic Policy* 9 (1985): 2–6.

"NEH at 20, How Much and So What?" *Change Magazine,* January/February 1986, 12–22.

"Great Walls and Running Fences." *Sewanee Review* 94 (1986): 384–417.

"Humanism and Its Discontents." West Virginia Endowment for the Humanities McCreight Lecture Series, 1986.

"On the Road Again with Recorded Books." *Washington Times Magazine,* 1 September 1986, M3–4.

"Politics and Culture." *SCAN* 1, no. 6 (1986): 1–2.

"Prosody and Genre." *Research at Georgetown* (Spring, 1986): 1–2.

"'Put Money in Thy Purse': Supporting Shakespeare." *Shakespeare Study Today: The Horace Howard Furness Memorial Lectures,* edited by Georgiana Ziegler, 153–67. New York: AMS Press, 1986.

"Robert Penn Warren: Bard for a Year." *Washington Times,* 12 March 1986, 1.

"Tudor Humanism and Surrey's Translation of the *Aeneid.*" *Studies in Philology* 83 (1986): 237–60.

"Shakespearean Tragedy: The Mind in Search of the World." *The Upstart Crow* 6 (1986): 71–82.

"At Stratford, a Surprising Summer Fest." *Washington Times,* 31 July 1986, B1–2.

"A Tree, a Streamlined Fish, a Self-Squared Dragon." *Georgia Review* 40 (1986): 369–403. (Chosen for Pushcart Press Prize Volume for 1986/87)

"Midseason at Niagara." *Washington Times,* 25 August 1987, B1–2.

"Stratford's 'Nothing' Is Something to See." *Washington Times,* 26 August 1987, B5–6.

"Drama and Ritual: European Religious Drama." In *The Encyclopedia of Religion.* New York: Free Press, 1987.

"Foreign Language Accents with Perfect Writer." *Profiles: The Magazine for Kaypro Computer Users* 5 (1987): 75–77.

"Humanism." In *The Spenser Encyclopedia,* edited by A. C. Hamilton, Donald Cheney, W. F. Blissett, and David A. Richardson, 397–81. Toronto: University Press, 1990.

"Humanities '87: Setting Some Priorities." *Georgia Review* 41 (1987): 679–90.

"The Disappearance of Man." *Georgia Review* 42 (1988): 679–713.

"Binding Proteus: An Essay on the Essay." *Sewanee Review* 96 (1988): 610–32.

"Machines, Metaphors, and Horizons of Invisibility," *Individuality and Cooperative Action,* Edited by Joseph E. Earley, 13–35. Washington, D.C.: Georgetown University Press, 1991.

Poetry

Poems in *Carolina Quarterly, Contemporary Poetry of North Carolina, Epoch, Esquire, Impetus, Lulibulero, New Republic, New Southern Poets, North Caro-*

lina Poetry: The Seventies, Parnassus, The Poet Upstairs, Poetry in Review, The Southern Poetry Review, Washington Dossier, Washington and the Poet

Book Reviews

Book reviews in *Books Abroad, Bulletin of the American Association of Higher Education, Cesare Barbiere Courier, Chronicle of Higher Education, Comparative Literature Studies, Criticism, Journal of Contemporary Psychology, Modern Language Quarterly, Modern Philology, New Republic, New York Times Book Review, Renaissance News, Renaissance Quarterly, The Sewanee Review, Speculum, The Review of Metaphysics, Thought, Western Humanities Review*

Contributors

JOHN F. ANDREWS is editor of the *Everyman Shakespeare* and the former editor of *Shakespeare Quarterly*. From 1974 to 1984 he was associated with O. B. Hardison, Jr. as director of Academic Programs at the Folger Shakespeare Library.

E. J. APPLEWHITE is most recently the author of *Paradise Mislaid: Birth, Death, and the Human Predicament of Being Biological* (1992). Long an associate of R. Buckminster Fuller, he collaborated with Fuller on his major work, *Synergetics: Explorations in the Geometry of Thinking* (1975). He was a long-time friend of O. B. Hardison, Jr.

T. V. F. BROGAN is an independent scholar and an electronic publisher. He is the editor of *The New Princeton Encyclopedia of Poetry and Poetics* on which he worked closely with O. B. Hardison, Jr. for four years. He has published widely on the history and theory of verse.

FLETCHER COLLINS, JR., was Professor of English and Drama at Elon College, 1936–42, Professor of Theater at Mary Baldwin College, 1946–77, executive director of the NEH film *Visitatio Sepulchri* in 1979, and from 1982–91 the editor of *Medieval Music-Drama News*. The Cultural Laureate of Virginia, he was the founder of three theaters. O. B. Hardison, Jr. participated in the making of Collins's theater-wagon documentary and in his medieval workshops in Staunton, Virginia.

CAROL DWORKOWSKI, a free-lance writer, part-time editor, and medical records clerk in Annapolis, Maryland, was a long-time acquaintance of Hardison.

LEON GOLDEN is chairman of the Department of Classics and director of the Program in the Humanities at Florida State University. He recently published a monograph entitled *Aristotle on Tragic and Comic Mimesis* in the American Philological Association's American Classical Studies series. He is coauthor of two works with O. B. Hardison, Jr.: *Aristotle's Poetics: A Translation and Commentary for Students of Literature* and a study of Horace's *Ars Poetica* and its tradition, Hardison's final book, which was published by the University Press of Florida in 1995.

JOAN OZARK HOLMER is professor of English and a former colleague of O. B. Hardison, Jr. at Georgetown University. She has published on William Browne, Robert Herrick, Thomas Nashe, Vincentio Saviolo, Shakespeare, and Milton, and on *The Merchant of Venice: Choice, Hazard, and Consequence*. She collaborated with Hardison on a Thomas More symposium in 1978.

RONALD HORTON chairs the Division of English at Bob Jones University. His dissertation, directed by O. B. Hardison, Jr. won the South Atlantic Modern Language Association Award Study for 1976 and was published by the University of Georgia Press as *The Unity of "The Faerie Queen"* (1979). He has published articles on Spenser and related subjects and is past president of the South Carolina Association of Departments of English.

ARTHUR F. KINNEY is Thomas W. Copeland Professor of Literary History at the University of Massachusetts, Amherst, and adjunct professor of English at New York University. He has written several books and essays on poetics, including *Humanist Poetics: Thought, Rhetoric, and Fiction in Sixteenth-Century England; Continental Humanist Poetics; John Skelton: The Priest as Poet;* and *Faulkner's Narrative Poetics*. With O. B. Hardison, Jr. he wrote the essay "Renaissance Poetics" for *The New Princeton Encyclopedia of Poetry and Poetics*.

LOUIS L. MARTZ, retired Sterling Professor of English at Yale University, is the author of several books on seventeenth-century English poetry, including *The Poetry of Meditation; The Paradise Within; The Wit of Love;* and *From Renaissance to Baroque: Essays on Literature and Art*, as well a numerous essays on twentieth-century poetry. He is the coeditor of Thomas More's *Dialogue of Comfort* and the author of *Thomas More: The Search for the Inner Man*. He was Hardison's colleague at Georgetown University.

JERRY LEATH MILLS studied Renaissance and modern literature as an undergraduate under O. B. Hardison, Jr. at Chapel Hill. After

graduate degrees at Harvard University, he returned to become
O. B.'s officemate and colleague at the University of North Carolina, where he is currently professor of English and editor of *Studies in Philology.*

ROBERT L. MONTGOMERY, Professor Emeritus at the University
of California, Irvine, is presently working on a book about Shakespeare's sonnets. He was Hardison's colleague in the English Department at the University of California, Irvine.

FRANCIS X. MURPHY, C.S.S.R., Medievalist and Professor Emeritus of the Academania Alfonsinna, Rome, participated with his
close friend O. B. Hardison, Jr. in the symposia on Thomas More
and on Petrarch at the Folger Library. He covered Vatican Council
II for the *New Yorker* under the pseudonym Xavier Rynne. He is
presently in residence at St. Mary's Rectory in Annapolis.

MARJORIE PERLOFF is Sadie Dernham Patek Profesor of Humanities at Stanford University. Among her many recent works on poetics are *Radical Artifice: Writing Poetry in the Age of Media* (edited
with Charles Junkerman) and *John Cage: Composed in America.*
Her *Futurist Moment: Avant-Garde and the Language of Rupture,*
initially reviewed by O. B. Hardison, Jr. in 1986, has recently been
translated into Portuguese. *The Poetics of Indeterminacy: Rim-
baud to Cage* (1981) was reissued in 1993.

PAUL RAMSEY was a widely published poet and scholar who recently retired as Poet-in-Residence and Guerry Professor of English at the University of Tennessee in Chattanooga. He was a
visiting professor at Cornell University and elsewhere and was a
research fellow at Yale University in 1982. A close friend of O. B.
Hardison, Jr. since their undergraduate days at Chapel Hill, when
they coedited the literary magazine *Factotum,* he died while this
book was in press.

RICHARD RESTAK is professor of neurology at Georgetown University. He is the author of ten books on the brain, including two
companion volumes to PBS television programs: the twelve-part
program *The Brain* and the ten-part program *The Mind.* Dr. Restak
was a friend of O. B. Hardison, Jr.

DAVID A. RICHARDSON was one of O. B. Hardison, Jr.'s last doctoral students at Chapel Hill; he is now professor of English at

Cleveland State University, where he directs the B.A. program in Liberal Studies. He initiated the annual session for "Spenser at Kalamazoo" and *The Spenser Encyclopedia* (of which he was managing editor) and has edited volumes on sixteenth-century nondramatic writers for the *Dictionary of Literary Biography.*

JASON P. ROSENBLATT, professor of English and former colleague of O. B. Hardison, Jr. at Georgetown University, has published numerous essays on Milton and the seventeenth century. He is coeditor of *"Not in Heaven": Coherence and Complexity in Biblical Narrative* and author of *Torah and Law in "Paradise Lost."*

MYRA SKLAREW, former president of Yaddo, is currently professor and co-director of the MFA Program in Creative Writing at the American University. Her interests range from cell biology to poetry. She has published seven collections of poetry, most recently *Altamira* and *Eating the White Earth,* and a book of short fictions, *Like a Field Riddled by Ants.* From O. B. Hardison, Jr. she learned to drive a car without brakes.

DAVID R. SLAVITT published his fiftieth book in 1994 with his most recent novel, *The Cliff.* His most recent volume of poetry is entitled *Crossroads;* his most recent translation is that of *The Metamorphoses of Ovid.* He was a fellow poet and close friend of Hardison.

HOMER SWANDER, professor of English at the University of California, Santa Barbara, is also artistic director of the American Shakespeare Company, founder and executive director of A Center for Theatre, Education and Research (ACTER), and director of Theater in England (TIE). During O. B. Hardison, Jr.'s directorship of the Folger, they designed several collaborative projects between the Folger and ACTER in Washington and elsewhere.

JOSEPH H. SUMMERS retired from the University of Rochester in 1985. He met O. B. Hardison, Jr. during his residency at the Folger Shakespeare Library in 1976 while writing most of *Dreams of Love and Power: On Shakespeare's Plays.*

PAUL TRACHTMAN, the author of *The Gunfighters,* was for twenty-five years an editor and writer for *Life, Horticulture,* and the *Smithsonian* magazines. Now a freelance writer, painter, and printmaker living in New Mexico, he founded with O. B. Hardison, Jr. the Quark Club, a Washington, D.C., group of humanists and scientists interested in issues and problems related to cybernetics.

EDWARD R. WEISMILLER, poet, novelist, and scholar, has taught principally at Pomona College and George Washington University. As a widely published scholar, he has specialized in the nature and development of English verse form and in Milton's prosody. "Rhymes and Reasons" was first delivered as a lecture at the Folger Shakespeare Library.